Lord of the years

To D.J. and O.R.B.
in gratitude to God

Lord of the years

Geraint Fielder

**Sixty years of student witness
The story of the Inter-Varsity Fellowship,
Universities and Colleges Christian Fellowship,
1928–1988**

Inter-Varsity Press

INTER-VARSITY PRESS
38 De Montfort Street, Leicester LE1 7GP, England

Unless otherwise stated, Scripture quotations in this publication are from the Holy Bible, New International Version. Copyright © 1973, 1978, 1984 by the International Bible Society, and published in Great Britain by Hodder & Stoughton Ltd.

First published 1988

British Library Cataloguing in Publication Data

Fielder, Geraint D.
  Lord of the years.
  1. Universities and College Christian
  Fellowship—History
  I. Title
  267′.61′09429   BV1430.U5/

  ISBN 0–85110–831–8

Set in Linotron Times
Typeset in Great Britain by Input Typesetting, London SW19 8DR
Printed in Great Britain by Richard Clay Ltd, Bungay, Suffolk

Inter-Varsity Press is the book publishing division of the Universities and Colleges Christian Fellowship (formerly the Inter-Varsity Fellowship), a student movement linking Christian Unions in universities and colleges throughout the United Kingdom and the Republic of Ireland, and a member movement of the International Fellowship of Evangelical Students. For information about local and national activities write to UCCF, 38 De Montfort Street, Leicester LE1 7GP.

Contents

Introduction

'I am sure that, over the past half-century, the impact of IVF/UCCF on the Christian life of the country has been enormous, but so diffuse and widespread as to be difficult to track down,' comments Professor John Paterson of Leicester University. My tracking down has been haphazard and limited, and I am aware that the impact of university and college Christian Unions upon the life of the country is far deeper than I have been able to assess. One of my original aims had been to put that impact in the context of the present secularization debate. It has been, I fear, an unfulfilled ambition, which someone more qualified for the task may yet take up.

This book is more of a popular history, by which I mean history written about people for people in a way that (one hopes) people will read! I have drawn on the reminiscences of a number of the men and women involved and they have been my main sources, along with earlier written material.[1] I have sought to tell the story through their eyes. This approach has its perils. It may, for example, put the 'wrong' people in the limelight. 'It is the same in war,' says a noble critic of this way of writing history. 'The Major or Captain in charge of the heroic unit sometimes gets the VC (for the whole unit), when really God alone saw the person who was most at risk and did most!'

I have sought, therefore, to guard against telling the story always through the eyes of 'majors and captains' (though there are many with those actual ranks in the story). Other ranks are

[1]See the Bibliography on pp. 247–248.

well represented, too, many unknown to most of the Christian public. Further, I have sought to keep uppermost what one former UCCF travelling secretary particularly requested; 'Like Paul and Barnabas reporting back to the church at Antioch that had commissioned them, we want our emphasis to be, "They . . . reported all that God had done through them" (Acts 14:27). We were thrown in at the deep end and were just so utterly cast upon the Lord that any glory must be *his*.'

Such a perspective requires us to remember that those quoted or referred to are but representatives of a work of God that is far bigger than all of them put together. They illustrate through the colour of their own lives what many another life could equally have shown. I see the book as the opening of a family photograph album where many faces are missing and many stages in the lives of those present are not captured. But the family story is still traceable. It is a book of related snapshots animated into life, rather than a continuous film projected on to a panoramic screen.

A word of explanation, too, about the extensive space given to the conversion experience of many individuals. The reason for this does not lie in the current fascination with 'experience' as such. The point is to highlight, not the experience itself, but the common thread of the saving truths of Scripture that produced those experiences. It aims to show that there is a body of truth in the Bible which centres in the fact that the cross of Christ saves sinners, and that the lives of those who believe this are changed by God himself. The personalities involved are as varied as any cross-section of students, and the details of their conversion have the variety that is part of the human story. The similarities are the recurring *truths* to which they bear testimony and which are objective to them.

It is also worth stressing that the fact that so many examples are given is not meant to imply that a dateable conversion experience is the necessary norm of the Christian's entry into new life. Most of those coming up to university as Christians would be from Christian homes and churches, so, for many, their turning to Christ as Saviour would have come as the slow opening of a flower to the sun. In the nature of the case the book does not focus there. The reason for telling the story of the way many found Christ in their student years is that we see the place and power of evangelism and so are stirred to continued faithful testimony to the gospel among non-Christian

8

students – for it remains the power of God to the salvation of those that believe (Romans 1:18). I believe that the book's method has a compelling way of demonstrating that we are dealing, not with a merely human story, but with plain evidence of the saving ways of God with human beings. Those interested in the contemporary situation, and the quest for biblical stability within it, could begin by reading the last two chapters, where the impact of the counter-culture is analysed. The rest of the book could well convey a stronger punch with those chapters digested first.

Any more ambitious attempt to relate the story of the Inter-Varsity Fellowship/Universities and Colleges Christian Fellowship to the wider history of the church, let alone society, would have taken us well beyond the bounds of the student world. But I hope the story will show that, though the Christian Unions (CUs) are not churches, they are concerned about the key issues with which the church has always concerned itself. The early-church emphasis, shared by the church throughout the ages, on witness, prayer and missionary outreach, is the abiding concern of CUs. Similarly, as the church had to defend itself against heterodox movements, so the IVF/UCCF feels itself called to be vigilant still in this area. Indeed, the CUs, in their lesser orbit, have tended to find themselves in the minority positions of the Athanasius and Luther and Whitefield and Spurgeon figures of church history, when the few had to stand against the slide of the many away from biblical truth. Lying beyond the scope of the book, though hinted at through some of the students described, is the whole area of biblical concern regarding the wider life of Christians in society, which is a constant challenge to the church. The significance of the student witness for later Christian influence on the professions, on social and ethical issues and academic life, cannot be exaggerated. The manifold flowering of Christian associations of all kinds linked with the graduate side of UCCF, especially in the last few decades, is an indicator of the enormous but diffuse impact of the graduate end of the student production line.

And now something that I hope will be specially borne in mind by Scots and Irish readers. This present book gives a tempting glance at the Scots and Irish CUs, but not much more. For example, Edinburgh, Glasgow and Queen's, Belfast, CUs, all highly significant contributors to the IVF/UCCF story, appear little after 1945. My motive is plain. Justice could be done to the Scottish and Irish stories only in books of their own. Someone please oblige! This story omits entirely any reference to IVF/UCCF in Wales for the simple reason that that story has been told in my book *'Excuse me, Mr Davies – Hallelujah!'*

The references to individuals in the text show how much and to how many I am indebted. Without their help a book of this nature just is not possible. I want to thank them all for their letters and comments.

Finally, very special thanks to my wife Mary, who bought me a word processor and then persuaded me that even I could learn to use it. And thanks to my son Robert and my friend Des Ruck for teaching me how.

Chapter One

A DOCTOR'S DILEMMA

It was a Sunday evening in an old part of London, south of the river near Tower Bridge. Down one of the narrow streets came a young man in a hurry. He pushed an old basket Bath chair. He halted at the door of one of the tiny terraced cottages lining the street. The door opened straight into the front room off a very narrow pavement. He greeted an elderly friend, helped him into the chair, and then set off along the way he had come. Arriving at the newly built Medical Mission he dumped the willing fellow into the care of others and was off again at a cracking pace to collect another passenger.

The area into which he disappeared was a rabbit warren of streets and passage-ways, some less than 12ft across from house to house, lying behind the Borough High Street. In the neighbourhood stood the Tabard Inn, famed from the days of Dickens. A little further down the road, on an island, is Little Dorritt's Church. The conditions Dickens described in *Little Dorritt* were, alas, in some respects, still applicable to the area in the early thirties. Squalor abounded. Men living in the district were badly paid, yet what money they earned often drained away in the local. Drunken brawls were frequent. Men and their wives stayed late at their drinking while the children, without knickers or shoes, would sit, bare-bottomed, on the kerbside. There they would fall asleep, only to be roused again when their parents snatched them up to take them home.

It was in this deprived south London ghetto that our young man, recently qualified as a doctor, pioneered a new work at the Landsdowne Place Medical Mission. Among the local people he was soon affectionately known as 'Johnnie'. Until he began there the community's medical needs had gone uncared for. He had long intended to be a medical missionary in Rhodesia, now Zimbabwe, but for a while he was instead to apply his medical skills in London's dockland. Experience gained while he attended dockers' meetings at Bristol, run by university surgeon Rendle Short, was a good apprenticeship. But even at that time he was involved in another work for God, and his life was at a crossroads, as we shall see.

His appointment at Landsdowne was the culmination of a step-by-step attempt of the Shaftesbury Society to offset the worst effects of poverty and neglect. Its Ragged School at Landsdowne Place pulled in hundreds of children. The voluntary workers used to hold daily sessions to teach them to read from the Bible. But the children were too hungry to concentrate, most having had no breakfast. So, with the co-operation of a national daily newspaper, the mission provided free breakfasts. Then they began a halfpenny lunch – nourishing soup and roly-poly pudding. Many had no shoes, so a boot club was started; then a goose club, so that Christmas could be a bit special. Nobody in the area cared about the children's teeth, so a dental clinic was started; or about their eyes, so an ophthalmic clinic followed. These amenities were all conceived and administered by voluntary Christian workers.

But when it came to attendance at Mission services, the adults, except for some old ladies, stayed away. It was the '*kids*' Mission'. The watchnight service was literally the only time that any man from those alleys set foot on the Mission premises. At about ten minutes to midnight, on New Year's Eve, a strange, superstitious compulsion brought crowds of them from the pubs. They were given black coffee, and Christ was commended to them. The leader of the women's meeting had been saved in this way and her life changed. It would be twelve months before the men came back.

But then Johnnie came. The Mission were persuaded that if they had a full-time medical worker with a concern also to bring the gospel to the adults, then they might begin to listen. A new worship hall was built, together with a medical wing consisting of a dispensary, consulting room and nurses' residential flat. At the inaugural meeting the new doctor was accompanied by Leigh Ashton, a friend who had been a houseman with him at Bristol. Memory of it brings a smile: 'Dr Stuart Holden, president of the mission, preached on the text, "All your robes are fragrant with myrrh and aloes and cassia" (Psalm 45:8). We were always thin on the cash line and I happened to know that even if his (Johnnie's) garments really were all that, his shoes were in dire need of repair.'

Johnnie was to use a lot of shoe leather as he busied about the area. But as he did so, that strange text from the Psalms came to life as Scripture so often does in God's obedient servants. He became a fragrant influence for Christ. During the few hectic years he was able to devote to the work, the doctor became also preacher, pastor, counsellor, friend. The apostle Paul makes the psalmist's imagery more specific: 'But thanks be to God, who always leads us in triumphal procession in Christ and through us spreads everywhere the fragrance of the knowledge of him. For we are to God the aroma of Christ among those who are being saved and those who are perishing. To the one we are the smell of death; to the other, the fragrance of life. And who is equal to such a task?' (2 Corinthians 2:15–16).

Johnnie's awareness of the task ahead of him came soon after the surgery opened. 'The first day was deceptively quiet. Only one old lady turned up – a bronchitis sufferer. She rushed off and told everyone: 'Come and see this new doctor; he listens!' 'So I did,' says Johnnie, 'to one patient!' Next day he got many more. A long queue of patients formed outside. Two Roman Catholic nuns came along armed with paper and pencil and took down the names of people in the queue. They were going to be reported to the priest if they entered this Protestant place.

From the start, the doctor's work in the area was tireless. It was often past midnight when he returned from home visits. As missioner he was ready to share the gospel with all who wanted to listen. He found that when a member of the family was very ill, custom dictated that all the other members would gather at the house. They would crowd around the bed. When the doctor had tended the patient he would quietly and warmly proclaim the risen Christ to them as their only hope in life and death. It had remarkable effects. He became a much-loved figure in the area. Many a patient would overflow with thanks for the way he had been cared for. 'If you really are grateful, then I shall know you really mean it if you come along on Sunday evening to the service.' For some three quarters of an hour before the start, that old Bath chair became a familiar

sight. It showed all with eyes to see that here was a servant of
God who was deeply in earnest that they too should share his
faith in the Saviour. Adults began to cross the threshold of the
Mission as they saw a dimension of faith and love that went
beyond the welcome medical care. From literally nothing, and
against so much deep-rooted prejudice, a Sunday evening
gospel service of 100 to 200 adults was built up.

For one contemporary, Alan Ramsey, a leader of one of the
Mission youth clubs, and later secretary of Rye Lane Baptist
Church, London, the memory of those years has never faded.
'In every way Johnnie was a most interesting character. The
Lord gave him a wonderful ministry. In some respects you
would have thought that perhaps his method of approach in
preaching would not have been right in such an area. His
sermons were long and he wasn't all that topical. But even in
this Johnnie was unique. The plain fact is that he preached the
gospel to needy people and the Lord's word did not return
void.'

But then came a crisis. After the first year the number of
patients rose to over 4,000. Even willing nurses found they
could not keep up with the pace and two or three had to resign,
literally unable to meet the physical demands. And then the
doctor himself sustained a suspected heart condition. The
warning light was there. With the greatest reluctance the
Mission council accepted his resignation. Prudence demanded
it. For although he had given himself to the work as if he had
no time for anything else, although his commitment was so
total, he was having to live a double life. For Douglas Johnson
was already involved in another work of God among evangelical university students to which, from now on, he was to
devote his full-time energies.

We celebrate the story of that work in this book.

Douglas Johnson had briefly picked up the nickname
'Johnnie' in the busy little world of the Mission. Known to his
friends as 'D.J.', he was involved up to the hilt in the Inter-
Varsity Fellowship (IVF),[1] a growing national and international
witness of evangelical students. Because of his unobtrusive way
there were some voluntary workers at Landsdowne who knew
nothing about it. They would not have thought it possible
anyway. As one recalls, 'He had really no time for anything

[1]Since 1975, the Universities and Colleges Christian Fellowship.

14

else. As far he was concerned it could truly be said, "This one thing I do." And he certainly did it.' But the other demands were encroaching. Over and above a ten-hour day at the surgery and on the rounds, he was doing three to four hours a day on IVF work, on top of which was the preaching at the Mission. 'It was clear', he says, 'that I couldn't keep faith with patients and emergencies in spite of three nurses from CIM.[2] Also, no-one should be trying to look after so many, even if underdoctored. I must have gone out one night at midnight to a case and gone instead to the Mission – for I woke up cold on the steps with the keys in my hand! Clearly the end was in sight!'

'Trying to put in a heavy day's work at the Mission and also then having to settle down to pressing and growing IVF work became an intolerable situation,' says his friend Leigh Ashton. In chapter four we shall see how the matter was solved and how he became full-time General Secretary of the Inter-Varsity Fellowship.

And what place, we might ask, has an excerpt from a medical mission in London's dockland in a story about students? Much in every way. The inevitable limitation of a story of student witness is that it is set in a three- to six-year period of a young Christian's life. We see little of their service to Christ in maturer years, except in so far as some of them came back to serve the student world as part of their professional life or preaching ministry. The Landsdowne tale serves, therefore, as an appropriate sample of what so many became, under God, in many a mission field or inner-city situation spread across the globe. It is a reminder that generations of Christian students devoted themselves, and still do, to a life of service to God and man, uniting in their ministry a concern for body, mind and soul, this life and the life to come. Constantly, as a direct result of their conversion to Christ in their student years and of obeying the call of God, young men and women have gone into secular society with the light and salt of the grace of God and the good news has spread. Our story looks at the preparatory years, in a context that is a mission field of its own – the secular campus. It is a tough training camp where the intellectual, moral and spiritual pressures upon young Christians are for ever escalating. Yet it is there that God has put them as a witness.

[2]The China Inland Mission, now the Overseas Missionary Fellowship.

So the time has come to tell the story of the IVF/UCCF and assess the nature of its evangelical student witness. We shall take up that story at a critical juncture as people returned from the First World War in 1919. Evangelical life was at a low ebb. But from then on, a small but committed band of students, which Douglas Johnson was to join in a year or two, saw the tide begin to turn. Under God a new, yet old, witness to the gospel gathered momentum in the universities, led to the founding of IVF in 1928, and strives to continue in the vigorous heritage of biblical Christianity to the present day.

PART ONE
1919–1939
VALIANT FOR TRUTH

Chapter Two

PRAYER LIKE APRIL SHOWERS

In his final year at school Douglas Johnson had a great disappointment. His intention was to take up a place at Emmanuel College, Cambridge, to study medicine. But there was simply no room in the college. Emmanuel was 'full up with heroes' – ex-servicemen back to their studies. So for Johnson there was a postponement of studies. It meant that, though he was aware of them, he missed being present at the crucial events of 1919 which marked a renewal of the student evangelical witness of the preceding half century, and which led on to the emergence of IVF in 1928. Renewal of that testimony was urgently needed. There had been something of a landslide away from biblical Christianity between 1900 and 1919. A shrinking band of evangelical leaders had been astonished, like Moses and Paul before them, at how quickly men and women could turn from God's revealed truth. The Student Christian Movement (SCM) had tragically been in the vanguard of this. The evangelical Cambridge Inter-Collegiate Christian Union (CICCU), founded in 1877, had, by 1910, dissociated itself from the rest of SCM on the grounds that the latter was denying basic Bible truths. That process had continued, and by the end of the first world war there was, for example, hardly any theological college that had not downgraded its view of the Bible and Christ.

The year 1919 is something of a special one in our story. A small group of students felt duty bound, under God, to make a Luther-type stand. We shall highlight seven factors.

First, the students themselves. Among ex-officers returning to Cambridge were a few tough evangelicals. War-weary though they were, they could see they had been flung into a battle for the truth of God. A group of students in London provided a second front in this spiritual and intellectual struggle, and by 1919 they were to be a united cause. Many of the men on the Cambridge front were recovering from war wounds in hospital tents pitched in college courts and on the 'Backs'. As they picked up in spirit they praised and prayed and planned for the future. Godfrey Buxton, Norman Grubb and Murray Webb-Peploe had accumulated between them four Military Crosses and some severe wounds. Basil Atkinson, a wartime student, had acquired a prison sentence for conscientious objection. He had been persuaded to join the CICCU by Webb-Peploe, in 1919. Webb-Peploe was to be, above all perhaps, a winner of others for Christ. The first recruit he won for the ranks of the CICCU, Basil Atkinson, the future underlibrarian at Cambridge, was to be CICCU's apologist extraordinary for over fifty years.

The second factor, which sets the backdrop to the whole of our drama, was the decision these students took in maintaining the CICCU's historic position. The overwhelming religious preferences of the day were against them. A very tiny 'remnant' of fifteen or so had kept CICCU's light burning during the war. Buxton and his equally small brigade returned to find that the chaplains, theology lecturers, and those of the student world still of a religious bent, all thought the evangelical faith outmoded. There was a strong anti-doctrinal mood. Christianity was seen as an ethical force whose energies should be directed towards social reconstruction. The evangelical Bishop of Durham, Handley Moule, had seen the trend coming and had written of 'a powerful drift of thought going in the direction of separating Christian theology from practical Christianity; the mysteries of our Lord's Person and Work from the greatness of his example. . . . Such a theory rends asunder the teaching of the New Testament and is a theory of (Christianity) started strictly *de novo*.' The accelerating effect of this was that writers and preachers seemed studiously to ignore the old Bible message of redemption from sin. To the Bible-believer the war itself had been the most harrowing demonstration of the fact of sin. But the message of what God had accomplished through the cross of Christ to set people right was being pushed aside. Leading religious figures rejected the idea that the atoning death of Christ was the necessary basis of our forgiveness and acceptance with God. In the summer of 1919 Norman Grubb saw clearly that this was creating another gospel that was no gospel. He was told by leaders of the SCM in Cambridge that the atoning blood of Christ was not necessarily central in the beliefs of the movement. That settled the matter for those who understood the Bible to teach that this was of first importance (1 Corinthians 15:3). There were no two ways about it. It could not be relegated to one alternative view among many without fatally weakening the gospel. To reject it altogether simply destroyed the gospel.

The reader may reflect at this point. Does this just seem like far-off days and battles long ago? Does it sound like an old, contentious debate from which we can now move on to more 'spiritual' things, such as love and fellowship in the Spirit, and worship of God, rather than definitions of truth? Careful, for those were the things the CICCU were told. Love, fellowship and worship were precious to them too. But they saw them as what bonded Christians together in the family. The issue here was the primary one of how someone entered the family; the fundamental one of how a person became a Christian at all. That is why Christ's saving work held for them, as it must for us, the central ground.

The third factor was the sense of empowerment from God they received. During that summer of 1919 something happened that ensured that they would not have just a defensive, 'dugout' mentality. It enabled them to move on to the offensive and show they were the true heirs of what God had graciously done through those earlier nineteenth-century student pioneers such as C. T. Studd, and the rest of the 'Cambridge Seven'.[1] At the CICCU camp at the Keswick Convention in July a good number had gathered to seek God's blessing. One evening their prayer time turned into an exhausting spiritual battle – but also a transforming one. 'One of the youngest present, who had come to university straight from school, began to pray. We had never heard prayer like it before . . . we began to do the same. We realized that something was happening to us and we did not break up till the small hours. The next day the whole atmosphere seemed

[1]Seven Cambridge graduates who offered to the China Inland Mission in 1884. See Oliver R. Barclay, *Whatever Happened to the Jesus Lane Lot?*, pp. 35–39.

different. Some went in the evening into the fields and woods to pray. There were various acts of self-dedication to God's service which subsequent history shows to have been fulfilled in our lifetime.'

The fourth factor arising from this was the effect on the immediate and longer-term witness of the CICCU. The next term saw signs following. 'The danger that we would be a hard, barren, defensive clique was over,' says Grubb. 'The spiritual temperature was magnificent. We were on fire for God and we daily got down on our knees and poured out ourselves in prayer, particularly, of course, for the university'. To the faithfulness that these leaders had shown in their determination to cling to the essentials of the faith was added the fire that came at Keswick. Some outstandingly gifted students were converted and the membership rose from the entrenched fifteen to fifty that session.

The fifth factor, again the result of the camp blessing, was the restoration at Oxford of evangelical student witness, which had collapsed before the war. Grubb singles out Noel 'Tiny' Palmer (he was 6ft 8ins tall), much of whose future lay in student witness in Canada, as the human instrument God used. In 1919 he was recovering from wounds at Cambridge but planning to enter Oxford. CICCU members befriended him. Norman Grubb took him to hear a CICCU speaker, Barclay Buxton. Soon he had come to know that his sins were forgiven in Christ. When it was learned he was going to Oxford there was some sympathetic banter! But there was no lack of seriousness when they gathered round him with fervent prayer before he left. 'I had the feeling I was being commissioned to go to start something new.' And so he did. But not immediately. It happened after he joined up with that CICCU summer camp and knew the enriching blessing from God that came through that spiritual breakthrough.

There was a whole bunch of strong evangelical ex-servicemen that carried the flame back to Cambridge. But Tiny wended a lonely path back to Oxford – a single burning coal from off the altar. Would he burn too low alone? 'One day, in the junior common room, to those who wanted to hear, I gave a testimony about what the Lord had done for us in the vacation. Within weeks we probably had as many as forty meeting in different rooms for Bible study. . . . Prayer would break out like April showers at all times.' He and a friend used to assist each other

22

to rise every day at 6 a.m. for a 'quiet time'.

And sixthly, the vision. Grubb tells us of another turning-point in 1919. It is the decisive factor as a pointer to the future. 'It was some time in the middle of the Michaelmas term 1919, that, in my room at Trinity, God gave me a clear vision of the IVF that was to be. I saw that not only must there be this witness in every university, but that *God* was going to do it. Probably the fact of Noel Palmer's prompt action at Oxford in getting to work to restart an inter-college CU enabled God to open our eyes to this much better thing.'

'God was going to do it'; 'God opened our eyes'; 'Palmer's prompt action' – divine promises, divine action, and human initiative in response. It led to the 'much better thing' that our story is going to relate. 'Much better' because of the clear-sighted determination of these young students to declare Scripture's own priority: 'Jesus Christ, and him crucified'.

To further this it was proposed that meetings should be held in London for all the universities. It led to the first Inter-Varsity Conference in London in December 1919 – our seventh and final event of this year of good seed, all of which came to a fruition in 1928. The name, Inter-Varsity, came partly from the fact that that December day was the day of the Varsity rugby match – it being decided that that would be the time when most evangelical students would be in London! In such ways does the marvellous majesty of God's purpose show itself to have a human face.

Chapter Three

THIS MUCH BETTER THING

London became the hub of reviving evangelical student endeavour. One of the factors contributing to this was that, at that time, Oxford and Cambridge sent all their medical students to the twelve London teaching hospitals for clinical experience. As the CICCU grew after 1919, so the reinforcements sent to London bolstered the already clearly defined hospital CUs. The London Inter-Hospital Christian Union had functioned since 1912.

London's student population was also a kind of microcosm of that in the rest of the country. As there were universities scattered across the face of Britain so it seemed that there were innumerable colleges dotted over sprawling London. CUs developed in the main colleges of London University. Consequently, when the hospital CUs merged with these other CUs to become the London Inter-Faculty Christian Union (LIFCU), it set a pattern of what IVF was to be.

It was a happy providence that placed Douglas Johnson at this doorway to the future. Because of the long queue everywhere for medical places, he accepted advice to enter University College, London, to study English. Quite a switch! It was part of the destiny that shaped his ends. He was in the right place at the right time. Early on in term he noticed a student saying grace before tackling a refectory meal. Together they eventually attended the 'freshers' squash' of the SCM. It became a dance – and definitely not of the praise and worship variety, unheard of in those days! It was a symptom of the time. The SCM, though numerically large, was in escalating crisis over its identity. What did it stand for? It had lost confidence in the message that, in earlier years, had given it considerable impetus. It tended to take its starting-point from contemporary attitudes, intellectual and social. One of the features of the immediate post-war era was a grimness from which people sought to escape into frivolity. 'Entertainment' was the big release of the twenties, and in opting for the dance there was perhaps an attempt to say that religion, too, was fun.

Johnson, no stranger to fun, decided to leave, along with two friends. 'The promptings of the Holy Spirit in my life', he says, explaining his reasons, 'were to thirst after Christ and to be obedient to his will.' These three formed a Bible study group, stirred like newborn babes to seek for food. In October 1922 they started the University College CU, already aware that they could affiliate with a growing London and Inter-Varsity movement. At the second Inter-Varsity conference in 1922, Johnson was made LIFCU secretary. A week before his BA finals in 1924 he sat and got a Warneford Scholarship for medicine, and later moved on to King's College. The following year, that scholarship was won by Stanley G. Browne, who was to become the world's leading expert on leprosy. Johnson, Stanley Browne and Peter Elwin were successive leaders of the CU that met in the vestry of the chapel at King's in the later 1920s. Little did he know it, but the die was well and truly cast for Johnson. He was to be around as a student for a long time to come, and in 1924 he was hijacked into taking on the developing Inter-Varsity Conference secretaryship. Never was there a more reluctant dogsbody, but the role stuck. No-one else would have the post because of the possible effects on academic work and the reactions of fee-paying parents.

London was host to the first six Inter-Varsity conferences. These conferences were non-residential. Christian families such as the Buxtons, Grubbs, Studds and others, aware of the reviving student witness through the Keswick camps, acted as hosts, some welcoming up to four students apiece into their homes. Then, in 1924, LIFCU started its first residential conference at High Leigh, Hoddesdon, Hertfordshire. It was a huge success, with over a hundred members present. A month later, when Johnson was 'landed' with the job of organizing the national Inter-Varsity conference, he said, 'Let's have it residential like LIFCU and try to help the distant university representatives to come.' High Leigh was booked for Easter 1926. Its significance was multiplied when, straight down from the first Scots evangelical students' conference, came one of the 'distant representatives' – medical student John Laird, later General Secretary of Scripture Union. The vision of 1919 was beginning to take shape. We shall give it substance by looking at some of the early unions in Ireland, Scotland and England.

Things were happening across the sea and over the border. The Scots and Irish play a very important part in the work almost from the word 'go'. It is a marvellous thing to see the way God has given these islands such a balanced human mix where English, Irish, Scots and Welsh complement each other. The empirical English, with their gift for the practical and a moderation which enables them to be truly tolerant; the warm-hearted, outgoing Irish with their strong missionary spirit; the perseverance and stability of the Scots, giving strength and depth to their theological outlook, the zeal of the Welsh, with their consciousness of the holiness of God – these combinations enriched the fellowship from the start. We have seen how the 1919 Inter-Varsity conference was concerned to see the witness spread throughout the country. Unknown to those who prayed, there was already a little stirring in the north and west.

In *Ireland*, the first seeds of a CU seem to have been sown in the war-torn fields of Flanders. A young soldier, Patrick Dixon, was huddled in a dugout, trying to read. In his post he had received a small khaki New Testament, sent to him by a student back home in Dublin. There, amidst the slog and counterslog of trench warfare, Dixon found Christ through the reading of the Bible.

On his return to Dublin, Dixon, son of the professor of anatomy and nephew of the professor of botany, began to study medicine in Trinity College. Along with another student he was assigned a spacious room, 'No. 40'. In 1920 he invited a number of his year to a buffet meal and nervously and blunderingly told his story. Out of that venture grew the CU. 'No. 40' became its name. The Inter-Varsity conference of 1919 had met with a view to 'enthusing other universities with a vision of starting their own evangelical groups.' 'No. 40', Trinity College, Dublin, seems to have been the first. (At this stage, southern Ireland was still part of the United Kingdom.)

1919 was a year of deep spiritual awakening in the north of Ireland, and a young man, led to Christ in that year, was to become a life-long friend of IVF. T. S. Mooney considered the time to have been 'the nearest thing to revival in Northern Ireland since 1859 and our university students shared in some of the blessing'. For example, Queen's University Belfast Bible Union was born in 1921. By 1926 it sent its first contingent of eleven students to the Inter-Varsity gathering at High Leigh. Queen's CU was to become one of the most spiritually fruitful in the whole United Kingdom. A work also began in Magee, Londonderry, where Mooney, a banker, had begun to befriend many of the students, some of whom had been converted through the unique evangelistic ministry of W. P. Nicholson, soon to make his mark in a mission at Cambridge University.

Back in Trinity, Dublin, 'No. 40' continued to see people converted. In his life story, *The Fibre Man*, Professor Denis Burkitt tells how, as a fresher, he was out one day on a cross-country run when he was overtaken by another student who invited him to a meeting at 'No. 40'. Burkitt describes how severely taken aback he was when, at a meeting there a few weeks later, a much older student cornered him with a question. Had he ever responded to the claims that Jesus Christ, the Son of God, made on his life? This, he recalls, was his first encounter with Christians who believed that what really counted was not what *they* did, but what Christ had already done on their behalf through his death and resurrection. Professor Burkitt pays tribute to the courage it took that student. 'Whether or not it was the right approach, I am profoundly grateful that God used this deeply committed student to crystallize my faith. Then and there, with very little understanding of the implications for my future, I made up my mind to follow the calling of Christ and be identified in the college as a Christian.'[1]

Scotland had a rich heritage of evangelical student witness. Edinburgh University students, like those at Oxford and Cambridge, had shown deep commitment to evangelism and missionary zeal in the previous century. But Scotland had suffered, too, the same eclipse of the great evangelical doctrines. 'The Bible is no longer looked upon as authoritative and the general eagerness was to study the ethic of Jesus and realize the kingdom of God among men,' said an Edinburgh student of 1919. But the eclipse was not total or permanent.

[1] Brian Kellock, *The Fibre Man*, p. 16.

A shaft of light came in 1922 when twenty-one students founded the Edinburgh University Evangelistic Association. From among the Edinburgh students came Eric Liddell, an Olympic sportsman and missionary whose lustre as a follower of Christ still seems to brighten with the passing years. The year after the Olympics and graduation he spent at the Congregational College in Edinburgh. During that time evangelical students held their first full-scale mission to the university. Their original plan had been to ask Noel 'Tiny' Palmer to speak. But that was deferred and it was daringly proposed to ask Eric Liddell, who must have been the youngest university missioner ever. A year later he was to sail for the Far East. A special kind of 'chariot of fire' lay ahead.

In Glasgow, students organized a prayer campaign among Christians in the city and then launched a postering campaign on campus. Professor Rendle Short was their first speaker, then Arthur Taylor of the CIM. It was during election week for the Rector and the posters for the meeting caught the eye of a high-spirited student body, who turned up to hear Taylor *en masse*. As was their custom in rectorial week they let their hair down. It is said that the noise could be heard a quarter of a mile away. Taylor took stock of the situation and stood on top of a table and told stories! But gradually he worked round to his subject and eventually a silence that could almost be felt descended as he spoke of things that really mattered.

Vastly encouraged by their start, a constitution was drawn up for the Glasgow Christian Students Fellowship (CSF) in February 1923. Most of the early leaders in Scotland, such as Laird and Cyril Nye, were from a Brethren background. 'Altogether they were great days and I recall them with joy and thankfulness,' says Laird. 'There was a flowering of evangelical life and power. We had a membership of eighty-two men and thirty women.' It reached a membership peak of 211 in the late twenties. One of the women, another medic, Winifred Anderson, found the strong Brethren ethos of the early days a bit restrictive. 'I was very much in at the beginnings of the IVF in Glasgow. I was a very raw Christian and the rigidness of the newly formed CU staggered me. I would in those days rather have preferred SCM! But looking back I realize my whole contact with IVF was a growing-up experience.'

In the Easter vacation of 1925 came the small beginnings of the Scots' own Inter-Varsity conference. It met around a picnic under a clear blue sky on the lee side of a haystack. There were students from Glasgow, Edinburgh, St Andrews, and, perhaps, Aberdeen. The witness in Scotland had its own identity and was developing along its own lines. But never in isolation. Within a year, Scots involvement down south in High Leigh led directly to the founding of a CU in Scotland's oldest university, St Andrew's.

But now let's see how well the *English* side of the family was growing.

Bristol CU's birth brings to our attention the most formidable character among the senior figures who supported the recovering evangelical movement between the wars – Rendle Short. We have already met him up at Glasgow in a typical role – first speaker at the founding of a CU. He was to speak at CUs all over the country.

As far back as 1910 this surgeon, later Professor of Surgery at Bristol, had organized Sunday evening meetings for students, along with his friend Dr Frank Bergin. Rendle Short was a smallish man with the toughness of a first-class surgeon. A marvellous intellect, an ordered mind, and a shining apologetic brilliance went hand in hand with a firm biblical faith. His great sweep of knowledge stood out in a period when there were hardly any evangelical professors. His capacity to answer questions off the cuff gained the ear of students, and many vividly recall their first encounter with him. His strong point was to bear witness to the truth of the Bible and he was highly gifted in marshalling evidence that confirmed its reliability. All this was combined with a concern for a person's relationship to God, not with intellectual questions in a vacuum. His men's Thursday evening Bible studies drew men from the St Phillip's district of Bristol. Over the years many were converted and some entered Christian work. He was generous in finance and hospitality, and nationally and locally the student work benefited.

In 1921 some medical students took over the leadership of the students' meetings and that was the pattern from then on. With little encouragement coming from local churches, however, the continued support of Short and Bergin was priceless. Dr Bergin provided the pitch for informal gatherings on Saturdays and weekend conferences by making available his large and delightful bungalow at Clevedon which overlooked rose gardens and the Bristol Channel. 'Bergo's Bung', as it was christened, was a centre of sustaining ministry in an unsympathetic religious world.

Not that they were an ingrown minority. Leigh Ashton indicated quite the opposite. 'One thing stands out very clearly in retrospect – the serious way the CU viewed our Lord's commission to go with the gospel to the world. A very high percentage reached the foreign mission fields. Among them was the sister of one of the CU founders, Roxie Dymond, who married J. O. Fraser of the CIM. Mike Wilde and Arthur Wright both went out with the Regions Beyond Missionary Union to the Congo, and Ted Gurney and Cecil Johnston to Burma. Lionel Gurney founded the Red Sea Mission Team; John Bates went to the Sudan and died in his early years of service there. Others went to Africa, Malaya, India, China . . .' Ashton himself went to Kenya and Thailand. Not a bad roll call for a small CU!

Their best efforts at evangelism, however, rarely drew more than sixty people and conversions were very few indeed. They managed to number a bishop (Taylor Smith), a professor (Albert Carless) and an admiral (Sir James Startin) among their speakers. The latter was a grand old seadog. The one history date he knew coincided with that of the Battle of Trafalgar! He startled his student audience by having chairs moved all round the room to show Nelson's battle formation in relation to the enemy. After some order was restored he proceeded with a talk based on battle and strategy in the Christian life. In those very formal days his illustrative method was something of a sensation.

Leigh Ashton's own story shows how fruitful even a tiny minority of Christians can be in recruiting the seeker or doubter. He had made up his mind to avoid the CU as, up till then, there had been no joy or reality in his attempt to live the Christian life. 'Through subtle liaison between Rendle Short and my father I found myself expected to attend the freshers' meeting. This I did. It only confirmed my conclusions that it held no interest for students, for the meeting was held in the large hall of the university club capable of holding over 1,000. Fifteen were actually present and five of those were on the platform. However, I was amazed to find that two of the leaders were both in the university rugby fifteen. I went again to spy out what these men had and found they had something I never had, but wanted, and found.'

Coming up a year or so later, Cecil Johnston, whose future was to include being a chaplain to Wingate's Chindits in the Far East, found that the CU was as difficult to find as the future enemy in the jungle. An early experience shows in a stark way just why the CU had been founded. While he was reading the Psalms in the common room, the SCM secretary looked over his shoulder. 'My dear fellow, Johnston, you do not mean to say you are reading that book. It's quite, quite out of fashion now. No intelligent person would read such a thing today.' Such were the high days of religious modernism.

Johnston, who helped to cultivate a more positive attitude to the Bible as post-war leader of Scripture Union in India, did track the Bristol CU down in time. His involvement was uneventful until one incident of blessing, rare at the time, showed how possible it was for the tide to turn when such examples multiplied, as they did all over the country, in the years after 1945. 'I lived in a hall of residence of about eighty. In a remarkable way a student called "Gus" Crane was converted and his whole life changed. He could not keep it to himself. "Look," he said to me, "We must get all the other men together and tell them that they can be saved." He shamed me into it. Each Sunday we had a squash in my room. I had learned from Bergin and Short that a very informal approach, with a firm Christian testimony, followed by questions and a very definite challenge at the end, could have a real impact. It was amazing how popular our attempt became. Many asked to be allowed to come, often we pressed men to come and all but a very few in the hall came at one time or other in that term. With great difficulty we persuaded two of the most outspoken agnostics in the college to attend – on their condition that they could argue and say what they liked. Near the close of the evening, one of them suddenly said, "If what you have been saying is true, then what must I do to be saved?" Later that evening he made a profession of Christ.'

In the city of Liverpool there was still evidence of its strong evangelical tradition from the days of Bishop Ryle. The appeal of modernism had not gone unchallenged and there were pockets of resistance in the churches. Also the para-church movement, National Young Life Campaign (NYLC), was strong. Evangelicals tended to regroup through such fellowships. It might therefore have been expected that the Liverpool CU would have emerged through local initiative. In fact the moves that set it on foot came from an ex-CICCU man who was doing further study at the Liverpool School of Tropical Medicine.

Once identifiable, the CU soon gained from the evangelical life of the area. Eric Richardson, who had been converted after just one visit to the Bible study meeting in Wallasey, was a mature twenty-three when he and his brother went up to Liverpool University together in 1928. It was his brother who first discovered the CU and, as Andrew introduced Simon Peter, so he brought Eric to see what he had found. Already keen members of NYLC, they found the CU met their needs. In its turn the CU gained an outstanding new leader and in later years the technical colleges nationwide found a vigorous champion of evangelical witness in Sir Eric, the future Principal of London's Regent Street Polytechnic.

While University College, London, and Bristol and Liverpool were getting going, Cambridge, under strong and incisive leadership, had not only seen growth from fifteen to over 100 in the four years after the war (thirty-five of whom went to the mission field), it had also firmly sorted out the matter of where it stood theologically in relation to the religious mind-set of the age. They were Bible people and gospel people and unashamedly so. Their position gave them great strength in proclaiming the truth and in producing a desire for godly living.

When Leslie Lyall went up to Emmanuel in 1924 he saw around him people who were, and continued to be, spiritual giants. One was Joe Church who, on sailing for Ruanda, became CICCU's 'own' missionary. 'Could we ever know', he wrote later, 'how much those prayers and the caring of generations of students during the following thirty-seven years meant in the outpouring of the Holy Spirit in Ruanda and Uganda?' Then there were L. F. E. Wilkinson, R. E. D. Clark, C. B. E. Harrison, Evan Hopkins, Max Warren, Arthur Casson, E. J. H. Nash ('Bash'), Hugh Gough and more. The daily prayer meetings in Henry Martyn Hall were well attended, the Sunday evangelistic meetings were full. Harold Earnshaw Smith, a college chaplain for a while and a much-used speaker among evangelical students, was 'unofficial' chaplain to the CICCU. Market Square was the scene of well-supported open-air meetings 'where I actually sang solos,' says Lyall. 'But I was terribly immature as a Christian in every possible way. A "quiet time" was always a problem with me and real intellectual issues never troubled me because I never gave them a thought. I didn't work very hard and I was a late developer in every way. Sport took too much of my time at Cambridge. I was in the hockey side that won the inter-college cup three years running, and captain during the final year. I went on a Kent and Sussex cricket tour and was president of a lighthearted cricket club for college athletes called "The Pagans". I sought to do all that was required of me as a CU man and became co-representative of Emmanuel with J. B. Phillips, the Bible translator. I attended an Inter-Varsity conference in the Church Army headquarters in London whence Wilson Carlile, head of the Church Army, used to lead us up to Hyde Park to teach us the art of open-air preaching. I attended the CSSM[2] camp under Clarence Foster and the CICCU camp at Keswick. So there were influences for good upon me that challenged my spiritual immaturity.'

There were also those about him whose later lives warned that collapse could be real if foundations were false. L. S. B. Leakey, the renowned anthropologist, was a CICCU member. Lyall's own school friend experienced a total spiritual collapse when CICCU president. But Hugh Gough stepped into the breach and was a wise and strong president. Lyall himself, though a self-confessed late developer, has stayed the race and run well, finishing what he claims is his last book, *God Reigns in China*, in his eightieth year. He was one of sixteen members of his day who went to the mission field. His call to the work was clear and he offered for CIM, sailing at the age of twenty-three for China.

Undoubtedly the most eventful occasion in the CICCU of those years was the mission led by the Irish evangelist Willie Nicholson. Lyall calls it sensational, and recalls how thrilling it was to see people being converted in more than twos and threes. In 1926, the years of the mission, CICCU was about 200 strong. Oliver Barclay in *Whatever Happened to the Jesus Lane Lot?* tells the story with great zest. The CICCU had a problem in this generation. Where were the evangelists who were both sound and suitable for a university audience? 'Willie Nick' was certainly sound about sin and salvation. But was this rough-and-ready Irishman suitable? The controversy raged both during and after the meetings. Some were saved. But

[2]The Children's Special Service Mission, now Scripture Union.

some were also scandalized. Some left the CICCU. But when the dust had settled, the stumbling-block was still seen to be what it had ever been – not the kind of man he was, but the nature of the message he preached. When, a generation later, God raised up speakers with all the polish and intellectual gifts necessary to be suitable to a university audience, the same antagonism to the message would still be apparent.

One of the books used by that new generation of gifted student evangelists in the 1950s and later was Norman Anderson's *The Evidence for the Resurrection*. A year after the Nicholson mission the future author and scholar began his undergraduate days at Trinity, Cambridge. 'When I went up I was a lazy Christian and something of a dilettante,' says Sir Norman. 'Next year I woke up.' In a quick summary of his ensuing years at Cambridge he says, 'They meant an enormous amount to me. The CICCU sermons set my standard for the content of the gospel for life and the missionary challenge changed the whole course of my life. I remember when I was president leading a small team of men to the (now) University of Reading. There was much blessing on that visit. We had a number of blues in the team as well as people who did well in the tripos. I especially remember small conferences in the vacations and particularly the contributions of C. B. E. Harrison.'

Norman Anderson, destined for a distinguished academic career, seemed to have no difficulty in gaining first-class degrees. But his description of his response on hearing that his was the only 'first' in Part 1 of the Law tripos shows how soon he became a wholehearted servant of Christ. In his autobiography *An Adopted Son* he recalls the moment when he heard the news. 'I remember walking round and round the garden with the words of a hymn ringing in my ear:

> And for thy sake to win renown
> And then to take the victor's crown
> And at thy feet to lay it down
> O Master, Lord, I come.'

He left Cambridge and went as a missionary to Egypt, returning to a very distinguished academic career after the war.

Now what of Oxford? The Oxford Inter-Collegiate Christian Union (OICCU) had a very chequered history after those great days under Noel Palmer. Yet again it lost its separate identity as an evangelical body. It was regained in 1928. And it came at exactly the right time in the history of the national movement, for it helped towards the fulfilment of the 'much better thing' that this chapter is heading for. OICCU's rebirth owed much to a young freshman at Oriel called Freddie Crittenden. He was instrumental in getting eighteen others to get the work going again. Their chief concern was 'God's honour in the university'. A meeting at the Town Hall was prayerfully planned. Its issue was decisive. Three members of the CICCU were invited to speak on 'What Christ Means to Me'. Large 6ft by 3ft posters in dark and light blue were put up all over Oxford. The hall was packed to the doors, the interruptions that had been feared were absent and a hushed audience gave ear to the three Cambridge students led by Kenneth Hooker. One of the other members of the team had come to Christ at the Nicholson mission two years before.

After the crowds had left, the small band of OICCU members counted the retiring collection they had ventured to take up. Expenses were formidable and they had prayed that they would be covered. There was ten shillings above the amount they were committed to pay. But just then the treasurer came in and reported he had given one of the town hall staff a ten-shilling tip! 'No-one present', said Freddie Crittenden, 'could believe that this exact figure in the collection was just a coincidence.'

So the OICCU was relaunched. A renewed confidence in God pervaded the crowded daily prayer meetings. More conversions were constantly reported, especially following the OICCU sermon each weekend. Twice the OICCU had learned by painful experience the consequences of failure to stand firm to its biblical calling. But it was not to repeat the mistake. It quickly became a robustly evangelical work again.

The stimulus of the vigorous delegates sent by OICCU to the 1928 Inter-Varsity conference at High Leigh was one of the decisive factors that turned it into a watershed. That gathering of CUs from all parts of Britain proved historic. It was plain to see that what was emerging was a spontaneous and renewed vision for biblical evangelism and fellowship among students in the older and the newer universities of the four home countries. LIFCU had been going from strength to strength under dynamic leadership. OICCU arrived on a wave of resolution. In 1927 Hugh Gough had completed two outstanding years as CICCU president and was now following this up with a twelve-month tour of the CUs. He had helped in the initial stages of some new ones, such as Manchester. Gough took a series of five evangelistic meetings in Cardiff, where the Evangelical Union had been a going concern for four years and was already sending regular contingents to High Leigh. During the year St Andrews, Scotland's oldest university, got its own CU going after eight students had travelled down to High Leigh in 1927, eager to find out what was happening elsewhere. They were stirred to the depths when they heard there of the solitary efforts of John Rollo, a former St Andrews man, who had been impeded, mocked and even locked up for a while by fellow students! They were fired to go back and see the matter through. Just before the 1928 conference Scotland had had its most heartening series of meetings since the huge turnouts of Edinburgh students to hear C. T. Studd and Stanley Smith in 1882. From 13 to 17 February 1928 Bishop Taylor Smith preached on five occasions to Glasgow students in the Union Debating Hall. On the last evening there were over 500 present. Taylor Smith was also a regular main speaker at High Leigh. Strong binding factors were at work, drawing people of evangelical faith and evangelistic fervour together. The time was ripe.

The moment of truth that probably settled the minds of many about the need for a new inter-universities fellowship had come some months prior to the conference when a few LIFCU members had met with the SCM General Secretary. There are parallels with Norman Grubb's experience in 1919 when discussing the CICCU's position. The SCM General Secretary made it plain that all schools of thought were welcome on equal terms and that the evangelical position was now irreversibly outmoded. On the pivotal points of authority and atonement he could not have been clearer. 'The doctrine of the verbal inspiration of the Scriptures is as dead as Queen Anne.' 'No theologian worth the name accepts the penal view of the atonement.' It was a candid acknowledgment that the SCM had moved from what once had been considered scriptural orthodoxy.

In fact, of course, the heyday of liberalism had arrived, and it had itself become the new orthodoxy. It was not the truth only that was at stake. It was abundantly clear that there was the need not only to proclaim the gospel, but also to defend it, and, as much to the point, to defend students in training for the ministry who felt they had their backs to the wall. There was a crying need to give some form of encouragement and support to ministerial students who were in a lions' den of criticism. Young evangelical theological students were under immense pressure to conform to the current consensus, and few during these inter-war years maintained their evangelical distinctiveness.

One who did, and who has lived to see the stand of his own church become more biblical again, is John T. Carson, a future Moderator of the Presbyterian Church of Ireland and a secretary of its historical society. He recalls how lonely a business it was sixty long years ago. He went up to Queen's University, Belfast, in 1927. His church's liberal stance on the authority of Scripture and the deity of Christ was evident from the way a Presbyterian professor of marked liberal views had been exonerated from error in 1928. 'With this background it was scarcely respectable for Presbyterian students to exclude themselves from SCM, which shared that liberal stance. That was the attitude when I went up and I felt it,' says Dr Carson. 'As a consequence there was little or no support for our Bible Union, especially from theological quarters, though our numbers were swelled from converts from the Nicholson missions. Our members were mainly medics and later converted sportsmen.'

There were therefore positive and defensive reasons for the decision of 1928. The growing feeling among CUs around the country was that evangelicals, though they were devoid of theological and official support, had no choice but to go forward independently on a frankly Bible-based platform. It was time to give more structural shape to the 'much better thing' that was already coming into being. Those present at High Leigh could see that the existing spiritual links between the CUs should be recognized in a more identifiable way. So, in the spring of 1928, led by their first chairman, Hugh Gough, the conference delegates from four Scots, three Irish, one Welsh and eight English CUs constituted themselves the Inter-Varsity Fellowship of Evangelical Unions.

Keen, dedicated and conscious of their biblical roots though they were, we must not forget that any religious authorities who might have noticed them would have regarded them as an irrelevant rump from bygone days. Our tribute to them sixty years on reminds us that the Lord of the years has, time after time, used a day of small things to begin again to restore the honour of his name.

It was six months later. On 5 October 1928, Alan Stibbs, one of the CICCU graduates involved in this evangelical students' resistance movement, boarded a ship bound for China. When he got to the Red Sea he posted a letter to the editor of an evangelical magazine in Wales alert to the significance of the founding of IVF. In it Stibbs reveals the intellectual and spiritual toughness that enabled him later to take on the all-pervading modernism of the day and help the young IVF to redevelop a Bible-believing scholarship. He was perhaps the very first young theologian to write in this way and his words capture as well as any what lay at the root of that 1928 conference:

'At Cambridge God allowed me to prove that his Word is trustworthy. I was led, quite unexpectedly, to read modern theology, only to be told by some that there was no place in the ranks of theological scholarship for those who would not accept modern critical theories with regard to the Bible. But I was led by God to the three men, to whom Nebuchadnezzar said that there was no place in his kingdom for any who would not bow to his image. And the same God, who kept them in Babylon, kept me in Cambridge. I learnt, from experience in the place of trial, that God's Word is to be trusted, rather than men's.'

In the month Stibbs sailed for China, a young Scot, F. F. Bruce, began his student days at Aberdeen. Years later they were to be involved, together with a growing number of others (there were certainly more than three!) in a revival of scholarship that had come through the academic Babylonian furnace and still believed that God's Word is to be trusted.

Chapter Four

GOD ON THE MOVE

Here, then, is a young movement, launched like a ship, with a new name, but with only a voluntary crew. It possessed nothing but its commitment to preach Christ and to be obedient to his Word. At the end of that High Leigh conference the small IVF executive committee were all students within eight weeks of finals or stiff exams. The big decision was behind them. It would not be long before they went for their trains, hoping for a clear run of exam preparation. Those were their hopes.

They had not bargained for Norman Grubb. He had just made the end of the conference, hot-foot from a tour of the Canadian universities, and he asked to see them urgently. At the very moment when his vision of 1919 had reached its clear fulfilment, he came with another one.

His appeal to the committee was this: 'We are now debtors to Canada. In only one Canadian university have I discovered a CU standing for the Word of God and atonement through the blood of Jesus. I believe God wants CUs on these lines in all the universities of the world. This should be the missionary outlook of the IVF. May it not be that God is now calling us to take the first step by entering the open door to Canada? A man of faith is needed for this opportunity.'

Those exam-conscious young students saw it 'as a definite challenge from God'. Who was it to be?

The executive committee invited Hugh Gough as their chairman to represent them in Canada. His bishop declined to release him. But Grubb's call was not to be gainsaid. It was as if the Holy Spirit had said, 'Separate out for me a person for

41

the work I have called him to do.' That person was already prepared.

Living in London at the same address as Douglas Johnson, 49 Highbury Park, the hostel of the Medical Missionary Association, was Howard Guinness, LIFCU president from 1926 to 1928. He was a highly motivated and extravert personality. He also had a passion to see people won for Christ. There is simply no other way of describing it. He would witness just where he was – to passengers on a bus, to members of the rugby team on the way to or from a match. He was fly-half and captain of the Bart's Hospital rugby team at a time when it contained several Christians, Bill Capper, a future senior leader of IVF, among them.

Guinness had the approach to life of a cavalry charge officer. He rode, not a horse, but a big motorbike with sandwich boards tied to the carrier. Doubtless this was one of his wilder student ideas, but few will forget the sight of his ride into Bart's, bike festooned with the text 'Prepare to meet thy God'. His life was all risk, attack, venture, daring. When he shared a meeting with other speakers he came over as the fast attack, the shock bowler. But he loved people, and his warm-heartedness came through. After public-schoolboys' camps he would write fortnightly letters of encouragement to some of the boys, such as A. J. (Jim) Broomhall and C. G. Scorer, both subsequent IVF student leaders. There was a love of music too. 'Howard at the piano was, for me, unique,' writes Jim Broomhall. 'His self-taught playing favoured thumb action, with the general effect of accentuation of the lower octaves where the melody appeared, while his right hand supplied harmony and air as necessary. I loved it.'

> Mine are the hands to do the work,
> My feet shall run for thee.
> My lips shall sound the glorious news.
> Lord, here am I, send me.

He did more than play and sing the chorus. Just qualified as a doctor in 1928, and with a saintly mother who prayed much about his future, he it was who donned the mantle of pioneer. Grubb's 'man of faith' was ready to go. Nothing less than the future work of the International Fellowship of Evangelical Students (IFES) was on the anvil. An enormous fur-collared overcoat was given him by Grubb; he could expect snow! The students gave him a pocketful of money, the princely sum of £14 scratched together from the sale of hockey sticks and the like. And the ticket to Canada, one way only, was paid for by Rendle Short. Howard exchanged his motorbike for an Atlantic liner, and medicine for a lifetime of preaching Christ.

He left on a bitter October morning on a small Cunarder from Liverpool to Montreal. 'The Atlantic Ocean is not to be recommended in a 13,000-ton boat,' he wrote in his diary. 'Two days out we ran into storms and I spent the following week mainly in my cabin. We disembarked on 4 November 1928 in Montreal.'

His intention to return in time for the next series of 'house jobs' at Bart's Hospital in March never materialized. That one-way ticket to Canada stretched and stretched – after Canada, Australia; after Australia, New Zealand; and then Canada again before turning for home after more than two years of rewarding and exhausting service. 'My feet shall run for thee.'

In the early morning of a foggy January day in 1931, Leigh Ashton and Douglas Johnson (by then medically qualified and both housemen at the Bristol General Hospital) awaited his return. They stood on the wooden pier projecting beyond the end of the main Cunard Line quay, listening to the deep foghorn of the *Berengaria* slowly coming up Southampton Water. At length, the ship's light lit up the fog and the bows suddenly appeared out of the mist. The tugs pulled her round rather fast and she hit the bumpers, slaking those waiting with an icy morning shower before easing off. Eventually a very tired Howard Guinness came down the gangway and the two friends saw him into a corner seat of the London boat train at the harbour station. He was utterly weary, but happily sure that in those last two years he had obeyed God's call. He was soon to be back in harness in the UK and Europe. LIFCU, especially, had missed his leadership.

However, in 1929, up to London to study medicine came Jim Broomhall, one of the schoolboys Guinness had helped on in the faith. They were later to be involved in a university mission that marked LIFCU's next great step forward.

In his early years in London Broomhall was to see at first hand something of the backroom work of that unobtrusive beaver, Douglas Johnson. Broomhall had first met him in 1925 at the age of thirteen when he had come back for schooling from China. 'A day or two after coming ashore I was taken to

"49". I found Howard and D.J. playing "tennis" of a sort on the "lawn". D.J. was still a student at No. 49 when I moved into the same hostel as a fresher and he took me up. I helped or hindered him in his little bedroom study when he was preparing mountains of envelopes and sending out the conference papers for High Leigh. Bed, table and floor were strewn with row upon row of addressed envelopes. They would get stuffed into the local postbox at eleven o'clock at night or later.' Johnson may have been an English graduate, but he was to give the phrase 'man of letters' a twist of his own!

By this time he was studying medicine, but the way he was caught up in the growth of IVF was turning a task into a hazard. He always seemed to be at the point where growth produced more work. The way the Guinness tour developed meant that the secretarial work took on the new dimension of the overseas vision. Not that Johnson harboured thoughts of anything grand. When the Canadian proposal had first come up it had seemed to him that it was as likely that students such as they could launch an international mission as that they could launch a Viking raid on North America. After all, Guinness had gone with only pocket money. But the more he considered his task the more Guinness knew that he had to scrap his timetable. 'What did a few months setback for my own medical career count beside the evangelization of the world in this generation, to which the completion of my job here would give such an impetus? . . . I found a great urge within me saying, "Stay until the job is finished." ' So, as Howard ventured on and referred back, the little committee at home found themselves increasingly involved in novel decisions relating to worlds across the sea that none of them knew. But financial support started to come from faraway places and Johnson found himself acting as an embryo missionary society.

At home the official launching of IVF in 1928 meant that Johnson, as student honorary secretary, was now increasingly sought after as new CUs got under way: Swansea, Sheffield (where he linked with a local stalwart minister, Joe Bryce), Birmingham. After some Birmingham students attended the 1929 conference they invited him to help them launch a CU. By 1930 he confessed to being dog-tired, bemused by the variety and extent of the calls upon his time and deep into the first part of his final exams. He failed in obstetrics. Professor Rendle Short heard the news from Johnson himself. 'Young man, you'll never qualify if you don't ease off. I'll arrange with your Dean that you come down to Bristol. That should cut off your CU contacts till finals. Just work. No Christian involvements except on Sundays.'

So it turned out that Johnson left London for a tolerable life at Bristol, qualified, and then found himself torn between various calls. Turning down two highly attractive professional prospects which opened up at the time, he had to decide whether to take tropical training for going overseas as a medical missionary, or to settle as IVF secretary. He tried to get a number of those with secretarial gifts to take on the student work, without success. 'It would ruin our careers,' was the general reaction.

But what of his own career? It was the natural expectation of friends and family that he would remain in medicine, for which he had long prepared. While he weighed up this sense of obligation on the one hand, and on the other the challenge to faith that the young student work presented, along came the pioneering opportunity at the Landsdowne Place Medical Mission in South London. Barely a few months after he launched out on this venture, which enabled him to keep body and soul together, he was persuaded by those interested to accept the newly created part-time post of General Secretary of the IVF, a role he had virtually already created by the volume of work he had done.

Soon the overwork pattern repeated itself, only more so. His crisis we have described in chapter 1. Even as the work escalated, Johnson had a pointer that IVF would be his future work. A suitable one-room office in a prime London square suddenly materialized.[1] It was somewhere about this time, too, that Rendle Short's decisive judgment helped resolve the tensions, which were added to by the fact that Johnson still felt himself under obligation to Rhodesia. The professor had come up to London to speak at the King's College CU. Johnson accompanied him to Paddington to catch the fast train to Bristol. Putting his head out of the window the professor said, 'give up the idea of Africa. Take to IVF and send someone better to Rhodesia.' He knew his man. Johnson was well able to accept that someone better than he could be found to go to

[1] See D. Johnson, *Contending for the Faith*, pp. 161–162, for the full story.

Africa! A substitute for Rhodesia was found, and a successor too for the Landsdowne, which eventually became a three-man Christian practice.

During the days of his Medical Mission commitment Johnson was writing long letters to Norway. His avid reading of historical and theological matters led to astute judgments. He seemed to see over the heads of his fellows, making decisions that really mattered. For example, he contrived to organize a visit to the 1934 IVF conference of the elder statesman of world evangelical mission – Dr Robert Wilder, now retired in Norway. At a stroke it linked the old evangelical movement of the nineteenth century with the new, and it further linked new initiatives in the old world and the new. A pioneer of the Student Volunteer Movement of the 1880s, Wilder had to his great grief watched that evangelistic passion die away. When he resigned as General Secretary of the SVM in 1927 he lamented that it had everywhere lost its original commission, which he saw as 'the spreading of the message of Christ's atoning death and his offer of salvation, together with his call for labourers to go to the uttermost parts of the earth'. He was not to hear of the IVF for some years until he was shown a copy of the *Inter-Varsity Magazine* in Egypt. It persuaded him that God was raising up the same standard in new hearts. That conviction enabled Johnson to persuade him out of retirement to travel to High Leigh.

Every word of his brief but telling addresses was heard in concentrated silence. People began to appreciate something of his first impact on the British scene in 1891. Students surrounded him. Many never forgot their brief conversation with him. He was asked to return for a tour of British universities in 1935 and nobly promised to come. In the marathon of witness the torch belongs to young and old. Young Guinness and elderly Wilder, each in his own world, showed that Jesus Christ is the same, yesterday, today and for ever.

The same continuity is seen in the couple Wilder brought with him. Carl (later Professor) Wisloff was engaged to Wilder's niece. On the way to London after the conference, Johnson was showing them around Oxford. 'While we were at lunch in the Cadena Cafe, Carl said, "Our two post-war movements were born at about the same time and we are of the same spirit. I am going to get our committee to invite six of you to come over and make an alliance between Britain and

Norway." ' In less than six months the alliance was forged. The International Fellowship of Evangelical Students was fore-shadowed.

Back in London, Johnson had arranged for a small band of student leaders to meet Wilder. They met at the CIM head-quarters where the IVF chairman, Arnold Aldis, was staying. Aldis tells of the great air of expectancy with which he climbed the stairs to hear Wilder's message. He remembers the text: 'A great door for effective work has opened to me, and there are many who oppose me' (1 Corinthians 16:9). 'Most men', said Wilder, 'would have said "But"; Paul says "And". Opposition to biblical truth must be seen as an opportunity to work.' Johnson took him at his word. There and then they worked out an itinerary for the following year.

There was opposition and opportunity everywhere. Two effects of opposition are that you look round for allies, and you look to your defences. First, allies. The European alliance put fresh heart into the IVF. For the next few years continental forays were very popular. The first came in September 1934 to Oslo. Johnson primed each party on what to expect and how to react. 'To travel with D. J. was an experience,' recalls Aldis. 'He was a voracious reader and could brief you on the country and sometimes knew more about the evangelical heritage and present scene than the locals. He knew the mistakes to be avoided.' Not everyone had the same sure touch. 'Lord, take these Finns and turn them into Finneys' (a famous nineteenth-century American evangelist), prayed someone in Helsinki in the hearing of the very serious locals, who already thought these English were too hearty and assured in their approach to the faith. When Aldis went through customs he had felt anything but assured. He was beckoned aside by an official and bidden by signs to sit down; the door was barred by two soldiers who stopped him leaving. When their interpreter eventually arrived, things were sorted out. The very red cover of Guinness' IVF book *Sacrifice* had been seen at the top of his bag. He had been suspected of bringing in unwelcome Communist literature! Even interpretation itself could sometimes be a problem, for, in one country, their talks were theologically reinterpreted! And it was a disappointment, too, for Guinness and three British graduates when their visit to Karl Barth at his home left them all floundering for the want of an interpreter.

But all the contacts through conferences did the work as a

whole the world of good, especially links with the strong Norwegian work led so powerfully by Professor Hallesby.

Though members had found pockets of allies abroad, IVF still found itself a tiny minority at home. A small work inevitably gets pushed on to the defensive and it is hard to see that the tide will turn. One of the sad things Wilder had witnessed in the wider student world was the wholesale collapse of nerve among evangelical students as the tide of liberal churchmanship and secularist advance had swirled about them. There were some CU groups that were very small indeed, and Aldis saw the LIFCU in his day as a kind of survival mechanism for Christians under pressure. This is where real leadership sometimes emerged and a good defence was made the base for later advance. For example, in Royal Holloway College the small CU was under pressure from the big SCM group to amalgamate with it. Dorothy James (later Mrs Douglas Johnson) went to the SCM committee and explained exactly why such a small bunch felt it essential to maintain a Bible-based and gospel-centred CU. More than half a century later, her son, Professor Alan Johnson, was the main speaker at a well-attended conference at Royal Holloway College. The position had been held and the tide had turned. At a similar time plans were afoot at the London Hospital to abandon the CU and the SCM and put in its place a kind of uncommitted discussion forum. Jim Broomhall felt obliged to say that whatever others did, he would be the CU at the London.

There were many Valiants for Truth of like resolution in the thirties. Some of them were to be instruments in the hand of God in taking up Robert Wilder's goals of worldwide student mission once more. We shall now take a look at a few at Oxford and Liverpool.

Chapter Five

FASHIONED FOR THE FUTURE

'I wouldn't go to Oxford, if I were you. The dangers of becoming "unsound" are so much greater than at Cambridge.' That kind of advice was heard often enough when six-formers gathered at Christian summer camps. It was a risky business to go to Oxford. The OICCU had, after all, folded up once or twice. So students tended to opt for Cambridge.

But some thought this betrayed a lack of faith in the Lord's power to keep. So they deliberately chose Oxford. Future headmaster, Tim Brown, for example. His Christian 'nursery' was the Varsity and Public School Scottish camps and the CU at Merchant Taylors' School. When he went up in 1933 he was quickly roped in by a small but strong CU group at St Edmund Hall, led by the captain of boats. Also converted at VPS camp in the Highlands (in 1932) was Tony Wilmot. He threw in his lot with OICCU and found in Tim a rock of stability. A third freshman, David Bentley-Taylor, had never heard of such things as VPS camps, CUs or evangelicals. He turned up at Oxford after living for a year with a Roman Catholic family near Vienna, immersed in the German language. But then God intervened. Through the eyes of David, Tim and Tony we shall watch some of the ways God forged and fashioned future servants in the Oxford of the mid-thirties.

David's roots lay in the soil of polished English paganism. He was very much at home fox-hunting, on the tennis court, playing contract bridge, at race meetings, on the dance floor, the cricket field and the golf course. But his study of Schiller in Austria had somehow given him an undefined longing. By the autumn of 1933 he was a seeker after something – no more tangible than that. Schiller's line, 'I am my own heaven and my own hell', had left in him a sense of the mystery of life – a void unfulfilled by the ample provisions of a privileged existence.

This, plus the sheer boredom of Oxford's first few days of term, which he spent reading poetry, made him look around for something else. On the Sunday he turned in to St Aldate's. Not one word caught his ear. But on the way out his eye was caught by some pamphlets advertising a Monday meeting in the church. 'What could they possibly do in a church on a Monday?' he thought. He went to find out, very much in the same way as he would have gone to a theatre. The preacher was the same, Bryan Green. Tim Brown was there too and was aware that God used the preacher that night. At the start of the meeting Green called those at the back to come and sit at the front. David went to the very front pew. The preacher then left the pulpit and spoke right next to him as he sat at the end of the row. He was born again through that message. He had no previous knowledge of the gospel whatever.

It was not an OICCU meeting, but Green told him about it. David discovered that there was only one OICCU student – Gerald Scott – at his college. He was away ill. So he fell in with the SCM and within a week was asked to lead a group on comparative religion. He was clueless. What could he do? He bought the first book he found. The gist of his talk was that 'what Confucius says negatively, Christ says positively'. Sitting there listening to him was the OICCU representative, Gerald Scott. On his return that day he had been told about David's conversion and that 'he's speaking at SCM tonight'. Scott took him to tea and gradually, like Apollos, the young undergraduate had the way of God explained to him more adequately. He was born to, and quickly grew into, leadership.

'David's zeal and enthusiasm for his new-found faith, and his own lively personality, certainly were not long in making their mark in OICCU,' says Tim. 'Early on he needed the steadying influence of mature Christians such as Laurie Woolmer (later Bishop of Lahore). But few can have grown so quickly in Christ, and his bright manner and infectious good humour, complemented by humble faith and burning zeal, made his presidency memorable, so much so that getting on for fifty years later fourteen of our vintage still unite through an annual praise and prayer letter.'

How does someone progress from colourful pagan to OICCU president? The stages in that story point up the personal fostering in the faith that the OICCU offered. The OICCU people thrilled him. He warmed to them. Their freedom from time-wasting and the current 'ballroom mentality' challenged his tendency to trivialize.

But one of the steps into normal Christian life seemed a giant one. When Scott told him that they had a prayer meeting every day he nearly expired. To him a prayer meeting was the last thing on earth he would want to attend. But he went. Daily attendance at the central prayer meeting was expected of everyone and the response was good. As he heard others pray, he thought, 'They must be using a book.' With a peep of curiosity the truth sank in. Their words came from the heart, just as his friend had said. This was a crisis for him. Gerald continued to nudge him along in his quiet, gentle way. 'You haven't prayed aloud yet.' He needed that push to get launched. On paper he put down a sentence or two of simple prayer and at the next opportunity 'did his bit'. His sails filled and he was away. Gerald was not really his type – not at all sporting and much more scholarly. But his discipleship was the quiet winning kind that involved the discipling of others. There was nothing prepackaged about it. Years later, in Java, Dr Rupert Clarke, a tough pioneer who sailed for the Far East on the same boat as David, testified that Scott had had the same sort of influence on him when they were at school together.

From early days David read Alford's Greek Testament. OICCU students of this period strongly motivated one another to get proficient in New Testament study. Tony Wilmot valued this reinforcement of his habit, acquired since his conversion, of getting up early enough to have what he calls 'a real feed on the Bible. By the grace of God no day has passed, as far as my memory goes, from my conversion till today, without my reading something from God's Word.' Happy the student group that gives such wholesome discipline to each other. Soon David had a two-hour study time before breakfast devoted entirely to prayer and Bible study. He carried around a small zip-fastener Bible in his hip pocket and would whip it out like a revolver. He took it everywhere and would read it on buses and trains. This appetite for Scripture led him to turn to theology for his degree. But he went into it blind, little knowing

51

that the course was almost exclusively literary criticism of the 'how and when the books were written and by whom' kind. He grew to deplore the impersonal nature of it. During the disappointments of the theology course, OICCU daily prayer meetings and the fellowship preserved him from spiritual dryness and helped him to hold firm. Reading authors such as James Orr was an additional anchor.

Solitary energies put into personal devotions need translating into service to others. Tim Brown was for a while the OICCU organizer of local activities, responsible for finding speakers for a number of Sunday schools and struggling missions on the outskirts. The experience of being an officer at an evangelistic summer camp for schoolboys helped students gain more than they gave. 'It was the camps that really made the difference in me,' says Bentley-Taylor. He was soon taken to meet 'Bash' (E. J. H. Nash). In the first five minutes he realized, 'This is the man who will help me.' Bash's limpid simplicity seemed geared to his needs and he went on nine camps.

At camp and OICCU there was a lot of stress on witness to one's peers and prayer for their conversion. But when this tended to be linked to a strongly negative view of relationships with non-Christians and few positive guidelines on how to remain in touch, it could leave Christians on a bit of an island. There was little fruit in these years, partly because there was so little real contact. The OICCU on one occasion prayed for forty conversions, but no-one was saved. At these meetings the students had done most of the speaking themselves. On another occasion they had a great concern for the Indians in the university. So they invited them all to hear Howard Guinness, just back from India. Not a single Indian came. So they prayed and ate the food.

One of their problems was that they tended to be a bit 'stiff' in going about things like this. Guinness, who undoubtedly had an exceptional gift for getting through to people, was looked on as a pattern for everybody. He used to stress that no-one should let the sun set without talking to a lost sinner. So David would find that as he got to the end of a day he would try to get hold of someone to talk to. It produced a tenseness and people began to avoid them. So despite a genuineness of dedication, the lifestyle and the approach could hinder rather than help. Sometimes intensity was confused for spirituality. But young Christians were helped in their faith and many were prepared for useful service in later and different days.

The next big question that filled the minds of this generation of students was precisely that: What does God want me to do in the future? In IVF at the time the major question was: Are you willing to go overseas? Why not? If you saw six people carrying a log, five at one end and one at the other, which end would you go and help? The logic was compelling. The OICCU missionary breakfasts conveyed this challenge consistently and it was a stimulus that David Bentley-Taylor enjoyed. At 'Bash camp' he devoured a copy of Hudson Taylor's biography, sold to him by John Wenham, who ran the bookstall. Thinking about 'overseas' was not strange to David. He had spent a long time abroad and his mother had an international outlook; her father had been Vice-chairman of the Suez Canal Board. So there was a congenial spirit in him.

But there was the matter of the 'call'. It was usually conveyed as a dramatic thing, probably because it had certainly been that for the great Hudson Taylor. But the exceptional had been made the expected. He read of Hudson Taylor lying on the floor, hearing a voice calling him to China. So he prostrated himself in similar manner. There was no voice. Did that mean that there was no call? He prayed about China for years, waiting for the dramatic moment that was the expected pointer. Eventually he decided – why not go ahead and apply? He failed his medical. CIM asked for another opinion. A Harley Street specialist reversed the decision with great alacrity. Surely, he thought, this was the sign he needed. He went on CIM's twelve-month training course and at twenty-three years of age he sailed for China. It was 1938.

Tony Wilmot also went overseas in 1938, but in a different direction – Africa, and in the colonial service. It led to a life of evangelistic fruitfulness, especially in the student world, that has helped give African Christianity a strong core of evangelical leaders. Is it more than coincidence that, in the years of Robert Wilder's final work for Christ in the United Kingdom, when so much prayer was made that God would restore lost priorities, David and Tony, two of God's most dynamic servants in the sphere of international evangelical student witness, were being awakened to their future callings?

Looking back on OICCU days Tony picks out the time when honest rebuke from Tim Brown pulled him down from a dangerous 'high' and helped to prepare him for better things.

Grace flowed from the wise wounds of a friend. That is how he sees it in retrospect. The incident brings to light the turmoil into which many were flung in the years between the wars over what to make of various teachings on Christian perfection and the work of the Spirit. His story is of a time in May 1935. 'A man met some of the OICCU exec. – but not me – and told them about the work of the Holy Spirit. I got the notion that God would fill me with the Holy Spirit "on demand" and unconditionally. It was supposed to be by faith. And then I presumed I had it. I got horribly bold and probably put a number of people off the gospel in the next few days. After one OICCU meeting Tim Brown took me for a walk and for an hour told me what an obnoxiously proud and self-assertive person I was. He left me outside Teddy (St Edmund) Hall to go back to his digs. I recall his last words: "What will you do now?", to which I answered, "Pray." '

'He didn't know that my prayer would be for God to bring comfort to my damaged ego. God did not give me what I asked. Every Bible passage I looked at convicted me horribly. I prayed on my knees until I collapsed with weariness, pressed beyond measure. On Monday, at the door of my tutor's house, waiting to be admitted, something happened. The words 'Not I, but Christ' hit me. It seemed both a revelation from God and a prayer forced from the bottom of my heart. I suddenly knew that I had the sentence of death in myself that I should no longer put any confidence in myself, but in him who delivered, does deliver and would go on delivering in resurrection power. I am not the person to judge the results. (No-one in the Bible ever claimed to be filled with the Holy Spirit – it is always the testimony of a third party, not of those who were filled.) All I know is that I had dismally failed to become perfect! But I knew a new peace and things were different.'

During his time at Oxford he found himself more and more drawn to work overseas. Gradually he set his sights on taking the gospel to areas of the world where unsympathetic influences prevented the entry of full-time Christian workers. A post-graduate course in colonial administration helped to open that door. In Africa he started, at Douglas Johnson's request, a prayer fellowship of IVF graduates in secular service abroad, from which seed grew the great tree of African Christian student witness.

From the Liverpool CU of the thirties two men emerged who were not only leaders exceptional among their contemporaries. They also were being fashioned by God for life-long ministry to the student world. The first, Eric Richardson, we have already met. Leith Samuel came up later.

'It was thought almost improper for a president to come from those awful engineers!' says Sir Eric. But his presidency of the CU lasted from 1930 to 1932. His leadership showed, first, courage. At one stage the Free Thinkers Society were intent on ridiculing the CU out of existence and challenged them to debate. 'This we resisted for a long time because we thought it would be undignified and we were fearful to face their intellectual superiority. In the end, as it led to the taunt that we could not substantiate our case, we agreed. They began with all guns blazing, but there was more noise than scholarly substance and it became a walkover for the CU.'

Secondly, he took a strong, clear-thinking line in defence of the CU over the confusing influence of the Oxford Group, later called Moral Rearmament. It was confusing partly because the Group had seemed evangelical enough to some early IVF people, especially at Oxford, when first launched by Frank Buchman, but it was now shifting a good deal further from a biblical stance. 'In 1930', says Sir Eric, 'some of the Liverpool committee came under its spell, and *this* was to be "it" for the CU. They resolved to lift the CU into this higher plane of living. Careful enquiry into what the Group believed and practised convinced me that they were doctrinally adrift and I was enabled by God's help to persuade the CU to remain outside. I will give an example. They followed a procedure which up to that time they called sin-sharing (later it was called victory-sharing). The idea was that they would publicly speak of their past sinful life – no holds barred – in order to show the wonderful power of the gospel to overcome sin. Sex sins so often came in, it became an embarrassment. My Bible studies included a series on sin under such titles as "What is sin?" "What has become of sin?", *etc*. The latter helped much in our defence against the practice of sin-sharing. That study gave no less than sixteen different pictures of what God has done with our sins, *e.g.* they were blotted out, put away, cast into the depths of the sea, nailed to his cross and so on. It therefore seemed wrong to be dragging them up and parading them before each other. We rejected the pursuit.'

Richardson's leadership also had a wider perspective – the good of the budding national fellowship. Liverpool representation was way above most others at the IVF conference. One fresher who went to High Leigh was Guy Timmis, a medical student. A letter from the CU had arrived at his home the day he started his course, telling students that their education would be incomplete if they omitted to study the claims of Christ. He had ventured to the CU, got a surprise welcome from a prefect of his old Birkenhead school and then found himself sufficiently interested to go to High Leigh. Its challenge led him some weeks later, in the quiet of his own room, to acknowledge his need of a Saviour. 'For years I had struggled to read the New Testament and could never get past Romans. Now it was all alive with new meaning.'

A further chain of events followed. When a younger fellow pupil of the Birkenhead school, Keith Cameron, caught up with Guy at university he was a bit taken aback when Guy, whose one consuming interest in school had been cricket, told him that he was so glad that he had received Christ as his personal Saviour. Keith too began to enjoy the company of CU members and 'it was not long before the Lord graciously spoke to me through the words, "This is my blood which is shed for you." Realizing then that I was a blood-bought, born-again child of God I sought to find service for him who had done so much for me.' He, in turn, began to recommend the CU to his friend Laurie Chandler, who has never forgotten his first visit and the sight of a dozen or so kneeling in prayer on the bare lecture-room floor. The spontaneous and earnest prayer was so different from the formal affairs with which he had so far been acquainted. Guy, Keith and Laurie all became long-serving medical missionaries, in Uganda, China and Northern Nigeria – each with an outstanding life story of his own. Laurie Chandler's call to Nigeria was partly the consequence of meeting some African Christian students, rare in British universities then. 'I found that they too felt there was need of help from Europe to open up the interior of the continent to the light of Christ's gospel.' Another student saved through the witness of such fellow students, having come up thinking all Christians were 'nitwits', and then called to service overseas, was Winifred Gass (though she did not get to Kenya till she was fifty-one years of age, delayed mainly by family responsibilities). In all this we see yet again how faithfuly student witness widens the global reach of the gospel.

Someone else who faced the implications of the call of God was Leith Samuel. One of the scene-changing advances in the post-war evangelical world was the number of people in the 'full-time ministry' equipped for a penetrative evangelism among students. The first of that generation of young preachers was Leith Samuel. He was to feel God's preparing hand in his student days at Liverpool. The moulding of a servant of God for future work takes many forms and many years. But sometimes a spiritual crisis shows how the battle for complete consecration to the will of God was decided.

One day a call came through to Leith from Douglas Johnson to arrange a visit of Robert Wilder to the CU. He was aware of a special insistence in Johnson's voice. 'See that you look after him properly and protect him from the cold and damp. Help him on with his overcoat when he has finished speaking. And get a taxi to take him to where he is staying.' Johnson was taking no chances. Here was an elderly statesman, who, under God, had done very special things in the student world.

'A day or two before Wilder's visit', says Leith Samuel, 'I received a letter from a Durham theology student, enclosing an article from the *Inter-Varsity Magazine*. It asked a question: "To what profit is it that we dwell in Jerusalem if we see not the face of the king?" It was based on Absalom's sad experience of distance and estrangement from his father. At the prayer meeting two mornings running this phrase had come into someone's praying. The idea of being "distant" from God's presence haunted me. And then Dr Wilder came. His theme was the challenge of that great first student wave, oft repeated, coming from the lips of men like C. T. Studd: "If Jesus Christ is not Lord of all, he is not Lord at all." As I knelt by my bed that night I felt convicted. I was busy serving the Lord. But how close was I to him, the King? Was he the Lord of my all? Many things I could hand on for him to keep or discard. The battle was really on when it came to my passion for athletics. I was eager to represent the university successfully and gain my colours. I reckoned it was good for the CU witness that I should. But supposing *he* did not want me to? Finally I got to the point where I could honestly say, "Lord, if you don't want it I don't either." As much of myself as I knew of myself, and the rest, were in the Lord's hands. I tumbled into my bed in peace.'

He gained his athletics colours. But after that night of wrestling with God he had come to see that he was competing by glad permission of the King, to whom he had surrendered his all. He had, of course, another race to run. Robert Wilder himself was soon to finish that race with joy in 1938, aware that God was raising up again the kind of work to which he had devoted his life. This sense of being involved in a task that had been handed on came home to Leith when he was on an evangelistic tour of American universities in 1951. It was at the home of Miss Lucy Haynes in Philadelphia. One evening he stood near a log fire burning in a large old fireplace. 'Years ago,' she said, 'Dr Wilder stood on the spot where you are standing and prayed. He asked the Lord to restore SCM to its former biblical outlook, or to raise up something biblical to take its place. I believe your coming to America is part of the answer to that prayer.' On that cold, damp Liverpool night in 1935 the old American who prayed with vision had preached with a mission: he was passing on the baton, and it was taken up.

Meanwhile, in London in 1935, Howard Guinness (by then IVF's university evangelist in Britain, a role that Leith was the next to take on) was engaged in the most significant United Kingdom mission of his ministry. We shall assess some of the impact of that, and then, to complete our look at the 1919–39 period, we shall return to Cambridge to see how things were faring with the original pioneers.

Chapter Six

LONDON AND LITERATURE

In 1935 Hitler was shaking Europe. After a Nazi plebiscite he had been declared Führer in 1934. Oswald Mosley led mass Fascist meetings in Olympia and Hyde Park. The unemployed were restless. Churchill warned against the German air menace.

The LIFCU leaders read the signs with the concern of youth, possessed not of fanaticism, but of faith and love. They saw the apathy of most of their generation at home and the misdirected fervour of their contemporaries across the water. They saw too their inertia in witness. Given in measure the mind of Christ upon the crisis of their day, they saw the need to call people, soon to be flung into a vortex, out of the impending chaos to Christ. In 1935 they settled on a major mission and gave it a dramatic title: 'Out of World Chaos'. One wonders how many of their friends mocked it as a bit melodramatic. It was, however, a well-planned bid to reach every university student. A copy of John's Gospel was addressed to each one individually – a major undertaking. Howard Guinness gave the main talks. The LIFCU leader was Jim Broomhall. There were some short- and long-term effects on IVF literature prospects arising out of this mission. So we shall look at books too in this chapter.

The sheer earnest endeavour of the 1935 mission caught the heart of Donald Wiseman, a student of King's, and one day to return to his old university as a professor. He looks back on it as a major factor in his life. 'The evangelistic fervour under the leadership of Howard drew me and many others to witness more openly. My own late brother-in-law, John Marchant, was among several converted then.' He traces two other benefits. The mission provided moral and spiritual preparation for the demands of World War 2 and it helped settle his own future direction in life, delayed though that was by the intervening war. Time after time during the discussions that the mission triggered off, the problems brought up were those relating to the Old Testament. The future editor of the *Tyndale Old Testament Commentaries* felt a strong call from God to devote himself to seeking the answers to such questions. It meant a change of subjects to Hebrew and Semitic studies.

At the Royal College of Music was Derek Kidner. The Old Testament was to be his domain too, and several *Tyndale Commentaries* bear his name. But the influence that led him into this speciality came later. The mission did not reach the depths in him that it did in Wiseman, and Kidner recalls his own college's effort with a certain puckish humour. 'Our most ambitious effort was to get Bishop Taylor Smith along on our home ground at RCM. We persuaded Sir Hugh Allen, the Director of the College, to take the chair. But that little triumph went astray in that the bluff Sir Hugh capped the gospel address with the summary, "So it all comes down to this – do your best here and you're all right hereafter, eh, Bishop?" Whereupon, to our dismay, the Bishop, who was by then a little hard of hearing, smiled his thanks for what he assumed to have been a few formal words of gratitude for his visit. It was a lesson to us about pinning our hopes on "posh" chairmen.' Despite his advancing years, Taylor Smith still got through to students in his vivid way, drawing them by his cheerful and obvious joy in Christ. Medical student Denis Pells Cocks recalls taking him that week to the refectory at Bart's, before the Bishop's mission address there. 'Quite soon he was surrounded by students as he talked so warmly of the Lord Jesus.'

Though writers such as Wiseman and Kidner were one day to help change the scene for evangelical literature, the 1935 mission highlighted the gaping holes in the fences. Future authors did not answer the present problems. The needs of IVF students in the thirties in the realm of relevant reading were so basic that it would have seemed like sheer indulgence to dream up the kind of post-fifties literature such young authors were to write. The year of the mission did see IVF publish a compilation of Wilder's evangelistic addresses, *Christ and the Student World*.

In the following year, another work was published which has long stood the test of time. During the run-up to the mission

Jim Broomhall called to see Douglas Johnson. 'Look, if we get any conversions, how can we instruct them in the faith? We need something to establish people in biblical doctrine.' It got an instant response from Johnson. He hammered together a full outline and then approached Canon T. C. Hammond to polish it up and put his name to it. So by March 1936 *In Understanding be Men* was born, a bestseller which has seen over twenty impressions. Along with *Search the Scriptures* it became basic diet for decades. The latter had also grown out of a student suggestion, and had appeared two years earlier. Geoffrey Lehmann, then president of OICCU, had been disturbed by the move away from the Scriptures to 'personal guidance' which the Oxford Group had come to represent. 'Let's get people to read the Bible more than books about it' said Lehmann. Johnson passed on the seed thought to G. T. Manley and Canon Guillebaud – two of the very few older scholarly supporters of that time. It grew into a scheme of Bible study built deliberately around a three-year course and so designed to correspond with a student's stay at university. In revised forms *Search the Scriptures* has had a life of more than fifty years. It was exactly the kind of thing required.

Johnson did much of the practical work on the manuscripts and sometimes 'ghosted' sections of other books, and it was rumoured that there were some nights when he virtually never went to bed! But help was at hand. When Johnson travelled home from that meeting in Birmingham that had launched the CU in 1929 he had grave doubts that it would last. No wonder. At the meeting so much opposition to starting a CU had come from the SCM that the president-elect became faint at the prospect, and, it is said, had to be revived with brandy to enable him to take the chair at all! 'Going back in the train to London the question in Ezekiel came to the secretary's mind, "Can these bones live?", and the reply, "Ah, Lord, thou knowest." However, as has happened so often before and since, the grain of mustard seed began vigorously to grow.' And it was from the Birmingham CU that Ronald Inchley came. He found his life's work in IVF literature.

'I remember that in the summer Crusader camp of 1935 D.J. was acting as medical officer. I attended as a camp officer. We all wondered why he kept so much to his tent. I found he was working on the proofs of *In Understanding be Men*. After that we talked about the possibility of my joining the team after graduation.' In 1936 he started – at £180 a year. 'It is difficult to imagine now how few of the Christian books then in circulation were suitable for students. The format was pretty grim and the range of subjects not really relevant. We concentrated first on Bible study aids, made an attempt at apologetics with Rendle Short's *Modern Discovery and the Bible* and attempted to stir up missionary interest.' But the spectre of financial losses would not go away. 'When I was engaged I was told that a married man could not be supported. You can see what confidence there was! In 1939 I was expecting to have to sever my links when war came and the literature programme was more or less put into mothballs. I transferred to John Laing, who needed administrative staff for new aerodromes.'

There is a gracious irony somewhere in the fact that as the IVF publications secretary lost his role and got taken up by Laings, so John Laing himself began to take up an interest in IVF. And even more ironically, his interest had all begun through reading an IVF book that looked a bit of a sales flop. The history of the CUs, *Christ and the Colleges*,[1] like many a Christian history book, was not exactly a sell-out and was judged a failure by many. But the ubiquitous Johnson had been present at a Crusader camp at the time he was working on that manuscript, too. It had been noticed by F. D. Bacon, a 'City gent', who later bought a copy. He it was who one day passed it on to John Laing. One copy of a loss-making book from a loss-making publisher fell into the hand of a man, John Laing, whose chief desire under God was to see young men and women brought to Christ. He did not need much persuading that here was evidence that God was on the move in the universities. The work became an abiding concern all his days.

As the story of IVF unfolds it is like watching empty spaces fill up slowly with familiar faces. A trickle gradually becomes a flood. There is one constant figure – Douglas Johnson – who always tried to keep invisible. It was immensely difficult, for example, to get him to speak in public. Arnold Aldis once challenged him about this and he replied that he would never do so while he could find someone else who could do it better. This appeared to be always! By keeping right out of the limelight, he succeeded in persuading all sorts of people from professors to school leavers, to do what needed to be done. In

[1]Edited by F. D. Coggan, later Archbishop of Canterbury.

this way he was the 'midwife' behind successive and significant evangelical ventures of the twentieth century. It is scarcely possible to exaggerate, says John Wenham, the importance of his amazing letters, his ability to stimulate people, his intellectual grasp, his diplomacy, his power to keep the boat balanced, and his brilliance as a secretary. He was a trainer of others in the art of taking decisions that always kept in view the spiritual and theological implications of what was said and done. And there was invariably a touch of fun about it too.

Broomhall, who acknowledges Johnson's lively influence upon him from 1925 through the thirties, left these shores for China in 1938. He had been sure of his call since childhood days. An episode from his time as a LIFCU leader shows how the burning issues for many of this era's young people was the question of personal holiness. In many ways the successes of the future were built upon the consecration of such people. Their earnestness exposes how 'laid back' our generation has become. Broomhall tells of how he had been encouraged by a friend to be completely surrendered to the Lord. 'For two weeks while I was living in the residents' hostel I used every moment I could spare to kneel before the Lord and examine myself, searching for sins unrepented of and unforgiven, for any kind of rivals to his reign in my life, anything that could prevent him doing whatever he wished in me. Was I willing not to have T.J.C. as my wife? Was I willing, if he willed it, not to get the FRCS? When I could find nothing that stood in the way, when all was forgiven and I was his entirely, he flooded my heart with such joy and peace as I have never known. To this day, being utterly at the Lord's disposal is, to me, the beginning of knowing his will in guidance and of confidence that he will lead, use, supply and protect.'

When Broomhall sailed he left with a party of ten others. They included Chris Maddox, Rupert Clarke (also doctors, both of whom remained on the field well into their seventies) and David Bentley-Taylor.

What an age away was their going! It followed Munich and Neville Chamberlain's 'peace in our time' with Hitler. Japan had invaded China in 1937 and it was a matter of getting in before they closed the way. 'We went to Vietnam and drove lorries and seven cars from Hanoi to Chungking. With us as companion was a man of over eighty – Sir Montagu Beauchamp of the Cambridge Seven. He was going to his son Ivor at the hospital in Paoning to end his days where he had been a missionary so long before, and where Charles Maddox and I were to spend the next few years too,' says Broomhall.

What a symbolic link there was in their going! Two waves of evangelical pioneering missionary spirit. It spanned a century's close, a world war and a theological crisis of cataclysmic proportions that almost destroyed that spirit. And now, once more, as the LIFCU mission had prophetically warned, it was to be world chaos and a second world war.

Back home the LIFCU itself plodded somewhat into the war era. Some of its members, though later to make their mark, felt little of the *élan* of those young and lifelong adventurers for God careering into China. But even that makes a point of its own about the variety of God's training ways for his people. There can be a call to faithfulness amidst the undramatic, and many would identify more with our closing testimony, which indicates that God's pace with and his purposes for his children have no regimented pattern. Douglas (later Professor) Spanner joined the CU at Imperial College on going up, and became its secretary. 'But my life as a Christian had no high points or golden hours. It seems to have been all plodding with nothing memorable. My Christian life had no sparkle to it. I remember the international conference at Cambridge on the eve of the war and I remember how I envied those students I saw who were full of joy and vision. I seemed such a stranger to these things. Our CU used to meet in the vestry of Holy Trinity, Prince Consort Road, jointly with the smaller CU of the Royal College of Music. David Hum (now serving as a university maths teacher overseas), Hugh Sansom (who was for many years in Africa), and others were the leaders. But I can testify that the CU meant a lot to me and kept the light burning on the altar.'

And that has never gone out.

Had we followed the then IVF travelling secretary Hugh Evan Hopkins around the thirteen LIFCU groups he visited in 1939 we would have seen a quiet, sometimes encouraging, sometimes depressing picture. The bright light was the CU at University College Hospital, where things were moving 'largely through the influence of the president, Paul Brand', noted the travelling secretary in his diary.

The casualty officer at UCH was Arnold Aldis. One morning in 1939 the Dean sent for him. 'The government is worried there will be heavy bombing in London. Cardiff Medical School is fully prepared for our evacuation. Will you take students with you and teach them there?'

'When?'

'The day after tomorrow.'

The CU and Paul Brand went too. For the Cardiff CU it meant blessing and a new era.[2] For Paul Brand it involved an instant freshers' address to the joint CUs in place of Arnold Aldis who had just got married and forgotten to go! Medical-missionary fame was to come for Brand with the passing years.[3] For Aldis the move meant a lifetime's career in the Welsh capital and increasing journeys to speak all over the country at CU meetings. He made up a thousand-fold for that one that got away.

[2]See my *Excuse Me, Mr Davies – Hallelujah!*, pp. 78–94.
[3]See J. Young, *Paul Brand*.

Chapter Seven

BASIL, BASH, BARCLAY, AND BENNETT

The thirties were an uphill climb for the CICCU. This chapter shows how hard-won ground helped others scale heights in later days.

Students love a character. Basil Atkinson was certainly that. He was loved and chuckled over by successive generations of students at Cambridge. He was consulted and revered too. As the thirties progressed, his constant advocacy of the biblical faith helped the CICCU to retain its evangelical identity when religious life was awash with liberalism. His long, almost patriarchal links with the CICCU from 1919 to 1971 gave to his perspective a unique continuity. He saw the thirties as a time when the CU had to hold on by its teeth to maintain its evangelical character.

The centenary of Charles Simeon's death in 1936 could hardly have marked a lower tide in the ebb and flow of fidelity to the Scriptures. Then, wearied by their own spiritual dryness, the SCM began to be more 'devotional'. They had always argued that evangelicals should be the 'devotional wing' of SCM while they pursued the main thrust of social and intellectual issues. They invited an Anglo-Catholic monk to lead a series on prayer. Some of the CICCU were extremely taken with his devout message. Basil, however, heard his alarm bells ringing. His assessment looks uncannily prophetic fifty years on. 'Immediately I foresaw a new danger of an ecumenism that would combine the Protestant liberal view of the Bible and the Roman view of the church'. Both options, apart or together, were anathema to Basil. For those who believe that an uncompromising stand for biblical truth is what the Scripture itself expects of us, it follows that here was clearly God's person for the hour to stand by the CICCU. He combined an excellent Greek scholarship with vast enthusiasm for biblical exposition. Each term he took three or four college Bible studies weekly, so most CICCU students benefited from his love of Scripture and never forgot his beaming face. 'I recall', says Roger Forster, a CICCU convert of post-war years, 'Basil preaching in the open air in Cambridge and mentioning heaven. A student shouted out, "What do you know about heaven?" With that seraphic smile he replied, "I live there." '

In 1932 F. F. Bruce, also a classicist, came down from Aberdeen to continue his studies. He had left behind a much stronger evangelical work in Aberdeen than the shy group, still on its way to finding its feet in university life, that he had joined on going up in 1928. The Christian Students Fellowship at Aberdeen had begun as a Bible class, inaugurated by two medical students, Albert Duncan and William Souter. The latter, after missionary service in China till the Revolution, attended the fiftieth anniversary conference of the CU in 1971. Bruce was president of the Fellowship, as it was called in its early years, when (Dr) W. Ingram Emslie went up in 1930. It did not have university status. 'But through the good offices of Fred Bruce and the high regard in which he was held by his professors, the Fellowship was recognized and called the 'Aberdeen University CU,' says Emslie. One enterprise which helped to establish the witness was a mission in 1930, the preacher being the veteran John McNeill, then aged seventy-six. Howard Guinness' visit the following year proved a tonic and would have served as a reminder in distant Aberdeen of the wider work. Dr Elmslie has had opportunity to revisit the Aberdeen CU in recent years. 'I have been impressed with the huge increase in numbers these days and the way spiritual standards have been maintained.' That part of the story we shall reserve till later.

In his autobiography, Bruce records his reactions on coming down to Cambridge in 1932: 'The CICCU struck me in those days (in contrast to later days) as being much less interested in the intellectual side of Christianity than its counterpart in Aberdeen.'[1] He noticed that they were encouraged to cultivate the company of 'toughs' – the less academic types who might

[1]*In Retrospect*, p. 70.

68

distinguish themselves on the playing field but who were unlikely to have the inclination to enter into intellectual argument. There was a 'plus' in this in that 'toughs' tended to make splendid pioneer missionaries, where the going itself was tough. The CICCU always provided its fair share of such people. In the 1938 mission when Evan Hopkins, a former CICCU president, came back as travelling secretary to help, he scribbled in his diary, 'There was a great readiness on the part of toughs to talk about Christ. In one squash the whole of the Cambridge Boat Race crew turned up. The inner circle of men are working hard to bring people along. A steady work was done and some were saved.' Raymond Turvey learned a lot from watching his contemporary Maurice Wood, future Bishop of Norwich, witness so profitably. 'He seemed to spend all his spare time talking about Christ to his friends. He led several, notably other members of the Queen's Boat Club, to Christ.'

One of the influences directed towards keeping the gospel simple was E. J. H. Nash ('Bash'), a CICCU student of the mid-twenties. Bash became as much a byword as Basil over the years. Many of the more evangelistically minded students in the thirties were products of his Varsity and Public School Camps, a department of Scripture Union, where they were trained in personal witness. It was also at such camps that student leaders were drilled in the use of SU Bible reading schemes. God honoured these young people and many post-war leaders looked back with gratitude to God for the way they were introduced to the Saviour. It is significant, too, that many who came to Christ 'the simple way' have become some of the most outstanding in their capacity to relate the biblical faith to the modern world; John Stott is an example. That development, however, had to await other maturing factors in evangelical witness, and the anti-intellectual bent tended to leave those with clearly academic gifts, like Bruce, feeling uncomfortable.

Much of the best work in the CICCU was done by the college representatives. They saw personal testimony as of paramount importance, and many gave sacrificially of their time in seeking out fellow students for Christ. Gordon Harman, who became a wartime travelling secretary, tells how he called on Robert Ingham in his room at Peterhouse twenty-four times to follow up a freshers' squash he had attended. He was always out. But they did meet up again. 'I appealed to him to turn to Christ.

"I'll try," was the response. I said that was no use. Months later, he came round to my room one evening to say he was wrong to drift and wanted to become a Christian. And he did.' Commenting on his years in the CICCU, Gordon Harman says, 'I think the spirit of prayer God poured out on some of the CU deserves emphasis. I remember one day, for example, going to see Tom Anscombe in his room. As usual we decided to pray together before we parted. We went on for two hours and it seemed like half an hour. We prayed alternately, the one taking over whenever the other had finished.' Their prayer partnership has lasted fifty years.

Jim Melville, medical missionary in India and Nepal, is another who has reason to thank God for a faithful college representative. 'My godly grandfather gave my name to the CICCU rep. of my college. He came to my room after a meeting and asked me if I was a Christian. I assumed I was, but when he explained what it really meant to be a Christian I realized my lack and asked the Lord into my life that night, though with little effect then. A year later a specific incident completely altered the direction of my life. I had failed the Lord and in considerable distress I asked him for forgiveness. Immediately I was conscious that he had done so, and at the same time I became aware that it was his purpose for me to serve him overseas. No such thought had ever entered my mind. But it was so clear I yielded my life to him in a new way as far as I knew how. My whole Christian life was changed. To serve him became my purpose and joy.'

And so it was for many others, fired for a lifetime of service in many different spheres, as this sample cross-section of Melville's contemporaries shows: Martyn Cundy and Jack Earl in education (one overseas in Malawi, the other staff inspector for religious education in England and Wales; David Adeney, worldwide missionary statesman who in Basil's judgment was the most outstanding missionary secretary of all and one who left his mark on the CICCU; John Wenham and F. F. Bruce, pioneers of a positive biblical scholarship that was rare or non-existent in their own student days; (Sir) Maurice Dorman, a leading overseas government official ('I learned in the CICCU that my life must be one of service'); Sidney Hamilton, bombed, sunk and rescued in the Far East ('Even in the big battle cruisers I found small bands studying the Bible'); Mary Isaacs, president of the small and, in those days, separate

Cambridge Women's Inter-Collegiate CU, who spent forty years in Iran as a missionary; (Sir) Kirby Laing who says that the CICCU gave him his first experience of management when he was made representative of Emmanuel. His involvement in the IVF preceded that of his father by several years. It was the publication of *Search the Scriptures* that was, for him, a spiritual milestone. 'Those three years of personal Bible study were invaluable. I am only sorry I can no longer put my hands on the notes I wrote out.'

One of the great CICCU traditions of student evangelism was the 'open-air' in Market Square which took the place, in the summer term, of a gospel sermon in church. There, people had to make a stand for Christ and were publicly identified in their allegiance. Basil Atkinson, who often preached there with great joy, tells of one remarkable consequence of its witness. A vicar visiting Cambridge told him how, as a student, he had been approached by a little fellow while passing the open-air. He was asked if he was saved. He felt so enraged that he knocked the man to the ground. Some time later he had to go to Australia. Left to himself during the quiet days of the passage he found that he could not get the man's question out of his mind. He yielded his life to the Lord while still at sea. Eventually he entered the ministry. Years later he was preaching at a convention and saw the little man he had hit to the ground sitting at the back. He went to him and greeted him warmly. 'I'm sure there must be a mistake,' was the response. But the clergyman explained what had happened and the man was transformed! Ever since the incident he had been afraid to speak to others about Christ.

By the time Derek Kidner came up to Cambridge from the Royal College of Music, in 1937, the summer open-air had been dropped. Some felt this to be a betrayal. 'So there were compromise experiments – groups of colleges running open-airs on Parker's Piece or by the river and occasional evangelistic garden parties – very stiff and shy occasions. An embarrassed president gave out a notice about one such garden party at a Bible reading, while at the same time trying to explain that it was just as valiant an enterprise as the open-airs of long tradition. The notice, trying to do justice to both, became so confused that when the speaker began he prefaced his talk with congratulations to the president for repudiating the idea of garden parties (spoken with blistering scorn; he was a rough diamond from the mission field) – of all namby-pamby notions! So there was even more embarrassed explaining to be done.'

How then shall we assess CICCU in the thirties? Basil Atkinson, who knew the thrills of the revival immediately after the First World War and the remarkable blessing of the era after the Second, accounts these years 'the CICCU in the doldrums'. But for those who were there it provided the staff of life, and future evangelical strength was growing beneath the surface in what were comparatively disappointing years. 'For me as a young Christian', says Raymond Turvey, 'these were my formative years in the Christian life, and a continual thrill and privilege. Scripture was expounded faithfully and fascinatingly. We were thoroughly enjoying being wholeheartedly committed to the Lord.' 'But the harvest from missions and Sunday sermons throughout my time was painfully small,' says Kidner, 'though attendances were good and prayer was earnest.' There were only twelve conversions known to the CICCU in the year of Kidner's presidency, a figure which, though not negligible, was disappointing to many. But there was a great harvest to come and the intercessor does not always see the reaping in his own day. So it is best to see it as a holding time. 'The grand presidents of those defensive days, right up to the war (from 1935 to 1939 they were all Bash men) must remember that their fidelity kept the Union on the rails and kept a firm foundation for the remarkable growth of post-war years.' That's how Atkinson saw it.

In 1938, Raymond Turvey noticed an outstanding young fresher at Trinity College – it was Oliver Barclay – who seemed uncertain as to which religious group to join. There was a long tradition of Quakerism in his family, reaching back to the seventeenth century. 'I went up as a young Christian who had been stuffed with liberal teaching since my conversion. I had friends in the SCM and played with the idea of amalgamating SCM and CICCU. I am not sure that I ever went to an SCM meeting. I did, however, in my first year or two, hope for that wider unity which soon I saw to be clearly impossible. I was at the same time immediately attracted to the CICCU by its spiritual life and vigour. I was amazed to find that they held these old-fashioned beliefs about the Bible. I did not know that any young people still believed these things. My own doctrine of the person and work of Christ was heretical and my understanding of the atonement almost non-existent. Before the first year was over I had been brought to a confidence in the reliability of Scripture (which had all sorts of practical consequences), the beginning of an understanding of Christ's death and the dawning of an ability to explain the gospel to my friends. In this process the college Bible studies and the Saturday expositions were very important.'

Almost twenty years after Douglas Johnson had stepped out of an SCM meeting in London, the one who was to succeed him as IVF General Secretary soon saw the need for decision over the same issues at Cambridge. We are on the edge of the next take-off in evangelical witness, with a new consciousness developing of the adequacy of biblical truth for the whole of life's challenge – the university challenge included.

Phyllis Bennett came on to the small IVF staff some years before Barclay and became something of a legend for her exertions on the women's side. It was while she was a student at Bristol University that the CU there was galvanized into new life by Ken Bergin, a Cambridge student who changed to Bristol to complete his medical studies. It was a turning-point for the CU at Bristol, for he brought with him something of the best CICCU commitment to 'think big' for God. When Phyl Bennett came up the CU was a small affair of about twenty, rather timid, meeting in a small room underneath a stage in the Victoria Rooms. In her third year, that changed through the sheer dynamic drive of Ken Bergin, son of Bristol pioneer Dr Frank Bergin. Ken was destined for days of valour in war and service close to royalty. He was soon co-opted on to the BIFCU (Bristol Inter-Faculty CU) committee. His reaction to its low visibility was swift.

' "What are you doing 'hiding' under the stage?" he exploded. "You have the greatest message in the world. You should be holding your meetings in the finest lounge of the Victoria Rooms, have the best speakers, the most attractive invitation cards. You should put on superlative squashes and expect up to 200 students at your open meetings." He insisted we had a prayer meeting at 7.00 a.m. once a week, this being the only time the whole committee could meet. Phyl Bennett dodged. "I'm not sure I can get there as I live in a suburb." "Yes you will," he countered. "I'll fetch you in my car as I haven't to travel to get to the prayer meeting." And he did. We then had breakfast with the Rendle Shorts.

'We prayed and planned. Howard Guinness came for a mission which was held in the main lounge of the Victoria. We had been deputed by Ken to get 200 spoons. Not all were used but well over 100 came – for us an excellent meeting. I had persuaded to come to this meeting a member of the netball club of which I was president. When Howard Guinness finished he invited people who wanted to hear more to go to Frank Bergin's home nearby. I turned to my friend, Betty Price, and asked, "Would you like to come?" "Yes." I was too shy to speak to Betty on the way home, but some time later she was converted and we did Bible studies together. Betty subsequently became president of the CU and eventually principal of a teachers' training college. After this time BIFCU did not look back. It put the CU on the map and our numbers doubled.'

Phyl Bennett we shall meet again as she served the wartime CUs. Ken Bergin left the student arena for the theatre of war and found himself brought through many a tight spot. Perhaps one story from his experience will serve for the many others who look back with gratitude that they were spared to serve God in post-war days. As medical officer he flew on one bombing mission into Germany to test the reactions of the crew under stress. Both the pilot and co-pilot were badly shot up. Ken, using his experience gained from Cambridge flying days, brought the crippled plane back home. He received a rocket from the commanding officer, tongue in cheek, as he was not supposed to have been on the flight!

Bergin's reaction to the 'invisibility' of the Bristol CU is reminder enough that the CUs were more or less unknown societies in the university life of the late thirties. That was sadly true of a wider context. A. M. Rennie, who was travelling secretary in Scotland from 1937 to 1940, points out that they were also hardly known to the Christian public at large. This was partly due, of course, to a general antipathy to the evangelical faith. But it derived too, from lack of information among those who shared it. Rennie asked for a few minutes on the platform of a meeting in Glasgow that had been called to pray for revival. 'It was enough to touch a chord in the hearts of those mainly veteran soldiers of the cross, who were perhaps surprised and certainly warmed to learn of the evangelical witness in the universities. One after another stood to pray with some emotion for the students.'

So why not have a public meeting specifically devoted to

prayer for the student work? Glasgow's Renfield Street church in the city centre was an ideal place for a public meeting. Chairmen such as Professor Donald Maclean of the Free Church College, Edinburgh, or Duncan Blair, Professor of Anatomy at Glasgow, assured a widening of prayerful interest. Blair really took up the cause. He had moved to Glasgow from a chair at King's, London, and it was there that Douglas Johnson had encouraged him to open support of the IVF. He dated his conversion from First World War naval days when he had been medical officer of a minesweeper escort off Northern Ireland. His commitment became clear-cut. He would sign the Doctrinal Basis of the Fellowship with great enthusiasm and say, 'I regard it as a running up of my ensign to the masthead in order to show where my allegiance belongs.'

A further way in which Christians at large became more familiar with IVF was through the growth of student teams leading church campaigns. These summer missions grew from humble origins. In 1933 eight students (six Edinburgh, one Glasgow, one Dundee) pitched their tents on what proved to be a wasp-infested site on the banks of the Tweed. Of the eight, one went to Peru, one to India, one to Arabia and three to Africa, and one became a professor of theology.

'The preparation of these missions could give a great sense of God's Spirit having gone ahead,' says Rennie. He remembers having a tight schedule to reconnoitre a town where he knew no-one. The first minister he found said he knew the SCM and the CU, but not the IVF. When he discovered the link he was ready to support the mission. A second minister said he had been waiting for, and his mother praying for, such a mission. The only other minister was met outside the railway station as he was leaving. He, too, was in favour. Three hours had set the project going.

As the Spirit of God went ahead, and as young people followed his lead, all sorts of projects were to get going in days to come.

PART TWO
1939–1945
INTO THE WAR

Chapter Eight

BRICKS WITHOUT STRAW

There had been a long-standing spirit of fear among evangelicals about biblical scholarship. The few hopeful signs before
the war that it was giving way to a sounder mind had more
than a little to do with the prayers of two girls at Ridgelands
Bible College – though that's not what they had in view!
Eleanor Wenham and Pat Givan prayed for the conversion of
Eleanor's brother John. 'They prayed me out to a VPS camp
in Leukerbad, Switzerland,' says John, 'where I got caught.'
John Wenham did great things in stirring evangelical students
into scholarly feats and helped in the founding, between 1941
and 1944, of Tyndale House, Cambridge, the evangelical centre
for biblical research. Pat Givan was to marry Norman
Anderson, who became its Acting Warden in 1945. It was at a
conference during the dark days of the war in 1941 that the
battle for the Bible took a turn for the better. We saw a
solitary intimation of it in Alan Stibbs in 1928. John Wenham's
schoolboy experiences in the thirties show us some more. We'll
start there.

When the schoolboy newly converted at Leukerbad thought
about returning to school as a known Christian his heart filled
with dread. There were thirty mocking 'varmints' to face in his
school house. It was then that the first Bible text came alive to
him and he knew the power of the Word of God. 'Be on your
guard;' he read in 1 Corinthians 16:13, 'stand firm in the faith;
be men of courage; be strong.' If it was a preparation for
facing the teenage terrors of Uppingham School, it was also a
commission for life. In his own tiny school study the Bible
literally became meat and drink to his soul.

When Wenham entered Cambridge there were no academically qualified evangelicals teaching in universities in the field of biblical scholarship. 'Today,' says Professor F. F. Bruce,[1] 'in British universities alone, there are between twenty-five and thirty teachers of biblical and related studies who are associated with the Tyndale Fellowship. We have ample cause for wondering gratitude to God.' For at least a generation before Wenham's day evangelicals had been warned off academic biblical research. It was seen as dangerous and valueless because of its negative approach to the Bible. By following Wenham's story we see how the problem began to be tackled at root. Whether consciously or not, that verse from 1 Corinthians was working out in practice, and he and others were given a mind that was unafraid to tackle the issues.

Wenham's passion at school was modern physics. But they had also to do divinity. Their teacher, a remarkable and gifted man, read them out the syllabus. It included Daniel and the Maccabees. 'None of us had heard of the Maccabees. They sounded interesting so we voted for them. We studied S. R. Driver, the doyen of British critics, and R. H. Charles, the supreme authority on pseudepigrapha. I drank it all in; the supposed prophecies of the coming great empires were not prophecies at all, but were written after the events had taken place – to be precise, in the days of the Maccabees, four centuries after Daniel; miracles were just legend.

'Up to this time my interest in the Bible had been purely intellectual, but during the next school holidays I was converted and the Bible came alive to me. I had no theory of biblical authority or inspiration, but it spoke to me forcefully, even some of the unlikely parts. But there was this cloud over Daniel. Then I came across a book by Sir Robert Anderson with the intriguing title *Daniel in the Critic's Den* in which Driver's arguments were taken to pieces one by one. I was just amazed. I had no idea that there was another side to the question. Though this book is not one which I would put high on a reading list now, it did me inestimable service; it made me critical of the critics.'

Upon his introduction to Genesis and Wellhausen he went through the same process, accepting the theory of the mutually disagreeing documents – JEDP – all written after the time of

[1]*In Retrospect*, p. 127.

Moses and explaining the composition of the Pentateuch. But a holiday reading of James Orr's *The Problems of the Old Testament* produced another reversal. Orr convinced him how unsound, slender and faulty were the argument, factual basis and logic of this theory. 'It involved processes psychologically incredible and it destroyed all hope of understanding the phenomenon of Israel. From that day to this I have known that whatever other views I might acquire I could never go back to JEDP. This despite all my gratitude and affection for my teacher.' So disillusion with Wellhausen further encouraged him to believe the Bible to be true, and even, in the end, to believe it inerrant. Avid reading followed as he tried to sort out some of his ideas. 'It became clear to me that the key questions were the deity of Christ and the authority of his teaching. The great watershed in theology was how one viewed the teaching of Christ – as trustworthy or not? With those of us who eventually plunged into university theology, this question was most pressing in the form: Could we trust the teaching of Christ concerning the Old Testament? We talked and prayed much amongst ourselves about these things.'

A few things happened around this time (we are thinking of the year 1935) which we can read as signposts to a qualitatively new future, especially in this area of Bible-believing scholarship. Isaiah speaks of God giving 'strength to those who turn back the battle at the gate'. There were those who were no longer prepared just to hope that the gates would hold. It was a kind of El Alamein. No further. Yet more retreat was just not on. The battle *could* be turned back at the gate.

In 1935 The Hayes conference centre at Swanwick was booked for the first time and it was to prove a marvellous post-war rallying point. In the same year the first small conference for those in teachers' training colleges was held. In London, during the LIFCU mission, Donald Wiseman committed himself to the lifetime study needed for a defence of the Old Testament. Travelling down from Scotland *en route* for Vienna, F. F. Bruce decided, in unusual circumstances, to take up an academic post in the University of Edinburgh, a firstfruit of what was to come. In Liverpool that year God touched the life of Leith Samuel through Wilder's visit, and an evangelist for the educated was born. In December Dr Martyn Lloyd-Jones was the final speaker at a public Bible rally in the Albert Hall. With exceptional force and persuasiveness he appealed for a return to the proclamation of the central evangelical doctrines of Scripture. Among those listening was Philip Hughes, who was to put his pen to weighty defence of those doctrines. His heart leapt. So did that of Douglas Johnson, for he was there, alert to the significance of what he was hearing, and now strategically settled into his first year as full-time IVF General Secretary. John Wenham had just taken over the secretaryship of what was soon to be the Theological Students Fellowship (now the Religious and Theological Studies Fellowship). According to Johnson from 1935 Wenham kept insisting on new books and more purposeful theological conferences.

Wenham picks up the story himself. 'In 1937 there were twenty-two present at the first theologs' conference at Digswell Park. We could find no academically qualified theologians to help us. We students read papers to each other. I cannot remember for certain about the others, but I read one on 'Our Lord's View of the Old Testament'. We earnestly prayed that God would bring his church back to the teaching of her Saviour. It seemed an impossible task. But we set to work to make bricks even though we had no straw.'

There was one senior figure they felt it crucial to incorporate. In June 1938 five men visited G. T. Manley at St Luke's, Hampstead: H. E. Guillebaud, Alan Stibbs, now returned from China, Douglas Johnson and two students, John Wenham and Norval Geldenhuys, a research student at Cambridge from South Africa. Manley chaired this meeting and from it emerged the Biblical Research Committee. Further 'senior' help came from the addition of F. F. Bruce and Dr W. J. Martin of Leeds and Liverpool universities. 'It is a commentary on the situation of biblical scholarship in IVF', says Bruce, ' . . . that a predominantly Anglican Committee should have to enlist two Brethren who were not professional theologicans but teachers in Arts Faculties in secular universities.' 'The prime purpose was to do something to roll away the reproach of anti-intellectualism which had so long been attached to English evangelicals.'[2]

So, bit by bit, scholarly straw for biblical-theological bricks began to be gathered. Derek Kidner had moved on to Cambridge and was to gain a first-class degree in theology during the war. He recalls how Wenham came 'and talked inspiringly to some of us about an evangelical return to scholar-

[2]*Op. cit.*, pp. 111, 122.

ship. I remember the thrill of hearing about the Biblical Research Committee. My own special gratitude is for the vision that Alan Cook, then at Ridley Hall, had along the same lines. He had a persuasive way of getting the vision of evangelical scholarship across, and I, for one, resolved to have a go at this. But it was wartime before I was available and research would not have seemed right at that stage. God has his time for everything, and knows our limitations as well as our aptitudes.'

With so many away in the forces, G. T. Manley, who had lived through the first war, urged that it was the duty of those at home 'to strengthen the things that remain'. And so they began to think of long-term strategy. In 1941 a group of leaders were invited to a two-day conference at the Kingham Hill School in Oxfordshire. It was a week or so after Hitler had invaded Russia. Reading the names of those gathered is like a roll call of the evangelical 'few': Manley and Maclean, Martin and McCaw, Bruce, Bromiley and Babbage, Wenham and Wright, Knox and Stibbs, Connell and Houghton, Lloyd-Jones and Johnson.[3]

Years later some of those present remarked, 'We had no idea at the time how important and fruitful those two days were eventually to prove.' Some decisions bore immediate fruit such as annual summer schools in biblical languages and two annual lectures in biblical studies (the Tyndale Lectures-to-be). Longer-term plans conceived at Kingham Hill were for a Bible commentary and Bible dictionary. One decade and then another were to pass before both saw the light of day (*The New Bible Commentary*, 1953, and *The New Bible Dictionary*,

[3]Rev. G. T. Manley; Professor Donald Maclean of the Free Church College, Edinburgh; Dr W. J. Martin, Rankin Lecturer in Hebrew, Liverpool University; Leslie McCaw, later Principal, All Nations Christian College; F. F. Bruce, later Rylands Professor of Biblical Exegesis, Manchester University; Geoffrey Bromiley, later Professor of Church History, Fuller Theological Seminary; S. Barton Babbage, later Visiting Professor, Columbia Theological Seminary; John Wenham, later Warden of Latimer House, Oxford; J. Stafford Wright, later Principal, Tyndale Hall, Bristol; David B. Knox, later Principal, Moore Theological College, Sydney; Rev. Alan Stibbs, later Vice-principal, Oak Hill Theological College, London; J. Clement Connell, later lecturer, London Bible College, A. T. (later Bishop) Houghton; Rev. Dr D. Martyn Lloyd-Jones and Dr Douglas Johnson.

1962). Finally there was a determination to secure a residential centre and library for biblical research. The centre was purchased in Cambridge in 1943. Oliver Barclay heard that a distant relative was thinking of selling property in Selwyn Gardens. John Laing, chairman of the Business Committee, was practical and generous in his help and offered £1 for every £2 raised by others. He footed one third of the bill. 'I remember how thrilled he was to be involved in the setting up of the House,' says son Kirby. Tyndale's name came readily to mind and Tyndale House was dedicated in 1945 to the extension of the kingdom of God. Colonel (later Professor Sir) Norman Anderson, came as Acting Warden after demobilization. The house started with a succession of people who had little claim to academic training in theology. Only later did members gradually gain academic status and attain quite important posts. In the meanwhile John Wenham and others went quietly on 'trying to emulate the B. B. Warfields', says Douglas Johnson, 'and seeking to neutralize by superior scholarship the effects of those weakening the scriptural position.' We give Wenham's own words:

'In the days when we were so starved of biblical scholarship, the writings of B. B. Warfield were a great find to us. He showed us the massive inductive basis on which the divine authorship of the Scripture was based. He argued further that, since God did not make mistakes, the God-breathed Scriptures must be inerrant. The solidity of this induction and the seeming inescapability of his deduction have had a profound effect on our work. We were unable to escape the view that Jesus regarded both the history and the doctrine of the Old Testament as true in a simple and straightforward sense.' Such were the foundations on which the living stones of Tyndale House were built.

Some years before John Wenham had started reading B. B. Warfield, another member of the Kingham Hill conference had stumbled across the complete ten volumes of Warfield's work in Toronto.[4] In 1932 Martyn Lloyd-Jones was on his way into the Knox Seminary Library when he caught sight of them on the 'new acquisitions' shelf. His feelings at that moment, he

[4]See Iain Murray, *D. Martyn Lloyd-Jones, The First Forty Years*, p. 286.

was later to write, were like those of 'stout Cortez' as described by Keats, when he first saw the Pacific. It was a transforming experience, for it drew Lloyd-Jones deeper into the Reformed faith and it was to give him a freshly invigorating perspective on evangelical trends in Britain. His assessment was given in the 1941 conference. We shall quote him extensively for two reasons. First, his comments cast light on what we have seen so far in the CUs. Secondly, his talk rings many bells today.

Lloyd-Jones' first experience of an IVF conference had led him to comment on how simplistic it was. We shall see what he was driving at in a moment. But Johnson was convinced that Lloyd-Jones was just the person to help improve things, and his persistence won. Perhaps one of the things that helped their pulses to beat in unison was that they had both seen the Word of God work in the toughest of arenas – Lloyd-Jones long-term among South Wales dockers, Johnson more briefly in London's dockland. This should help us to remember something very important. The subject of the Kingham Hill conference was 'the revival of biblical theology'. That would necessitate a revival of evangelical scholarship. But it was not a purely academic issue in the specific sense that it was desirable to have more evangelical lecturers in university theology departments. That, of course, was highly desirable, and was one of the priorities to be aimed at. There was, as F. F. Bruce says, a reproach to be rolled away. But behind that aim to restore confidence in the integrity of God's Word was a desire to see its power let loose among the people – docker and student alike. In other words, a disciplined means (believing scholarship) was to serve a greater end (a believing church with a gospel to bring to the world). A conservative biblical scholarship that would strengthen the preaching ministry of the church and defend the faith against its critics was a noble aim. The conference was outstanding. But it also showed that that aim brought with it tensions.

The task assigned to Lloyd-Jones at this gathering was to diagnose the cause of the contemporary lack of evangelical scholarship. It would be impossible to do so, he said, without being provocative and even polemical. It was observed that as he developed his argument, the Grand Old Man of evangelical scholarship and missionary vision, G. T. Manley, turned round more and more in his chair until he almost had his back to the speaker. What were the shock waves that produced such a response? As Lloyd-Jones probed away he reopened deeper wells of biblical heritage than evangelicals of Manley's era had been accustomed to. In many ways the speaker was querying the frame of mind that evangelicals had been in for half a century and more. No doubt Manley's long-life perspective showed him what was happening – thus the seismic effect.

Evidencing first some general causes of the lack, Lloyd-Jones reminded them that evangelicals such as Charles Simeon and others, whom they all acknowledged as their forefathers, had a somewhat different outlook from what now prevailed among them. The first difference related to the link between evangelicals and scholarship. Simeon made it abundantly clear that true conversion normally took place through the continual sowing of the appointed seed in the form of accurate and persuasive exposition of Scripture. Hence to Simeon the fundamental essential in the training of theological students at Cambridge was in the scholarly exegesis of the text, so that it would be given due application in its context when preached to their future congregations. 'Alas, in many present-day evangelical pulpits, this practice has become not merely a lost art, but a lost aim. Biblical theology and accurate exegesis have been neglected and regarded as "too heavy".' Much of this Lloyd-Jones saw as an understandable reaction to the barren intellectualism of liberal preaching. But it had been an over-reaction. He asked if the cure for bad theology was no theology. Church history had often shown a pendulum tendency – an alteration between what could loosely be called 'Puritanism' and 'pietism'. For example, the Puritans of post-Reformation times had been followed by an arid intellectualism of the late seventeenth century, later to be corrected by the pietism of the eighteenth. Something similar had taken place in the next swing to Simeon and then back to the pietism they themselves were facing.

The speaker proceeded to mention four movements in particular which had tended to discourage scholarly enterprise. He was well aware of the positive side of their achievements. What he had in his sights was the side-effects on scholarship of their main emphases.

First, the interest in prophecy. Amidst the distress of the Napoleonic Wars and expectations of Christ's return a number of erudite men had met together. Out of their dialogue had emerged the Catholic Apostolic Church of Edward Irving, and the Brethren led by J. N. Darby and others. Irving believed that the church's charismatic gift of prophecy, in the sense of new knowledge, was being restored. This led to a dependence on the promptings of the Holy Spirit while one was preaching. The worship practice of the Brethren, too, though differing radically on prophecy, also encouraged a dependence on the dictates of the Holy Spirit regarding what to speak on as a meeting proceeded. These factors, along with the expectation in both movements of the imminence of Christ's return, left a legacy which was hostile to patient scholarship in the service of biblical theology.

Secondly, there was the higher-life movement. This teaching emphasized holy living and led to the Keswick movement. No Christian would deny the call to holiness. But what happened was that the movement isolated the doctrine of holiness out of all proportion and thus falsified it. The approach became passive with an emphasis on a false simplicity. Consequently, it tended to be anti-theological.

Thirdly, evangelism had lost its base in sustained exposition and had also been isolated into special activities. More stress was put on method, technique and psychology than on careful sowing of the seed from a properly prepared biblical base. The careful exegete of the Simeon stamp was eclipsed and this ethos took its eventual toll of the thirst for scholarly attainments in biblical exposition.

At this point the speaker paused. 'You asked me to diagnose the reasons for the present weakness and I am doing it. If you teach young people that there is little need for preparation and that the Holy Spirit will give them the right words when they stand to speak; that the second advent is so close – which, of course it may be – that there is no need to bother about hard, deep, scholarly work; that the one gift and technique that matters above all else is a particular style of evangelism; and that sanctification consists of "letting go" and letting the Holy Spirit (either once for all or from day to day) do all the work, then do not blame me if you have no scholars!'

He then proceeded to a fourth side-effect emerging from a movement of rich blessing. The student missionary movement under the saintly Robert Wilder and others had led to hundreds of graduates going overseas. No words could do justice to the self-sacrifice and devotion to Christ of such people. But, if 'keenness' in the CUs was then graded, with missionaries at the top, any graduate who said he was going to stay on to pursue postgraduate work in order to lecture came to be highly suspect and thought to be in danger of spiritual shipwreck.

The cumulative effect of all these trends was to demote the due evaluation of the work of the biblical scholar. Evangelicals had tended to sidestep the attack of rationalism rather than meet it head-on by seeking proper equipment for the task. Since evangelical theology was derived from the Bible it could only be revived by a return to the Bible. Scholarship is needed precisely at those points where there is need for the greatest degree of certainty about the text, exegesis, translation and exposition of the Scriptures. It is the evangelical who has the biggest stake in preserving and advancing the most accurate Bible scholarship, concluded Dr Lloyd-Jones.

It is not difficult to recognize some of these characteristics in the CU story as we have outlined it. There is not much you can immediately do in response to such a talk. It was profound. In its wake lay changes of mind-set that were later to surface, and our generation has seen, in measure, the Puritan/pietist pendulum swing again. But the conference proceeded with the possibilities of what could be done. Dr W. J. Martin of Liverpool University advocated the desirability of a postgraduate centre. The idea was taken up and discussed in some excitement over a meal. Then, says Douglas Johnson, Dr Martin plunged into an illuminating and awe-inspiring description of his experience in such first-class theological halls as Princeton (before it fell to liberal influences) and the world-famous schools of the German critics. 'Dr Martin in full flight on scholarship was as Olympian as Dr Lloyd-Jones was on biblical theology.' Martin laid down a dozen principles necessary for establishing an all-round technical standard in biblical scholarship to a university level.

It was now Lloyd-Jones' turn to feel a little discomfort. He endorsed entirely Dr Martin's plea for university standards. But he wished to apply a corrective to what he saw might easily become over-specialization in isolation. This could so easily become the master rather than the servant of the gospel. Ultra-specialization had the great danger of losing the perspective that sees the proportions of the whole case.

When this happened in medicine the patient was at risk! Their 'patient' was, after all, humanity in need of the gospel. Technical experts are often poor theologians, and sometimes, after contributing their own piece to the puzzle, seem largely uninterested in the task of putting it in its proper place. There must therefore be equally trained and gifted theologians to make due use of the total result. It was therefore also of the highest importance (and many at the gathering stressed this) that the leader of any such research centre should be one with a pastoral heart and a real feeling for younger members in lonely research, and that he himself should be supported by a team for his own spiritual and intellectual health.

And so, hardly aware of how much they were formulating the problems and the growth of future days, these people sharpened each other like iron upon iron. One thing is sure. The kind of things they were thrashing out never go away. Diagnosis and treatment are always with us. The patient certainly recovered, though he has picked up both anticipated and unforeseen complications along the way.

Chapter Nine

LIGHT IN THE BLACKOUT

There were probably very few students aware of what was being prayed and planned for among the theologians. But just as no general's plans can come to anything without those in the front line, so any evangelical advance was dependent on what was happening in the CUs. The tale of two CUs from 1939 to 1945 will suffice to show what the prospects were. Historic CICCU saw exciting new potential that was realized after 1945. The struggling Birmingham CU, though small, got to its feet and many of its members were later to grow tall in the service of Christ.

For many years the witness of CICCU had been brave and faithful, but not all that fruitful. It now began to take off again. From 1940 to 1945 Oliver Barclay became the backbone of the CICCU. That was the judgment of its most experienced observer. With his long family tradition of Quakerism, reaching back to the seventeenth century, he received an absolute exemption from military service. Consequently he remained on in Cambridge engaged in doctoral research of national importance. In 1941 he struck up a friendship with a freshman at Trinity College named John Stott, who had been converted at Rugby School through the influence of Bash. The doldrum days of the CICCU were beginning to pass away. It was as if a cloud, the size of a young man's hand, appeared on the distant horizon.

But when Stott went up to Cambridge his father's last words to him were hardly complimentary of the body his ministry was to do so much to strengthen. ' "You will find a society in the university called the Cambridge . . . er . . . Inter-

Collegiate . . . er . . . Christian Mission. Don't join it! They are a lot of anaemic wets!" So, respectful of parental authority, I did not join it. But I went to the meetings and found great blessing there.'

Meanwhile Barclay, the CICCU president, drawn both by ties of friendship and the outstanding qualities of the younger man, spent a lot of time with him. 'Oliver and I met frequently at college prayer meetings, sat next to each other for meals and both sang in the college choir. We often walked round and round the Great Court of Trinity or along the Backs or in the Trinity Fellows' gardens, "trying to solve all the problems of church and state" as I have sometimes put it. We were both pacifists and had conscientious questions about Christian participation in war.'

A friendship so congenial and formative helped to gel some of the best in parallel evangelical strengths and to be constructively critical of some of its weaknesses. It was becoming clear that Oliver was Douglas Johnson's heir-apparent, and John Stott seemed set to follow Bash. 'D.J. and Bash did not see eye to eye with one another, Bash regarding D.J. and the IVF as too intellectual, so that he did not want his officers to attend IVF conferences; while D.J., though admiring Bash's evangelistic zeal, felt he was unbalanced in some of his emphases. But Oliver and I did not share the mutual hesitations of our respective bosses. After two years of modern languages I switched to theology. I saw then the need to develop an adequate intellectual basis for an evangelical faith. On more than one occasion I sought help from D.J. regarding the right approach and what books to read.' This influence, wedded to the fellowship of the CICCU, helped to hold Stott to a strong commitment to Christ and the Scriptures while he came to terms with liberal theology. He was set a good example, which he was to follow, by the older than usual CICCU president of 1939, Derek Kidner, who had gained a 'first' in theology, and was to write IVP books outstanding for their biblical scholarship and their sharp eyes for the contemporary world.

Though speakers were less available during wartime, the number of conversions rose. Old Testament Jonathan was not the last to discover that 'nothing can hinder the Lord from saving, whether by many or by few' (1 Samuel 14:6). The Sunday night CICCU sermons were now attended by students from evacuated London colleges. Barclay and Stott were ushers at these events. Early on in her first term Shirley Johnson of Queen Mary College, London (later Mrs Bill Lees of OMF), had been invited to the sermons. She soon noticed how graciously the two ushers smiled at all the men, 'but when the girls came in, they showed us to our places with their eyes to the ground. I tried to get one of them to smile at me, but I did not succeed; and when Bill told John this some years after we were married, his comment was, "Oh, Bill, aren't you glad I didn't?" ' At least this careful reserve, a fence against over-familiarity typical of the CUs of that day, did not deter her from regular attendance. That term she did not miss one Sunday night sermon. During the Christmas vacation a friend wrote to her, and she replied saying how much she was missing the sermons. 'During the next term a non-Christian friend and I decided to go to see some Shakespeare, but found an enormous queue. We wandered round to a tiny cinema in a small side-street off the Market Place. The film was called *Escape to Happiness*, and, as the lead was being taken by Leslie Howard, my then favourite star, we decided to go inside. The theme was of a man going off with a pretty girl for a "wow" of a time on the continent. But the final scene was of the man opening the door of his home as his wife came down the stairs to welcome him back. There had been no "escape to happiness".

'As I put my light out that night a full moon shone on to the corner of the wall in my bedroom; it seemed exceptionally bright. I kept on looking at it. I "saw" a figure in the brightness, and the Lord seemed to say to me, "That is what you are trying to do – escape to happiness. You will not find happiness, unless you find it in me." I got out of bed, knelt down and repented of my rebellion. Next day I told my friend and she nearly died of shock. But she too professed conversion by the end of term. The friend who had been taking me to CICCU said, "I knew something was going to happen when you wrote to say you were missing the sermons. It encouraged us to go on praying for you." On my next vac. I read Hudson Taylor's biography and I told the Lord I would be a missionary if that was what he wanted.'

Researching the sources of a movement of God is every bit as exciting as seeing the first pictures of earth taken from an orbiting space craft. The overall pattern emerges. Had we called in at Clare College in 1943 we would not have seen what

93

we can now see, looking down from the hill of history; for there we have the source of more rivulets of evangelical influence. John Collins arrived as a short-term RAF cadet. He had been converted at a Bash camp in the summer holidays before going up. When he returned for his main course of studies after the war he showed an outstanding gift of winning others for Christ. From Northern Ireland came Fred Catherwood (now Sir Fred Catherwood, Member of the European Parliament, and treasurer of IFES). He came from a predominantly working-class church and was well used to enjoying fellowship with Christian working men. But they were not equipped to solve the problems that cropped up at school. At Cambridge he began to meet, for the first time, people who were in a world of learning who were also Christians. 'But far more important, they prayed for and expected conversions and their prayers were answered. I too prayed for a friend's conversion and, much to my surprise, he was converted. Now I knew what it was to take the initiative with other Christians to roll back the tide of unbelief. It was an enormous encouragement.'

John Lefroy of Clare (later a London evangelical vicar) was among those converted. So too was John Marsh (later a surgeon and for many years chairman of UCCF Council). A daughter of the one and a son of the other were to be on the Durham CU executive committee together – just one illustration of how a wave of blessing in one generation swells the tide of belief in the next. John Marsh was on the wartime four-terms-a-year medics' course. His story tells us a lot about why and how people were reached for a life-time for Christ. He came up a seeker, having already had experience of what he later knew to be the conviction of the law of God, but having no understanding of the gospel.

'One of the disasters of my teenage life was that I expected confirmation at school to do something for me, and when it did not, I was pretty shattered. When I arrived at Clare, an old school friend, Frank Stallybrass, invited me to the freshers' sermon. The preacher was Canon Warner, a quite elderly man by then, chairman of the Ruanda Council. He was described by Earnshaw Smith as "an evangelist of whom there are all too few in the Church of England – a man privileged to see men and women won to Christ, Sunday by Sunday, through the clear preaching of the Word of God." So it was for me. At that freshers' meeting he preached on John 3:16. I sat there thinking, "This is what I have wanted to know for years." I went to collect a New Testament offered to any who wanted one. I went home in joy. I remember sitting up late reading the epistles and being amazed that they made sense. Every word rang true. This to me was, and still is, a tremendous confirmation of the truth of what I had heard in that very simple message of Warner's.'

In the weeks that followed he found that it was not easy to stand up for his new faith with old friends. But new CICCU friends helped to nurture him. He had his failures and watched one friend go through the introspective agonies produced by the confusions of perfectionist doctrines. But Basil Atkinson's Bible readings were a source of constant stimulus and they tended to be the pattern by which his generation judged everything else. 'I could not work out for some time what Bible version he was using. Then I realized that he came equipped with his Greek New Testament and that was all. But it was enough.'

Wartime stringencies tilted student lifestyle in the direction of discipline. There were two compulsory Home Guard drill sessions a week which most students did on a Sunday. Some Christians opted for a week day so as to keep Sunday free for worship and witness. This tightened up their work schedules. Then there was college fire-watching which involved sleeping in a duty room three times a term. It made life quite a serious business.

It was certainly a grim day for Helen Roseveare when she turned up at Cambridge to begin her medical training in 1944, having travelled through a doodlebug (flying bomb) raid on London on the way there. It left her feeling strained and tense and she arrived for her first day at Newnham nervous and lonely.[1] But a welcoming homely gesture was to leave its mark on her life. A note on the mirror of her room invited her to coffee in Room 12 at 8.00 p.m. The cheerful, helpful friendship begun there led, for example, to an invitation to hear Ken Hooker. It made her vividly aware of something radically new. As a nominal Anglo-Catholic she had never heard anything like his preaching on "There is . . . one mediator between God and men, the man Christ Jesus' (1 Timothy 2:5). She began to

[1]See H. Roseveare, *Give Me This Mountain*, pp. 19–32, for the full story.

read the New Testament for herself and found a great longing stirring in her soul. Nowhere in the New Testament could she find anything about a human priest who could act as a go-between between man and God. But was there really a God anyway? The other interest which competed for her support at this time was Communism. On a Saturday early in term she helped out as hockey goalkeeper for Newnham. Overnight she became goalkeeper for the Cambridge University women's team. Her captain and friend was the leader of the university women's Communist party.

So Sundays became a three-cornered battle – Anglo-Catholicism in the mornings, Communism in the afternoons and evangelical preaching in the evenings. As with many thoughtful seekers, known and unknown, it was the epistle to the Romans that settled the matter. Persuaded to attend a Bible training conference she bought a copy of *Search the Scriptures*. After supper she curled up by the fire in the lounge and started the study of Paul's letter. She studied each suggested question and wrote answers in the margin of her newly purchased Bible. Time ticked by and with a satisfied sigh she completed her task and went up to bed. As she made her way up the stairs she met some girls. To her astonishment she discovered that they were getting up for kitchen duty and she was going to bed at 5.30 a.m.!

The Word of God had done its work. Later in the same conference she came to know that she had entered into a new and living relationship with God by faith in Christ. The epistle to the Romans has remained her favourite ever since. Witness to her hockey captain followed and eventually she too yielded her life to the Lord and the Communist became a missionary for Christ, as, of course, did Helen Roseveare, known the world over through her books about the Congo (now Zaire).

Nearby, in Homerton, another young missionary was in the making. Heather Masterman (Mrs Denis Osborne) came from a non-Christian home. But an attractive dimension of life in a new friend drew her to the CICCU. The sheer joy and reality in the singing amazed her, as it had done Helen. One night, the preacher, using 2 Corinthians 5:14–15, drew vivid pictures of someone living to himself and the difference when he began to live to Jesus.

'I realized I was in the first category and I wanted to be in the second. For about a month I tussled with myself as I knew

96

I would be ridiculed at home. Then, one Sunday evening, cycling among the beechwoods, I asked Jesus into my life – and spent twenty years in his service in Ruanda. From God's love and grace in speaking to me that first term there are now three Christian homes of the next generation where they too are seeking to live "to Jesus".'

A CU is like a hub and its members like the spokes going off in all directions. In any one particular year that hub may be very small, but the wheel's circumference can encompass the world. Members of the small wartime Birmingham CU were flung far and wide.

'One memory leads to another, like pulling spaghetti off a plate', observes Honor Ward (née Shedden). 'IVF began opening so many new doors to me that, in a sense, I am still going through them.' Her BUECU days were to lead to thirty-five years in the universities of three African countries along with her husband, Dr Alan Ward, who was converted partly through the influence of the CU.

But it could have been all so different for Honor. The CU encouraged its members to join their own local church. For someone in Honor's position it produced a catch-22 situation. She belonged to the Exclusive Brethren and if she were to become a full member she would not have been allowed to attend CU activities. Because a tendency to an exclusivism on a narrower basis than the gospel has again reared its head in some newer church groups, this episode still has its lessons. She was told by her assembly leader that she had no option but to leave the CU because such interdenominational evangelical bodies could not be in full agreement with the teaching and practice of the Exclusives. She was then asked about her plans for the future. 'I told him I hoped to work with delinquent girls. His reply, under the hand of God, helped me immensely. "What a thing for a respectable girl with your upbringing to think of doing! Would you try to grow beautiful flowers on a dunghill?" By sheer weight of age and experience he bore me down. I was crying too hard to get on a bus, so I walked home. On the walk of three miles or so the Lord spoke to me. Of course beautiful flowers grow on a dunghill. Where else would they grow better! And isn't that exactly what our Lord did? He came to a dunghill when he came to earth and he grew beautiful flowers on it. I decided to take my stand with the CU.'

Thankfully, the CU, which had begun to give her a wider window on the evangelical world, now became her refuge and resource, a warm nest that saved her from cold disillusion, a storehouse from which she gathered strength to cope with life. The close friendship of the CU was life-saving. 'I well remember the way Norah Nixon,[2] the travelling secretary, listened when I sought to tell her the problem. I have tried to hand on that sort of listening counselling.'

There were, of course, other local Christian bodies who fed in their young people to the CU with enthusiasm. For example, the Solihull Crusader group supplied Bill Lees, Frank Rhodes, Jill Dann (née Cartwright), and (to Oxford) Raymond Johnston. Few would look back without an immense sense of gratitude for the help given by the vicar of St John's, Harborne, who was 'a source of ever-ready strength', and by some of the university staff. Peter Gray (now Professor of Child Health at Cardiff) recalls to this day the first CU talk he heard in 1942 given by Birmingham surgeon, J. B. Leather. The occasional visits of Gordon Harman, the travelling secretary, did them all the world of good and Peter Gray derived much personal blessing from his ministry. Bill Lees, a fellow medic, remembers the lessons they learned from wrongly putting him on a spiritual pedestal due to his reputation as a speaker. Having heard much about him, they booked him to speak at two evangelistic meetings. So confident were they of a good meeting that little prayer was made. It turned out to be a disaster. The rather struggling CU dreaded another flop and so for the next three months prayer was anything but routine. They worked hard to get people along, trusting God to make a difference for his own name's sake. And he did. Gordon Harman spoke in the power and demonstration of the Spirit. They had begun to learn that, whatever a speaker's gifts, it was God alone who gave the blessing, and prayer was never dispensable. It helped to mature them as leaders, and in the process many had got to know better the ways of the Lord.

Bill Lees soon found that he was in demand as a speaker himself, and contemporaries remember him as an outspoken advocate of the gospel and also a fine speech-maker. When Anthony Eden was a guest speaker at the Birmingham medical

[2]Aged ninety-three at the time of writing, and still serving the Lord in her local church.

98

students' annual meeting, he remarked that Bill's presidential address surpassed most speeches he had heard in the House! It was preparation for preaching that helped formulate his Christian thinking; he discovered and developed gifts in the process and found a way to keep at it when tired. Sometimes, when hard pressed in his final hospital year he would deliberately accept a commitment to give a series of Bible expositions. He got to know that otherwise he would argue to himself that he was too tired to study the Bible.

Both Bill Lees and Peter Gray opted together for medical service in the newly released island of Singapore. Bill got there and later spent many years further east in Borneo with his wife, Shirley.[3] His friend was turned down for Singapore as 'category 4 or whatever was the lowest grade possible for mankind'. Since it transpired that the rejection was solely due to an error in assessing his eyesight it can only be assumed that a higher providence intended to keep him for Cardiff rather than to send him to the orient.

The 'shining witness' by common consent among the wartime medics at Birmingham was Ruth Watson. Her future, too, lay in the Far East. But she was for long in two minds about the path God wanted her to travel. It was very much her ambition to be a surgeon. It proved a great struggle for her as she thought about offering herself for missionary service. She chose the latter. Her story as 'the kanchi doctor' – one of the early missionary doctors into inaccessible Nepal – is fascinating and heroic.[4] She later testified that God gave her both her desires as she undertook a major surgical programme in Nepal. In a moving tribute the Royal College of Surgeons of England granted her an Honorary Fellowship in the latter years of her shortened life, in recognition of the pioneer work she had undertaken.

As a student she liked to make her own little claim to fame. Her father was a chief executive involved in the design of the Whittle jet engine. Ruth used to tell of one weekend in the war when he worried the whole time. He could not solve a particular equation which was necessary for the correct functioning of the engine. Ruth triumphantly gave him the answer. This she regarded as her contribution to jet propulsion!

[3]Some of their story is told in their book *Is it Sacrifice?*
[4]See David Hawker, *Kanchi Doctor*.

One of those who helped give the BUECU a missionary vision was Mrs Alexander Dixon, the widow of Mr Alexander of the Torrey/Alexander mission team of the early 1900s. From the founding years of the CU it had held conferences at 'Tennessee', her huge Victorian house, where in pre-war years they were fed and watered for a weekend, waited upon by maids, and didn't pay a thing. 'It was a different world,' says Ronald Inchley. Mrs Dixon was one of the Cadbury family. 'She passed through the eye of a needle with a great freedom and grace and used her "chocolate money" liberally in the Lord's service,' recalled Honor Ward. 'A conference centre had been built in the grounds by our time. As we all turned up for a houseparty she would walk, pained with arthritis, down the path from the big house to meet us. "Before the war, my dears, I used to have you all to sleep in the house, but now you are such a big group . . . Never mind. And now I want to introduce you to . . . " And our vision of the world church would widen further as we met an African with, to us, an unpronounceable name. Africa began to loom very large with me. There was a memorial study in that conference centre to Mr Alexander and we used Alexander No. 3 hymnbooks quite often in BUECU. Thirty years later, when we arrived in the University of Swaziland, I was amazed to find the student Christian group using that very Alexander hymnbook!'

And so we end the tale of two CUs in wartime. Meanwhile, Douglas Johnson, holding the fort in an evacuated office out of town, kept in touch all round and did his own bit of 'war correspondence'. Some ex-CU men wrote to him from aerodromes, garrisons and camps, enclosing gifts 'to help keep the work intact after the war'. Many had become chaplains, including Howard Guinness at Tangmere aerodrome, and Maurice Wood, decorated with a DSO, having landed with the Commandos on the high casualty raid at Walcheren. One chaplain in north Africa wrote asking for some Greek New Testaments to help officers planning to enter the ministry after demob. Two were later spotted – one being studied by an officer sitting on his tank, another being read, more symbolically, in the shade of a rock in the desert.

The traumas of wartime experience overseas were a factor in leading some to offer for missionary service when war ended. The Royal Army Medical Corps (RAMC) had a fair sprinkling of ex-CU men; for example, Dennis Burkitt and Guy Timmis. Timmis, at Liverpool, and Burkitt, at Dublin, were, as we have seen, both converted as first-year students within months of each other. They met up when pursuing further studies together at Edinburgh.

Timmis had several close shaves during the war. 'It was during an air raid on Malta when I asked the Lord to keep me safe if he had something useful to do through me after the war. His answer seemed to come when my unit was moving up the toe of Italy from Reggio. At the last moment the C.O. ordered me to get out of the medical truck with which I normally travelled and join the surgical team. I was a bit annoyed at the time. An hour later the medical truck went over the edge of a cliff. I have never learned why the C.O. gave the order. Towards the end of the war, Dennis Burkitt was serving with the RAMC in East Africa. (He was to continue in East Africa for many years.) He wrote to me suggesting that a useful form of service for Christians after the war was in the Uganda Medical Service.'

It was the kind of guidance Timmis was seeking. He spent sixteen years in Uganda and fourteen in Hombolo Leprosy Centre in Tanganyika.

This chapter has touched on enough to remind us that the war years were years of colossal disturbance, both on the surface of everyday life and in the depths of the nation's psyche. As women moved increasingly into jobs in factories, or became members of the armed forces, so their roles became more onerous. Adapting bravely to wartime emergencies were women travelling secretaries Norah Nixon and Phyl Bennett. Travelling often in blackout conditions, sharing packed-out trains with troops, they penetrated into the far-flung corners of the country, helping to breathe life into the embers of smouldering CUs. 'Is your journey really necessary?' asked the big wartime hoardings. An episode from one of Phyl Bennett's long tramps north shows how God had his ways of showing how valuable they were.

'At Leeds University, the secretary of the CU explained that they were expecting a Roman Catholic to come (very rare in those days). She came to talk to me after our Bible study on John 3:16. She understood clearly that Jesus had died on the cross once for all and that through his death she could have forgiveness. She left knowing that she could receive him as

101

Saviour. This she did on the following day.

'On Monday morning she came to see me off on the train about 9.30 a.m. She asked me questions about how the Bible and Roman Catholic beliefs tallied. I answered as well as I could, but remarked, "How I wish you could meet Canon T. C. Hammond," who had written on this subject, and who I knew was then on a speaking tour of CUs. As we talked, a train drew in from London, and, to my amazement, from the compartment directly in front of us, stepped Canon Hammond. "Canon Hammond!" I burst out, "What are *you* doing here?" "I'm going to speak at Hull University CU, but I've an hour or so to wait for my connection." I looked at my friend. "Have you a lecture?" "No." So I introduced them and left them talking.

'The next morning I sat in the office next to D.J. I noticed on his prayer leaflet that on the previous day the main topic had been "TS" (travelling secretaries). "Did you pray for me about this time yesterday?" "Yes." I then told him what had happened.' Such a small compact staff team were aware of constant prayer support.

Uppermost in Johnson's mind was the need to rebuild this team as war ended. He kept in touch with Ronald Inchley, who returned in 1945. They soon began to make the literature side hum, and as the influx of ex-servicemen, with their experience of leadership, had a profound effect on the speed of CU growth, so it became obvious that a full-time accountant would now be needed. Over in Washington DC, George White, a member of the RAF delegation, began to pray about his peacetime future. He had married Muriel Fowaker, a friend of Johnson's wife from CU days. 'The hall we had intended getting married in had been struck by a bomb the week before the date. The fire-fighters included my fiancée, who emerged from the debris to become my bruised and battered bride. When the war was nearing its end and I was on the demob list I got in touch with D.J. and was taken to lunch by him and John Laing. I dithered long over guidance. "The need constitutes the call," said my wife. I joined the IVF in April 1946. It was a bit of a shock after Washington not even to have a typist and to have to do the donkey work myself. But it proved a marvellous experience to watch those pioneers at work and to know they laboured indefatigably for tiny salaries. I count it an outstanding blessing to have worked in the back room with them.'

102

The blessing was not one way. 'Dear George White,' recalls a staff member about one who is now with Christ, 'with his great concern for each one of us. He gladly gave up much of this world's goods to serve the Lord with the IVF.' The hand-written, highly individual and very brief personal notes he added to the standard 'thank you' letters gave recent news, especially of the donor's former university CU. This helped greatly to make scattered graduates feel that they still belonged to the Fellowship.

Johnson also knew the crucial importance of persuading a few professional people to give their priority voluntary time to serve the witness of the CUs. He wrote and asked Brian Harris, an ex-CICCU member with a great business flair, to consider slotting IVF into his plans for post-war Christian service. He has been involved up to the hilt and without release until 1987, always in the back room, keeping the financial score. Such wholehearted commitment has come, too, from Dr J. T. (Jack) Aitken, then Senior Lecturer and later Professor of Anatomy, University College, London. These are two of the forerunners of many who have given unstintingly of time and talents to the development of the work from 1945 to the present day.

Out among the unions all kinds of encouragements were beginning to flow. Though many CU men of promise had been lost to the future of the work through death in war service, others had matured and rededicated themselves in the stresses of war. The student world was now to feel the impact of their quality of life and testimony.

PART THREE
1945–1949
THE GOOD FIGHT OF FAITH

Chapter Ten

CAMBRIDGE MISSIONS

'I feel that the Barnhouse mission in November 1946 should be held to mark the start of the evangelical revival in the universities which was a feature of the 1950s.' Such is the judgment of John Pollock, writing forty years on. War had concentrated the mind. The peace left many non-Christians in a vacuum. But for many Christian ex-servicemen it left a mature urgency to concentrate on fighting the good fight. Evangelical life gathered momentum in most universities. We shall start in Cambridge with the period of 'the great missions'. In 1946 and 1949 they were led by Dr D. G. Barnhouse of the United States.

The mission of 1946 had about it a thrust of evangelistic power that had not been seen in British universities since the nineteenth century. We have watched some of the leaders in training. Behind the scenes there was a gathering of strength. Suddenly the 1946 mission seemed to give it face and front. Whereas, at the end of the first world war, CICCU had been holding on by its teeth, this time its hold was firm. John Pollock, an ex-Coldstream Guards officer, was CICCU president in 1946. He had already been involved, as assistant missioner, in a wartime CICCU mission led by Colin Kerr a few months before D-Day. It had the title 'Life's Ultimate Realities'. The team included an army major, a pilot with a DFC, and a commando chaplain, soon to gain the DSO. Now those hazardous days were over, and Pollock was back, along with many others, alive and well, but still concerned with life's ultimate realities. But what about the hardened crowd of ex-combatants who were now the student generation? Would they listen to the gospel? The quiet, cultured tones of CICCU Christianity somehow needed sharpening. Men accustomed to the bark of barrack-room and battlefield could take a more trenchant edge. While up at the Keswick Convention Pollock went out of curiosity to hear Barnhouse. He sensed that here was a man with a strong element of attack in his ministry. He was pugnacious, witty and sincere. This was their man. 'If he was rough,' recalls Barclay, 'it was a language that the men of the time understood.'

The mission committee could hardly have been more in the mould of the English public school. It included a future bishop and suffragan bishop and two future public-school headmasters. But most of them had been staff officers. Only one of them – Timothy Dudley-Smith – was straight from school. 'Though the CICCU was still comparatively small and not considered intellectually respectable,' comments John Marsh, 'those returning from the war did not care much about the tastes of chaplains and dons in the way we who missed war service did.' Publicity for the mission was just a bit reminiscent of victory celebrations. Confident young men in their mid-twenties toured the little city in loudspeaker vans, and coloured streamers hung in Petty Cury, a short, narrow street off the Market Square. The gloomy realities of post-war Britain had not yet caught up with people and the methods fitted the mood. Things were to calm down as the enthusiasms of ex-servicemen waned, and the publicity of 1949 and 1952 owed much to the tasteful work of Dudley-Smith.

In both Barnhouse missions professions of conversion were more numerous than in pre-war missions. Some college CUs were high with thanksgiving. Peterhouse, for example, had seven members at the beginning of a year and ended with over thirty. One man, ex-army, a strong drinker and intellectual and reputed to know more dirty stories than the rest of the college put together, was soundly converted in the mission, and is now a Christian lawyer. The event produced a kind of emergency panic meeting among members of the college rugby fifteen. 'If a man like Colin can be converted, none of us is safe!' one was overheard to say.

After such a mission there would usually be some who professed conversion who would subsequently sink without trace. Others, though maintaining a Christian profile, eventually took a higher view of churchmanship. For example, one young atheist science student, converted in 1946, became an

Archbishop of York – John Habgood. He began to be won round after a combination of logical argument and straightforward confrontation from two assistant missioners. His biography *Living with Paradox*[1] tells of his talk with Barnhouse and his conversion to Christ on 28 November 1946. Other student converts fully embraced the more doctrinally alert evangelicalism that was emerging. As we follow the story we shall see that the biblical message, when faithfully adhered to and passed on, produces a continuity of witness and consistency of response that links one generation to another in a fellowship of truth which creates the true community of saints. Bearers of the message are links in a chain.

Sociologist Steve Bruce has noted how this freedom from the fad of the 'new' has prevented a constantly recurring generation gap in evangelical student life between past and present.[2] If the older generation remained true to the biblical gospel they were asked back again and again. It was a thrill to the 'few' – the pre-war students who had stood firm in times of evangelical ebb – to see God use their ministry to advance the work in more propitious days. Hugh Gough and L.F.E. Wilkinson and others were part of more reaping days in post-war Cambridge. 'What! Thirty conversions, Basil!' said Gough, 'It would have been a nine-day wonder in our time if there had been three.' The students, of course, were grateful for the support of the older leaders.

There is also a very characteristic chain of personal relationships as people were won for Christ out of friendship and a careful, unhurried approach. The gift of clarifying the issue, one to one, in a straight and friendly manner is seen at its best in John Collins.

It was a November day in 1949 when Collins, a theology student, first met David Sheppard, a freshman, in a game of squash. Sheppard had arrived in Cambridge with a county cricket cap and England caps not far ahead. He was also churchgoing, and by the time of the Barnhouse meetings Collins knew him well enough to invite him to attend. But for that he would never have thought of going. He assumed he was on the religious road already. 'The idea that I might not be on the road at all never occurred to me. It needed a blunt

[1] By John S. Peart-Binns.
[2] Steve Bruce, *Firm in the Faith*, p. 90.

preacher from the United States to jolt me into thinking. He aroused strong feelings. . . .

'But on the first night that I listened I realized that I was facing God himself, was judged by his standards and that I desperately needed to be forgiven . . . because I had turned my back on God and gone my own way. Again and again Barnhouse returned to his great theme that no-one can climb up to God by his own efforts to be kind, neighbourly or religious. Only by the totally undeserved grace of Jesus Christ can anyone be accepted.'

As the two friends talked, it was brought home to David Sheppard that his idea of trying to get to God by following Christ's example did not tally with the Bible. 'Once I had come this far I listened with quite new urgency to what John told me about Jesus. Numbering himself with sinners, deliberately walking to a criminal's death, going out as far as the furthest sinner is from God, he tasted the blackest moment of the sinner's experience, as he cried, "My God, my God, why hast thou forsaken me?"

'I understood the force of the words I had heard many times in the communion service, "He made there a full, perfect and sufficient sacrifice . . . for the sins of the whole world." If Jesus Christ had taken our place on the cross he has made it possible for us to be forgiven and for us to be sure about it. . . . The Christian's claim that he can be sure that God has forgiven him is not boastful, because it is a matter of accepting something we can never deserve. We accept it, or better, we accept him. That evening in Cambridge I heard a verse from the Bible for the first time, which in picture language seemed to make this all so clear – Revelation 3:20.

'I walked back to my rooms in Trinity Hall that night knowing it was more important than anything else in the world that I should become right with God. . . . I asked Christ to come into my life. Perhaps the first difference was to think rather worse of myself than I had before. Some weeks later I joined a Christian houseparty. I said to myself, "I didn't know there were people like this." I did not mean they were perfect: they were ordinary men of my own age trying to work out the friendship of Christ for every day. Discussing the problems of Christian living and simply sharing a common life with other Christians, particularly those in the CU, made the idea of the church as the family of God come alive.'

Meanwhile, a Clare man, Nigel Sylvester, had begun going nightly to hear Barnhouse. Till then he had been a regular at the 'Heretics' – the Rationalist Society. But he was a church-goer of sorts, and as the mission was on every night, he decided to go. He kept on going. 'The only thing I remember under-standing was that he said we could be sure we have eternal life. This seemed odd, because I had always thought of heaven as a reward for the faithful. . . .

'On my way out of the church one night I ran into a man who had taught me at school and was now back in Cambridge training for the ministry. He asked me what I thought of the service. For some reason I replied that I thought it needed talking over. I remember him explaining that eternal life is a gift that we have to receive. I dug out a Bible and saw it there. "The gift of God is eternal life" (Romans 6:23). "He who has the Son has life" (1 John 5:12). We then read from Revelation 3:20, "Behold, I stand at the door and knock." It was a simple idea to understand.' That night, in the quiet and solitude of his own room, he fought with indecision. He knelt by a chair and asked Christ to come to him and give him eternal life. Though it was only later he began to realize the extent of his own sin and the mystery of Christ's atonement, straight away life began to change. There was the further excitement of realizing that he was but one among many. He recalls twenty to thirty still active in Christian leadership today. One of them, John Dean, is International Training Consultant with Scripture Union. Nigel, after Scripture Union work in Africa, and a spell as General Director of the movement, is now its International Secretary. Conversion of such people in university helped to intertwine and consolidate ties between IVF and other expanding evangelical movements. We shall see something of the same at Oxford.

Chapter Eleven

OXFORD SEVENS

The leaders' meeting drew to a close. 'Keep looking up,' said the Group Captain to his team. It was second nature to an airman. The Wing Commander grinned. It reminded him of recent briefing sessions that were thankfully a thing of the past. Both former airmen were now students at Oxford and the team leaders' meeting was an OICCU executive committee meeting. The call to 'keep looking up' was not a reminder to keep alert in the cockpit. It was the oft-repeated phrase that the now demobbed Group Captain (acting Air Commodore) Donald Wiseman used in order to encourage his post-war OICCU committee to keep their eyes on the Lord in the spiritual battle they were now engaged in. The ex-Wing Commander, Branse Burbridge, found Donald's personal example inspiring. So did others on the executive committee of OICCU; Roy Stillman, for instance, an ex-Royal Marine. 'He was the one who helped me most by his disciplined Christian life. I was missionary secretary and I remember how insistent he was that all members should have prayed over the agenda for the weekly meeting which consisted of half an hour prayer and half an hour business. Sometimes it was literally that. I have been to numerous committees since those days but none to match it in keeping to the point.' One of the advantages that former senior officers brought to the CUs was that administrative tasks could be done efficiently without any distraction from the spiritual essentials.

Wiseman, who became OICCU president in 1947, had two main essentials in view. He, along with Burbridge and others, was very influential in stimulating evangelistic awareness. They were the mainspring of the T. C. Hammond mission in 1948.

College groups varied in strength and effectiveness, but there were as many conversions from their steady influence as from the Sunday evangelistic services (held then in St Martin's in the High) and the mission. His second concern was the advancement of evangelical biblical scholarship. It was now over ten years since the LIFCU mission 'Out of World Chaos'. He had been challenged then to give himself to the study and defence of the Old Testament. To equip himself for the task he had flung himself into conquering the mysteries of, among other things, the Sumerian, Hittite and Akkadian languages. 'We were active, too, in Oxford, in supporting the new Tyndale House work. We saw it as a source of academic encouragement and contending for the faith. It persuaded IVF men to aim for university appointments in relevant subjects and provided a background for the Theological Students Fellowship in making it not a matter of derision to be a Christian and a scholar. I formed the Old Testament group of the Tyndale Fellowship, of which I was secretary after J. Stafford Wright in 1948.' During this time he was also giving a vigorous lead as IVF student chairman.

As an expression of his own pre-war concern to see evangelical scholarship flourish, he gathered a few folk around him to pray. They prayed for an 'Oxford Seven'.[1] This they never made public. They were bent on looking to the Lord to bring it to pass. 'Looking back now over the years it is clear that the Lord answered in abundance and three times over. From that generation of students, seven went into full-time service at home, seven went to the mission field and seven went into full-time academic work, five at least becoming professors. This penetration of the university senior world had been my own special prayer interest. At our OICCU reunion twenty-one years on, the main note was that of praise to God for his glorious keeping power. We could think of only a very few of the then quite large OICCU who were not still active in the Lord's service.'

David Ingram, one of the many future professors, remembers those OICCU days as somewhat muted as far as his own witness was concerned. 'I was then among the Exclusive Brethren; they did not encourage active interaction with other Christians.

[1] A counterpart to the 'Cambridge Seven' missionaries of 1884; see above, p. 21.

114

Despite this disapproval I was a fairly regular attender at Northgate Hall (where the OICCU held its Bible readings and prayer meetings) and very much enjoyed the times. Jim Houston, who had then become a Fellow in the Geography School, stood out as making the deepest impression on me. It was a unique time with the mixture of returning ex-servicemen and eighteen-year-olds straight up from school. Among the former, Donald Wiseman particularly impressed me as one of the very mature wise men of that generation.'

Another of that age group, Branse Burbridge, belongs to the group of seven who went into the full-time home ministry. He confesses to feeling 'slightly elderly' on starting his undergraduate days in 1945. He was also obliged to run from publicity. Like Old Testament David's heroes, he was marked out as one among the 'Sevens' who had performed great exploits. As a Mosquito night-fighter ace he had come out of the war much decorated (DSO and bar, DFC and bar, American DFC) but also much pursued by reporters. Like many others in his situation he wanted to forget. 'I was determined to avoid further publicity (I had suffered a little) and live a different life now I was at Oxford. I'm afraid I had been rather brutally silent to one reporter. I might have become a bit of a recluse but for a firm knock on my study door, and I warmed to the cheerful face beaming out of an RAF greatcoat like my own – the face of Douglas Milmine.' Milmine was to become one of the seven who went overseas. He later joined the South American Missionary Society, becoming Bishop of Paraguay, and was made CBE in 1983. They were in the same college, St Peter's, and rowed together. It was Douglas' friendship that helped Branse eventually to commit himself to OICCU.

He had been advised differently on coming up, as he explains. 'On arrival I was encouraged by a senior Christian to take an interest in SCM. To be fair, I think he was genuinely concerned that it was losing its way, and that participation of "older" people could pull it together. I endured the tobacco smoke in committee meetings for a term, but when I could no longer see across the room I gave up.' He saw the value of a generous spirit, but he did not want it to cloud over his Bible-based convictions.

On going down he saw the need to establish a clear evangelical work in the schools. In 1948 he helped found the Inter-School Christian Fellowship, which, though independent of

IVF, was to do a substantially similar work with a younger age group. The ISCF was jointly sponsored by IVF, Scripture Union and the two Crusader Unions. Branse was greatly encouraged by the enthusiasm of Douglas Johnson. 'I lunched with him on the day of my first school meeting in Surrey. It was a sort of commissioning. . . . We parted and I got into the car, with plenty of time to make the journey from London. Before starting the engine I opened my bag to check the travel instructions, and was astonished to find that it was a lunch-hour meeting. It had just about finished. My profuse apology was generously accepted. I wrote a rather red-faced letter to D.J. because I thought he'd enjoy the joke. His reply was a sort of lament to the effect that "even as ISCF was brought to birth a school group languishes and dies". Fortunately it was a rather healthy group which was probably stimulated into a good DIY meeting.'

Out of these three seed-packets of seven, more vigorous new growth was to come. It reminds us that the prayer of the righteous avails much. Raymond Johnston has been sadly missed since his death in 1986. He was a key figure and was to be a Barnabas and a stimulus to others throughout his Christian life. In teaching and then lecturing in education, he was a moving spirit in the founding of the Association of Christian Teachers. Later he sought, from a biblical base, to address the social and ethical problems of the seventies and eighties and was at the roots of CARE Trust (Christian Action Research and Education; formerly the Nationwide Festival of Light). He is remembered with great affection. Burbridge recalls how he became a great Goon fan, and sometimes his antics reflected it. 'Some of us were on a mini-mission together, sharing somewhat Spartan accommodation in a church hall. Four of us were sitting two and two on the sides of adjacent camp beds, chatting before turning in. Raymond entered, making a third on one side, sat down and instantly broke the bed. It didn't help that he was carrying a mug of cocoa and went down in a scalding sea.'

For others the diversion of life could be chess or jazz. For Val Grieve it was chess. He more or less revived the Oxford University Chess Club and the annual match against Cambridge. When he came up he was a convinced atheist, but the faithful witness of Rolf Hjorth, a fellow student at St John's, got through his defences. 'At times I began to have a sneaking suspicion that the Christian faith was true. I was actually converted on an Easter Sunday while at home and I met the risen Jesus. This is why I have been talking about his resurrection ever since and have spoken at twenty-five universities and over 200 times on it.'[2]

Over the chess table he met a West Country student from Corpus Christi called Jim Packer, clarinettist in the Oxford Bandits jazz band. 'I always say he was not very intellectual,' quips Val, 'because I was able to beat him.' Before coming up Jim Packer had met an old school friend who had become a Christian while at Bristol University. He tried to explain to Packer what had happened to him.[3] But the latter had remained in complete perplexity about his friend's experience during the remainder of his school days. He did, however, promise to contact the CU when he got to university.

By the time he went up to Oxford in 1945 he wanted reality. He went to OICCU evangelistic services as promised. The college representative, Ralph Hulme, had helped him in his search for faith. 'Listening one night to Earl Langston of Weymouth the scales fell from my eyes . . . I saw the way in.' It was, he remembers, an 'ordinary conversion' – nothing spectacular – but it made him realize 'where I wasn't and where I ought to be'. He identified heavily with the OICCU. Even his beloved jazz went. Both OICCU and band met at the same time on Saturday and his changed priorities showed when the music stopped.

The other great love in his life was books. Here, happily, there was no clash of allegiance. His loss of the jazz outlet made him, maybe, more devotedly intellectual. Certainly the egghead in him revelled in the fact that when the OICCU was presented with a very big library of theological volumes, he was appointed their junior librarian. It was to be a major event in his Christian life, and subsequently in the life of so many more he was to influence. It demonstrates yet again the impact of the written word. Among the volumes, he found copies of John Owen, a former Vice-chancellor of the University of Oxford in the Cromwellian era and probably England's foremost theologian. Owen met his need and did him good. So did

---

[2]He has also written an evangelistic book on the theme: *Your Verdict* (IVP/STL, 1988).
[3]For a fuller account of what follows, see Christopher Catherwood, *Five Evangelical Leaders*, pp. 169–171.

much else, like Bishop Ryle on *Holiness*. Most of these books had been out of print a long time. He and others in their circle were fed in mind and soul as never before. The prevailing evangelical suspicion of what theology did to its students had got through to Packer within weeks of his conversion, namely, that it was 'bad for one's soul'.[4] It was now beginning to dawn on him that it depended entirely on what was meant by theology. For Packer himself the discovery was initially the realization that 'doctrine', which tended among so many Christians to be neglected, was no mere arid science, but the totally practical study of the living God.

It was the reading of Ryle and the Puritans that brought him into close friendship with Raymond Johnston. Packer remembers Raymond returning to OICCU from an IVF annual conference at Swanwick, raving about a speaker he had heard there called Lloyd-Jones. Elizabeth Lloyd-Jones, an English student (now Lady Catherwood), found that she had not only her father's word for it that these books were the thing to read. Here were student contemporaries who had been bitten by the bug themselves. Meeting regularly in the British Restaurant, they engaged in theological debate, stirred by the renewed interest in Puritan writings. A breath of reformation was in the air. When Raymond Johnston went on to do a diploma in London he got the bright idea of holding an annual Puritan studies conference there. He took his friend Packer to meet 'the Doctor', as Westminster Chapel's medically trained minister was usually known, so that they might enlist his help in setting something up. 'Raymond was regularly the quick one', says Packer, 'and saw before others what was needed to be done, and by sharing his vision motivated and encouraged others to take appropriate action. Such he was as a student and ever continued to be.'

Meanwhile OICCU pursued its richly varied life. David Morris, later of Nigeria and then Principal of All Nations Christian College, was one of the few married students in post-war OICCU, and he and his wife exercised a considerable pastoral role, opening their 'semi' to all who needed counsel. Maurice Wood held many gatherings for OICCU at St Ebbe's Rectory, as did Montagu Goodman in his home in Davenant Road. Doing a doctoral thesis on the Second Evangelical Awakening

[4]J. I. Packer's Foreword to Bruce Milne, *Know the Truth*, p. 5.

was an older student, an American, J. Edwin Orr. He was a rare and fascinating individualist, and the OICCU committee, led by steady and conservative people such as David Mullins, David Turk and Laurie Binder, were unfamiliar with his style. He approached the leaders one day about a friend of his, who was visiting Oxford and suggested that he should speak at a special meeting of the OICCU. He was sure this young man had a great future ahead of him. When he mentioned that he was an American evangelist, the committee felt it ought to decline the idea. And so it happened that Billy Graham had to wait for a new decade to speak at OICCU.

These are vintage years and only a taste has been possible. Many a quieter OICCU member, too, like Gordon Landreth, was to put an enormous amount into varied spheres of service to Christ. So, from a relatively small batch of post-war students we see representatives of those through whom the base of evangelical theological competence was strengthened (Packer), and the technical and linguistic expertise necessary for the recovery of Old Testament credibility among scholars was laid (Wiseman), how a new generation of science professors arose who were to widen the apologetic thrust of CU witness (Ingram), how a renewed evangelical concern in education and social concern was nurtured (Johnston), and how a nationwide network of schools ministry was established (Burbridge). It points thankfully to a governing hand and the goodness of God to his people.

Chapter Twelve

PREACHING AND PREACHERS

Wartime London had been no place for large public meetings. Helen Roseveare's nerve-rending experience while travelling through to Cambridge reminds us of what the residents had to endure. But with the peace, attendance at church became a less risky business. Some central London churches like All Souls, Westminster Chapel and St Paul's, Onslow Square, were to have a great influence on students. This is an interesting contrast to pre-war days, when such evangelical churches as there were seemed inappropriate for students to bring non-Christian friends to. Post-war students developed a much more positive attitude. At Westminster Chapel, Martyn Lloyd-Jones began to draw ever larger crowds. John Stott had gone as curate to All Souls (then meeting at St Peter's, Vere Street) in 1945 and was to become its youngest ever rector. The Lord had set up his banner amid high places. All Souls sits next to the BBC; the Chapel is the nearest church to Buckingham Palace. As students joined the throngs going up the wide steps to hear 'the Doctor', they came to an oasis of spiritual life. John Marsh moved from Cambridge to continue his medical studies at St Thomas's. 'We realized that we were privileged, but just how privileged we were came to us only later as we realized that we had been present near the start of the great expository ministry as he preached through 2 Peter.' There was one postgraduate student who recognized it instantly. On first hearing, the preaching came to Jim Packer 'like an electric shock'.

The moment is worth recording, not just to benefit from Packer's assessment of what he heard, but for two other reasons. First, it gives us an understanding of why so many young men from the CUs felt stirred and called to be preachers in these years. Secondly, it marks in some ways the theological coming of age of IVF. It is now 1948, twenty years since its birth. Lloyd-Jones and Packer were soon to enter into a period of fruitful co-operation and their speaking and writing filtered through into CU leadership and thence on into many a pulpit. Lloyd-Jones, who had regularly chaired the TSF conference, later suggested that the younger man took his place. Perhaps we could say that the older 'Luther' figure and the younger 'Calvin' figure had met. (The originals sadly never did.) The actual first meeting came the following year, as we saw in the previous chapter, and it had quite momentous results.

Packer's recollections of his first visit, when he had slipped away to the Chapel one Sunday night during a temporary period of lecturing at Oak Hill Theological College, were given nearly forty years later at an evangelical assembly in which he shared the platform with Elizabeth Catherwood, his intellectual sparring-partner of OICCU days and daughter of the preacher he is describing. He introduces his theme by quoting 2 Corinthians 2:17: 'As men of sincerity, as commissioned by God in the sight of God, we speak in Christ' (RSV).

' "In the sight of God" is the phrase I want to underscore; in the sight of God we do our preaching. . . . We speak to make others realize his presence, we speak in order to tell them that God has come, he has come in Christ, he is coming right now by his Spirit, as we, weak human instruments that we are, preach his Word. God has come, God is coming, God is here – meet him. That's what preaching is about.

'In Westminster Chapel I experienced Lloyd-Jones doing it. . . . He would announce his text and then start talking about some aspect of human life today, some problem that human life today raises, some issue on the human level, which he would then turn, step by step, into a spiritual question – a question about man's relationship to God. And then he would practise in 101 different ways the 'Isaianic inversion', by which I mean this. Isaiah has and communicates a tremendous sense of the greatness of God and, by comparison, the smallness of man. 'All men are like grass.'' "Man has but a breath in his nostrils." He is weak, puny, trivial. He doesn't think that. He thinks he's marvellous, big, strong, wise, competent. But view him as he really is, in the light of God, and you'll see that it is only God who is great. Again and again, Lloyd-Jones practised this inversion, bringing that vision of reality on the scene by contrasts with man's pretensions and his belief that he has got things in hand and can manage his life and the world. It was overwhelming to me to hear him doing it, and there was no question, when he brought God in, that the presence of God in the congregation was an experienced reality. It was a marvellous thing. I asked myself, "What is this man doing?", and I thank God I was enabled to see what he was doing.' Later we shall see for ourselves what God was doing through it in some of the student listeners of the 1950s.

Over at All Souls, student evangelism advanced apace, and as John Stott established himself, he too had a big effect on students, making the ministry a priority calling from God. As early as 1946 when still at Vere Street the concept of student guest services was developed. The LIFCU also had its own evangelistic Sunday service, though these were eventually dropped when it became obvious that students were getting their friends to church on Sunday anyway. However, student services were much used. George Duncan 'expounded a very thrilling and challenging message from Romans 1:16' at Vere Street; Alan Redpath of Richmond Baptist Church spoke to a large congregation at All Souls. There was a 'wonderful testimony to God's faithfulness by someone who knows' said the minutes about Pastor Alf Schultes. LIFCU was a buzz of variety and life. An ever-increasing supply of younger speakers from the academic staff of the university came into the pipeline, speaking at lunch-hour meetings, helping with LIFCU houseparties. Names appear on student committees who were themselves to be CU speakers of later decades. The impetus is one of constant advance.

The post-war years saw powerful preaching ministries emerge in Scotland too. They were every bit as influential north of the border as the London axis in the south. The formative years of two of the most significant of Scotland's evangelical ministers lie in the Aberdeen student scene. William Still went up to Aberdeen in 1939. It was a year after Lloyd-Jones began his London ministry and a year or two before Stott began his studies at Cambridge. Still and Stott began their post-war ministries at just about the same time.

Being about eight years older than most students, Still took

123

some time to be aware of the Christian Students Fellowship, the evangelical student group at Aberdeen. Alec Crockett, later to be a city engineer, went up to Aberdeen in the same year. One day he asked Still a question. 'Have you not been to the CSF?' It was a question he himself cannot remember asking. But Willie Still says that university life became a different thing for him after that. Coming up at that time, too, was a classmate of Alec's at the local grammar school, James Philip. As a result of Willie's influence life was to be different for him too, and not just at university.

William Still had a background in the Salvation Army and a strong liking for music in worship. As university chapel organist he transformed a dreary college chapel turn-out of two or three into a crammed service called 'morning song'. It became a wartime focus in the university. Still's leadership qualities were evident on a broad canvas. He was on the Student Representative Council, was director of publications, was in charge of music, and conducted his own music show. When it became known that he was to enter the ministry, a music critic commented, 'You are wrong! You ought to go in for a musical career.' As a CU member he found himself unhappy with the negative attitude to cultural expression, and once walked out of a meeting in protest.

It was Still's musical interests that brought him into touch with Jim Philip, a younger man who was also to have an immense influence on CUs and evangelical life in Scotland. Philip was also a singer and pianist, with a Salvation Army background. What actually cemented their friendship was Willie Still's weakness in maths! Jim gave him valuable help here. 'We never mentioned Christianity until Jim was knocked down by a bus,' recalls Still. Jim had been watching his older friend closely, and after the accident rang him up and asked for a visit. Willie walked into a lounge, empty save for the ashen figure of Jim Philip. 'It's my sins, it's my sins,' he muttered to Still. It was the start of the road to forgiveness. It was said in Scotland that 'Jim led Willie through to maths, Willie led Jim to the Lord'. There was much more than a mathematical equation in that!

Still was far from sorted out theologically himself. The CU helped and so did some of the Brethren. It was mostly lay people who helped. 'Forty years ago,' said Still in the 1975 IVF presidential address, 'most evangelical students were faithful mission-hall types, interspersed with a few Brethren folk, Baptists and Scottish Free Kirkers – all honour to those who kept the flag flying in darker days. I will never forget what I owe to some of those dogged souls, for they banded themselves together in various universities under different names for prayer, Bible study and outreach. They joined the IVF bandwagon.'

In the early war years some of the fine young minds among Christian students in Scotland, disillusioned with liberalism, were much taken up with the perspective of Karl Barth. Still recalls an IVF Scottish conference in the early war, attended by a hundred or so, called 'Witness for the Future'. Tom Torrance and Professor Alex Ross were among those present. There Douglas Johnson's warnings about the pitfalls of Barthianism were heeded by some, not by others. The Aberdeen CSF changed its name to Evangelical Union after that conference. It was the influence of IVF that helped to turn most Scots evangelicals back to their own roots in conservative Reformed Christianity. 'I want to testify', says Still, 'to what I have seen the IVF do in Scotland to help her recover her ancient faith.'

In 1945 William Still began his longstanding ministry at Aberdeen and became himself one of the instruments God has continued to use in the recovery of Reformed Christianity.[1] Gilcomston Church, very down at heel when he started, became a student church. It was during 1945/6 that Tony Dann, later a prominent lawyer and a mayor of Chippenham, came to Aberdeen along with a number of cadets training to be military officers. What happened was a foretaste, and but one colourful example, of what student witness combined with that of the local church has accomplished in Aberdeen.

'I remember Tony Dann's serene assurance that several in his dorm would be converted before the year's course was out,' comments Still. John Boxhall, one of those who was converted, tells his story:

'On the very day the second world war ended thirty eighteen-year-old army cadets were called to the colours to begin their training in Aberdeen. Among them was one Christian. A year later there were five Christians among them! Tony's attractive and consistent witness led to several visiting Gilcomston South

[1]See Sinclair B. Ferguson's fine introduction to the *Letters of William Still* for a fuller picture of the ministry in Gilcomston.

Church in the centre of the city to hear the dynamic new minister. Under his flamboyant yet faithful ministry and deep conviction of the Holy Spirit, conversions took place, the result of which are still to be seen today.

'These student cadets were full time in the university, and so they threw their weight in with the EU whose very able president was Jim Philip. This illustrates the combination of sound Bible ministry and vital church base in a university city. The EU gave the equally necessary stimulus for living and witnessing as a Christian in the university.'

As in other parts of the country during post-war days, a perceptible change was coming over the theological student scene in Northern Ireland, which was later to follow through in preaching and church life. The position of evangelicals in, for example, the Presbyterian denomination has changed greatly since Dr John T. Carson found himself so much out on a lonely limb at Queen's University in 1929. Some have become Assembly moderators and many take a decisive part in Assembly debates. In the twenties and thirties T. S. Mooney would often watch young evangelical students leave Magee for theological college in Belfast. Very few maintained their clear stand. But then a few found that it was possible 'to finish the course *and* keep the faith' (quips Mooney). A thin red line of evangelicals began to appear at the leaving end of theological college and has thickened ever since. It is no longer the case that there is an inevitable link between theological training and a loss of confidence in the truth of the biblical gospel.

The story of Herbert Carson catches one of the moments of change. When he went to Trinity College, Dublin, in the war years, the EU was quite small. 'The prayer meeting had shrunk to a tiny handful and there were less than ten at one evangelistic meeting,' he recalls. 'A number of us met one afternoon in a man's rooms in college to give ourselves to prayer. We spent the bulk of the afternoon crying to God to come to us in blessing. God began slowly to work. By my last couple of years we had a daily prayer meeting which reached up to eighty or ninety.' As with Scotland, the province saw its own spontaneous recovery of evangelical life, but again it came in step with IVF developments at large. Herbert Carson, for example, was Irish representative on the IVF student executive committee when Oliver Barclay was chairman. History smiles

126

at the role reversal of a later period, when until his retirement in 1988 Carson was minister at Knighton Evangelical Free Church, Leicester, where Barclay is a church elder.

Carson describes some of the pressures and helps during his earlier years of training for the Anglican ministry. 'Studying as I did before the emergence of Tyndale Press I was badly shaken intellectually by my postgraduate time doing BD. I believed with my heart but my head was full of doubts and queries. I remember talking at that time with James Barr whose doubts obviously took him much further down the road! There were few around to help as I struggled to get on firm intellectual ground. I would like to pay tribute here to Douglas Johnson, especially his help at the IVF staff conference.' (Carson became a travelling secretary in 1948 to 1951.) 'Our reading for the conference one year was Calvin's *Institutes*, Geerhardus Vos and Carnell's *Apologetics*. The substantial diet and the stimulus of D.J.'s lively mind were a great boon.' This stabilizing experience of Herbert Carson was shared much more widely in Ireland and elsewhere as IVF and TSF gained in theological weight.

Those who trust the Scriptures preach it in a way that helps the hearers trust it too. Carson had joined another Irishman, A. W. (Bertie) Rainsbury (1946–51), on the IVF travelling circuit. Bertie gave most of his energies to the Scots scene and few who heard him can forget his passionate preaching. 'I had the unforgettable experience of being assistant missioner to him when he led the mission at Stranmillis College of Education in Belfast,' recalls Donald English. 'I will never forget that experience. Bertie had such a lovely cultured Irish accent. He was a fine-looking man with his auburn to fair hair. And he spoke with the passion of a prophet. His evangelistic addresses were extremely sharp and to the point. He exposed human sinfulness as few preachers have done whom I have ever heard. He reminded me of a twentieth-century Amos. Yet the graciousness of the gospel shone through on every occasion. He was truly a man of God, and if at times he seemed to be restless I think it was because he was restless for more of God's grace and a greater experience of holiness in his service.' Death brought rest in Christ in 1986.

Although churches in London and Aberdeen were beginning to show the way, there were still very few post-war university cities which had much in the way of fruitful local-church ministry among students. Douglas Johnson saw how strategic it would be to have a gifted teaching evangelist who could be set free to work in the university world. He could roam even wider than travelling secretaries like Rainsbury and could give his time entirely to evangelism. Leith Samuel, already experienced in evangelism, seemed to be the man. In 1947 he joined the IVF staff as full-time university missioner. One of the factors that led him to move into this arena and out of city-wide campaigns was his uneasiness over making appeals for public response, now becoming common practice, partly through the post-war visits of American evangelists. As Samuel's name cropped up more and more in CU evangelistic weekends, Douglas Johnson, spurred on by John Laing, moved to invite him. He gave five years that were to include missions in Canada, the States and Switzerland, as well as almost every British university. He was a genuine evangelist among educated people and he was game for a fight too. Like Howard Guinness before him, there was a bit of the untamed warrior in him. Students were wont to change his name to 'Lethal Sam'. One CU president recalls being warned, 'Bring him in on the last train and let him leave on the first; he will deeply touch people with a good sermon, but he is likely to break some furniture!'

His versatility was legendary. He was equally at home in a small evangelistic Bible study, leading students into city campaigns, the open-air service LIFCU took at Hyde Park Corner at bank holiday weekends, or debating anywhere a crowd could be gathered. His adaptability was an asset because wherever he went CUs were inspired to take the offensive and to carry a Christian presence into parts of the university which had hitherto been immune or untouched.

He served as a splendid complement to John Stott who was soon to have such an effect in the older universities and in the Anglican 'religious' situation, where formal services were the outward clothing of dynamic evangelistic content. Leith enjoyed the greater freedom of the Mars Hill situation which many of the newer universities, with little or no religious background, gave him. He revelled in the give and take, in answering questions flung at him at the end of a talk. He was adept as a witness in the market place of competing voices. At a mission in the University of Glasgow in 1952, a number of students who would probably have not otherwise attended came to hear how he would deal with leaders of the Rationalist Society during question time. Often it was the knockabout with rough and ready engineers, rather than the more prepared ground of those already half thinking, maybe, of ordination in the church that raised his mettle.

Other staff, as well as students, learned a lot from him 'Almost my first task', says one of them, 'was to assist Leith in a mission. The main meetings were hour-long question-and-answer sessions in the main hall of Liverpool University, Monday to Friday. What a dedicated gift he had for that. And no wonder. Before the first session he asked me to make a list of every question asked and when I handed it to him on the train home I asked him what he was going to do with it. "First thing tomorrow morning I shall mark off the ones I felt I did not answer satisfactorily and work on them so as not to be caught out by them ever again." It was he who encouraged me into such evangelism in informal groups, often into the early hours, by assuring me there were really only about a dozen basic questions the students would ask. "So be patient, answer them, and then fire your question at them – such as 'What do you think of Christ?' " It was fascinating watching him doing just that at my first mission. On its last day an older man, sitting next to me among the hundreds of students, turned to me after it was all over and said, "How utterly incredible!" "I'm sorry, I'm not with you. What is?" "Well, I've been here all five sessions and that man has never once contradicted himself." "Oh," I said, "I don't find that so incredible. Every answer he has given he tried to base on Scripture, that's why." '

It was this characteristic trust in the truth of the Bible and the growing capacity of preachers to let loose its powerful message in a relevant way that lay at the heart of the evangelical comeback into the university scene in these years. One example comes from the mission led by Leith Samuel in Queen's University, Belfast, in 1948, where he shared the ministry with Herbert Carson. On the first Sunday evening Carson preached in Fitzroy Presbyterian Church and Leith followed at an after-meeting. Herbie sat next to a student who was evidently gripped by the message, 'Almost or altogether for Christ?' He was a research student named Dennis McDowell, who had already been contacted through meetings at Belfast College of Technology. He picks up the story:

'Herbie, who had been sitting beside me, took me to the

vestry and pointed me specifically to the Lord Jesus and helped me in my wrestling into personal commitment. I then emigrated to teach in Toronto University. In 1951 Leith Samuel conducted Canadian university missions and was brought round to my home. On hearing my story he said that it was the first fruit that he had heard of from that mission.' In 1978, thirty years to the day of his conversion, Dr McDowell penned a note to Herbert Carson, recalling the moment he had come to Christ in that vestry in Belfast. He has, in all the succeeding years, seen it as God's specific calling to witness for him in the academic scene.

Chapter Thirteen

PROFESSORIAL PIONEERS

Let's imagine we were on a tour with one of the very solitary travelling secretaries in the post-war era. His assignment on this occasion will be the universities of Manchester, Liverpool, Birmingham, and Leicester. Before going he would no doubt have gained some background detail about the CUs. What sort of history did they have? Two things in particular would emerge: the initiatives taken by local individual student leaders with vision, and the help that older CUs gave to get the young ones on their feet. Post-war Manchester and Liverpool are examples of the former. Let's go there first.

John White, who would one day write books read worldwide, had settled back home after service in the Fleet Air Arm and got down to medical studies. The CU at *Manchester* was small and persevering but had seen no growth. In 1947 White (later IFES worker, pastor and associate professor of psychiatry) became president. It so happened at that time that the warden of Hulme Hall was worried. When men of the armed forces invaded the student world and its halls of residence they tended to bring their wartime morality with them. Hulme Hall was an Anglican establishment and the warden an ordained man. Chatting one day with the Dean they milled over what might be done to improve things a bit. 'I know of a medical student, one of those Plymouth Brethren chaps; he might be a good influence. Certainly do no harm.'

At this point I, the writer, must intrude. This morning I picked a book out of a batch that had just come in the post. It was John White's *Excellence in Leadership*. I opened the book and my eyes fell on words relating to this very incident.[1] 'God was not long in convincing me about my neglect of the students living in residence halls. There were three halls of residence and only in the largest were there two Christian students. . . . I prayed about the matter and God put the thought in my mind to suggest to the warden that one of those two students live in my home while I took his place in the residence. Nonetheless I put it in the back of my mind. . . . But God refused to let me go. Within a couple of months the warden wrote to me asking whether I would be willing to live there and "provide some leadership".' Those are John White's own words describing his (and God's!) side of this incident.

When he left, years later, a very high percentage of the residents turned up to hear him speak at a farewell squash. Many had come to know Christ, all of whom, except one, went into full-time service. White had a marked gift for getting alongside people and staying with them, and also for getting others to work with him. He led the CU from 1947 to 1949 and in 1951 became national student chairman. Manchester CU nearly doubled its size in one year when it really got going in the halls of residence.

Another advance in witness came through better contact with the mass of students living in digs. Brian and Olive Clarke (parents of travelling secretary Rosemary, now Mrs Monty Barker) lived in a strategic position, being just off the bus route from the university and about fifteen minutes away. Hospitality for student squashes caused some domestic chaos, Mrs Clarke recalls. 'Our dining-room table was rather a lovely rosewood oval one. That table has been wheeled, on its side, out of the dining-room hundreds, even thousands of times! We used to take the dining-room door off its hinges and put it down in the cellar for big occasions, enabling the speaker to be seen and heard by all the folk sitting up the stairs and in the hall. When someone like John White came to speak my husband and I would not want to take up valuable space and so we seldom heard his message. But his very presence was a benediction.'

Over at *Liverpool* was another small and struggling CU. A few months previous to coming there as a student, Verna Wright (now Professor of Rheumatology at Leeds) had been converted

[1] Related on pp. 40–41.

at his home town of Bedford. 'We like to think at Liverpool that we were the first to introduce Saturday night fellowship as a regular part of the programme. They were modelled on the Friday night meetings that Young Life ran in Bedford. We began to meet in the basement of a house in Liverpool, sitting on orange-boxes. They were marvellous times.' The idea caught on in most other 'redbrick' universities, where it gave a needed fellowship focus. Saturday nights were a bit of a vacuum for Christians. Nothing to do except go to the dance or the 'flicks', which they could not afford anyway! Once the Saturday night meeting became established it developed into a programme for consecutive teaching.

Liverpool was also among the front runners in outreach. It followed Sheffield as the second university to hold a mission after the war. Both were led by Leith Samuel. 'What a great time it was,' Wright continues. 'We had a series of teaser posters in the weeks before. They just contained the title of the mission, "In Search of Truth", and a picture, for instance, of Rodin's "The Thinker" and under that, "Philosophy?" Another showed devotees gathered around a sacrifice and underneath the word "Religion?" A third showed typical white-clad, egg-headed scientists with their fuming retorts and underneath "Science?" There was an excellent provocative opening lecture on "The Impossibility of Agnosticism" which led one bemused student to exclaim, "I always realized agnostics were impossible people, but I never realized till now that agnosticism was impossible!" The lectures drove home the challenge of biblical truth under the titles "The Truth about God", " . . . about Christ," " . . . about Man," "The Truth on the Scaffold", "The Truth Triumphant" and "The Truth Shall Make You Free". They were followed by the most vigorous public question times, which added to the interest. In that forum, Leith Samuel was at his very best and was much used.'

From that post-war group came several missionary leaders; for example, two field directors of the Sudan United Mission in Nigeria, Maurice Cottam and Tom Owens. 'Another marvellous person of that era was Ursula Lowenthal,' recalls Professor Wright. 'She was a medical student in the same year as myself – a Hebrew Christian from an orthodox Jewish home. She had all the dedication of her race, insisting on walking to the University Hospital in order to save bus fares, and similarly insisting that I should eat sandwiches she brought, rather than spend money on lunch at the Students Union. She went on to become one of the rugged pioneers of the gospel in Thailand where she is still battling away.'

At *Birmingham* the CU had a rare kind of maturing experience. The president's leadership gained in spiritual stature via the testing path of grief – the death of his fiancée. Honor Ward was a student at the time. 'We had planned a houseparty in a remote youth hostel. It snowed badly and Freddie Crittenden, who was due to speak, could not get through. BUECU president that year, Frank Rhodes (now President of Cornell University), had recently been through a shattering experience. His fiancée had contracted polio and an iron lung was the last hope. Much prayer was made, but she died a few months before the conference. When Freddie failed to get through, Frank offered to give the talks on the subject of 'Death as a Christian Sees It'. He had been searching the Scriptures and what he had to tell us was fresh from the heart. It was a very moving ministry. The Lord met with us as we were brought very close to realities. I told Freddie some time later that, for BUECU, the best weekend conference he ever took was the one he failed to reach.'

Jill Cartwright (now Mrs Tony Dann) was a very timid fresher in Rhodes's day. 'I owe much to him. As almost the only girl reading law at the time I remember drinking coffee with others (non-Christian friends) in my year – virtually all ex-servicemen. I felt very, very young and diffident and indeed was wondering whether to keep quiet about my Christian commitment, when Frank came into the refectory, told everyone about a freshers' meeting, came over to me with the invitations and asked me to give them out. My colours were nailed to the mast and, thank God, there was no looking back. Later I served on the CU executive committee when Derek Burke was president'. (He is now the Vice-chancellor of the University of East Anglia.) Linda Barnes (now wife of John Taylor, Bishop of St Albans) was another of this generation. She outlines three areas of blessing from her CU days. 'I'm sure the best thing we learned was the need to link with a soundly biblical local church when we entered upon our careers. And I think my memories are of a clear, purposeful, joyful and quietly peaceful sense of relying on Jesus and living for God, which was extremely catching. John and I met several years before we were finally engaged. What one learned in the CU of being prepared to trust God and be obedient and wait, helped us to be led imperceptibly but quite definitely along a path which allowed both our paths to converge and then we became very firmly bonded in the same direction. It led to a confidence that God would give the best and never in thirty years of marriage have we lost this sense of God's purpose for us in a partnership working together for him.'

'Take two men and go to *Leicester* and show them how to organize a CU'. The words were spoken in Cambridge, but their effect in Leicester was decisive. Leicester was the last of the redbrick university colleges exisiting at the end of the war to have a CU. There was prayer throughout IVF for Leicester. Then, in 1947, everything seemed to gel. Some forty years later, Ivan Homer, one of the students involved, made contact with Oliver Barclay 'to express my thanks as I look back to those thrilling days at Leicester – a wonderful training for later ministry', spent partly in Burma.

In 1947 the names of six Christian freshers bound for Leicester (Homer's was one) had been sent to the IVF London office and they were put in touch with each other. On 20 October 1947, Homer recorded in his diary: 'Got together folk for our first CU prayer meeting. Grand time together.' But then the question arose, 'What were they to do next?' They wrote to the office for ideas. Four days later, neither of the two travelling secretaries being available, Ronald Inchley deserted his manuscripts and travelled there for the first open meeting. Barclay contacted Lieutenant-General Sir William Dobbie, the hero of Malta, who did sterling work for CUs all over the country. His personal testimony was crystal clear, and ex-servicemen especially were impressed by him and made no argument. On 15 January 1948, eighty students turned up to hear him. Then, a fortnight later, came the turning-point.

On Friday 30 January Homer recorded, 'Went out to friends' house in Leicester and met with ten CU members and the three fellows from Cambridge.' What were 'the three fellows' up to? The office had sent Leicester's letter asking for help on to the CICCU. Though the small full-time staff strove to do its bit and very much more, there was never a better principle than that students can best help students. And so one afternoon late in 1947, when John Paterson was on the Market Place in

Cambridge, he was stopped by the CICCU president, Geoff Grobecker. With something of the authority of the angel to Peter, he said to Paterson, 'Take two men and go to Leicester.' Coming from an ex-Life Guards officer, the tone was more of command than request. Paterson got his two men (both of whom later went on to make their mark in their Christian careers) and went to Leicester for a long weekend. Homer's account of their get-together tells its own story.

'We had a terrific time there in that little room. Truly the Lord was with us as we prayed together and sang. Then one of them told the story of entry into the promised land after a time in the wilderness, the crossing of the Jordan, the doubts and fears as an illustration for our own lives. Praise God for such a fellowship together. Then we returned and found a great crowd at Middlemeade (hall of residence) discussing religion after the news of the death of Gandhi' (assassinated that day).

Ivan Homer unavoidably missed the rest of the two days. But the blessing did not evade him. 'Monday 2 February 1948: Note on breakfast table – "Rennie converted last night." "O for a thousand tongues to sing our great Redeemer's praise, the glories of our God and King, the triumphs of his grace." Tremendous joy at the prayer meeting. Fourteen present and many of the girls joined in prayer. Surely our Father is working out his purposes among us. How many prayers have been answered as a result of this weekend!'

More was to come. Returning to his hostel during the evening he was asked by a friend from his old school to pray together. The weekend's meetings had sealed his conversion too. 'What a moment as we opened our hearts to God.' The next day his friend asked to join the CU. God's blessing continued. Off they went to the Swanwick conference, which they found an inspiration. The photos of the CU taken annually indicate the rapid growth. In 1948, nine; in 1950, seventeen 'including Donald English'; in 1951, thirty-seven. Three of the original six went overseas.

In 1975, when John Paterson moved to Leicester as Professor of Geography, he was in a sense coming back to familiar territory. The following year the office of what was now the UCCF went there too.

Although all these CUs were never controlled from any centre, there was a great sense of family provided by the national conferences. This became even more valuable as the fellowship grew. The inspiring experience of the Leicester folk is typical of what it did for new, small groups. The wartime conferences, held in Oxford and Cambridge, had been a huge consolation.[2] Dr Martyn Lloyd-Jones, both during and after the war, had a widespread influence through his expositions at these gatherings. 'He taught people to think, and think biblically. It was evident that a diet of purely devotional ministry was not enough. It was quite a discovery that doctrine was the basis of true devotion and of practical Christianity, and he showed the way.' Raymond Johnston was not the only student to return from a conference ecstatic at this discovery. The sense of pulling together under the Word of God gave the scattered fellowship a sense of belonging.

In 1947, conferences began again at Swanwick, and the IVF was the first to use it after it ceased to be a prisoner-of-war camp. That winter had witnessed one of the freeze-ups of the century with huge snow drifts immobilizing vast tracts of the country. Many of the central-heating pipes had burst at the conference centre, and when up to 500 students arrived they were met by piles of bedroom furniture in the entrance. It was then that the ex-servicemen came into their own and every one was organized cheerfully to beat the chaos. Co-operation in practical emergency unfroze human barriers and it proved an outstanding conference.

Lady Catherwood, then Elizabeth Lloyd-Jones, tells of the significance of that conference for her. 'The cold and the muddle were indescribable; some of us in the girls' corridors packed ourselves in twos in the narrow hard single beds just to keep ourselves from congealing overnight! But what I remember above all was the sense of the glory of God that was present among us and the wonder of his plan of salvation. My father gave the conference addresses on the basic truths of the gospel. On the night when he expounded to us the doctrine of justification by faith, using as his text Romans 3:26, ' . . . that he might be just and the justifier . . .' (AV), many of us understood it as we never had before. Some of us agreed afterwards that we almost felt we were in heaven as we listened.

[2]For example, for the exhilarating effect on the contingents from the Cardiff University College CU, 1941–3, see my '*Excuse Me, Mr Davies – Hallelujah!*', pp. 96–98.

'The Rev. Alan Stibbs gave the Bible studies on 2 Corinthians 4 and 5, and his profound and moving expositions perfectly complemented the addresses. I shall never forget how he compared Paul's words, 'The love of Christ constraineth us' (2 Cor. 5:14, AV), to the waters of the Yangtze river being forced into a rushing torrent by the walls of the great gorge. We students had seen God's plan in Christ, and we went back to our universities and the uncertain post-war world realizing afresh what it meant to be a Christian and, because of this, wanting to share our faith with others.'

Honor Ward tells how her widowed mother sacrificially paid for her to attend this and later conferences. 'They were food and drink to my heart. At the first post-war one in Swanwick I remember the broken windows and the biting cold and I remember the love and the joy. There was a German pastor there who had come to visit the remaining German prisoners of war, now housed nearby. He said, "I thank God we lost the war." This shattering admission impressed me very deeply. It taught me that Christian brotherhood was stronger than national pride, and that a German Christian and an English Christian were 'born again in Christ' and therefore brethren. I owe a lot to that brave man.'

By 1948, when there were not more than 2,400 CU members in the universities, about 500 of them came to the central conference. Most CU members came at least once. It helped give the realization that the Fellowship was in a battle together. This was one of the features of these years when numbers were growing, but when the overall Fellowship was small enough to feel they needed each other. This sense of battle was very biblical of course. It was a fight for God, and positive witness to his truth lay at its heart. The Doctrinal Basis was very much a centripetal force in this.

The Fellowship was bound together, too, by its awareness of its common disciplines. At one of the big conferences at Swanwick, it was obvious that some would have to sleep on the floor, a cleaners' nightmare. One of the cleaners commented happily, 'You can always tell when it's going to be a well-behaved conference – there are lots of Bibles about in the bedrooms.' The 'quiet time' was a major emphasis at the conference and many learned its importance there through teaching and the example of others. They would then bring it back to their own fellowships. At one Swanwick conference travelling secretary Michael Griffiths waxed so enthusiastic about the 'quiet time' that he took nearly twenty-five minutes, though his brief had been to be brief, because he was on before the annual presidential address.

Conferences were also good times for giving guidelines on personal relationships, and here humour (and 'Swanwick' was famous for its laughter) could often reinforce a point. Sometimes perhaps not. One of the problems tackled at one time was the tendency of CU committee members at Keele to be so tied up in pairing off that they neglected leadership responsibilities. Imagine therefore Professor F. F. Bruce introducing the solemn presidential address with this: 'I was a student in Aberdeen. I was president of the CU. I was one of those presidents who didn't marry the vice-president.' (Laughter.) 'The secretary had her'. (More laughter.) 'He was welcome.' (Bedlam!) 'I married the vice-president who was vice-president the year after.' Everyone was laughing except the poor travelling secretaries, who could be excused for thinking that their work was being undermined.

A word about the IVF Keswick camps. There were separate camps for men and women. When Bill Batt was commandant and Freddie Crittenden adjutant, the men's camp boasted two army majors. The women's response to their benign military precision was ambiguous. Says Marjorie Telford, 'Ours was never quite so tidy as the men's. Gladys, who looked after our catering, returned from a visit to the men one day and said she didn't want all the teapot handles facing *exactly* the same way, but it would be nice if they could face a little more the same way.'

Bill Batt's morning Bible readings at the camp were a marvellous model of how related to life accurate Bible exposition can be. Many valued them more highly than those at the big tent. How much time, too, he and others have given to listening to individuals and leading them into more Christlike ways as they relaxed amidst the beauty of the hills.

Major Batt had never been a student but, with this camp involvement and regular participation in missions, he probably had as much experience of personal witness to students as any. He assisted at nine CICCU missions, certainly unparalleled. Oliver Barclay talks of his 'wonderful way of finding points of contact and getting alongside people. He had an interesting mixture of reliance upon the transforming work of the Spirit and a vivid sense of good and evil, which meant that you needed to put the challenge bluntly to people in black and white. He had no sympathy with the devil. His evangelistic gift stemmed from his confidence that someone ought to be converted. Yet at the same time he had a great consciousness of the sovereignty of God and would never be tense in a mission when nothing seemed to be happening.' He created great team spirit and people pulled together when he was with them.

PART FOUR

THE 1950s
AND BEYOND

THE FUNDAMENTALS
OF THE FAITH

Chapter Fourteen

THE SCOTS CONNECTION

It was a Sunday evening during the snowbound winter of 1947. Hilary Woodward sat at home in Bradford and fiddled with the wireless set, trying to find the Scottish Home Service. Its reception in the north of England was not very good in those days. But eventually she found the wavelength and waited for the Sunday evening religious broadcast. It was being taken by members of the Edinburgh University CU. She recalls little of the service until the sermon. It was on 1 Corinthians 1:18–31. From then on she sat glued to the set. 'For the message of the cross is foolishness to those who are perishing, but to us who are being saved it is the power of God.'

Some months before, Hilary had gone to study at Edinburgh College of Domestic Science (now Queen Margaret College). Her religious inclination was high church and, though she got to know half a dozen of the CU members there, she was very sceptical of their activities. Then, in January 1947, she was whisked off to hospital to have her appendix removed. To aid recovery she was advised to take the rest of the term off. She got home just before the big freeze-up began. Then came a letter from college friends, telling her of the CU broadcast.

'While I listened,' she says, 'the Holy Spirit spoke to me and convinced me that all the trappings of my way of worship were nothing when set against what Christ had done for me on the cross. I came to Jesus as Saviour that night. I told my vicar and he said that I would get over it when I was fully convalesced. The lovely part of it came when I returned to college and told those girls. They were especially thankful because they had been praying for me.'

Marriage to Godfrey Dalton led to Sierra Leone, Zambia and Queen's University, Belfast, where he has held lecturing posts and they have continuing involvement with overseas students. Rather than 'getting over it' she has 'got on with it'!

The preacher at that student broadcast service from the Edinburgh CU was one of the young Torrance brothers. They were an exceptionally gifted family, destined to make a considerable contribution to the religious life of Scotland.

Scots, we have noted, have a great taste for theology. As a disillusionment arose with liberalism, there were some who felt the intellectual pull of the theology of Karl Barth. He seemed to rescue Christian preaching from the dead hand of modern unbelief. They saw his understanding of Scripture as a contemporary statement of historic and Reformation Christianity, profound and uplifting in his doctrine of God and devastating in his critique of liberal, man-centred religion. But some saw other nuances too. For example, Barth was subtly but definitely sceptical of a historical view of Christ's resurrection, and his strong view of authority was nevertheless slippery and equivocal about the Scriptures' objective inspiration and authority. Everyone could agree that he was an enemy of the subjective liberal religion which had taken over in the church. But could his system truly be recognized as a modern foundation for the evangelical faith? Was it fully consistent with the Doctrinal Basis?

In a way unknown in other CUs in the UK, the debate raged in parts of Scotland, especially in Edinburgh. Which way would the CUs go?

The Scots IVF conferences of the early fifties showed all the signs of recovering evangelicalism. But also the theological tensions that had begun to emerge in the conferences of the war years now came to a head. By 1953, 150 or so would gather from the four Scots universities at the Easter conference at Bonskeid, 'in a riot of woodland glory'. It was a great occasion. Among the theologs were ex-servicemen, some of whom were dominant figures by virtue of age and experience. The medics, too, were senior students; and the tensions were most obvious between some of the older theologs, who were being trained by Barthian or liberal teachers, and the medics who were not confronted by their kind of problem, though they had problems peculiar to their discipline. The medics sometimes felt that some of the theologs were wavering from the truth. The difficulties were further heightened in 1953 when there were conversions of people attending the conference, some of whom had an SCM background. Some maintained that these people were Christians already and were not happy with 'all this emotionalism'. The people involved, of course, did not see it that way! (The same had happened in Wales during a time of blessing among students in 1947–8.)

The serious upshot of the theological differences was that the Edinburgh CU became divided and diverted. Leith Samuel, who took a mission in Edinburgh in 1953, remembers how preoccupied many of the men were with theological issues, and rightly so, as they were urgent to safeguard the future witness. It turned out that the mission became mainly the province of the women students. It became clear that the Edinburgh CU leaders did not stand by the Doctrinal Basis. The very difficult decision had to be taken by the IVF student executive committee, under the chairmanship that year of Michael Griffiths, to disaffiliate the CU. They were sadly strained times. But the direction that IVF in Scotland maintained, and which the Edinburgh CU itself subsequently reverted to, has led to a consistency, depth and spread of biblical witness in the churches that is a stirring example to the British work as a whole. We shall follow a mere sample of the wider story.

First, *Aberdeen*. Some of the post-war stalwarts here were Ian Lawson, now a prominent doctor in the States, who managed to combine the presidency of the CU with that of president of the Students Union. His maturity was a great help. George May became CICCU president in the year of the first Stott mission. Laurie Campbell became a headmaster; the two Philip brothers, Jim and George, took pulpits in Edinburgh and Glasgow that have had a decisive bearing on Christian faith and life north of the border. Howard Marshall, who is now Professor of New Testament Exegesis at Aberdeen, shares some of his sense of gratitude for these days.

Marshall, influenced by IVF books even before he went to university in 1951, wanted, as a result, to be a biblical scholar and do battle against the opponents of the evangelical faith. He had the gifts and dedication that those of 1941 had prayed for. In 1949 he bought *In Understanding be Men* at Keswick. F. F. Bruce's *Are the New Testament Documents Reliable?* set him an example of biblical scholarship. H. W. Cragg's *The Conqueror's Way* taught him the need for and the possibility of holiness, 'but, I fear, did not make me holy: I'm still trying to understand the doctrine and the way of holiness.

'My first contact with IVF was when a student friend took me one evening while still at school to a Leith Samuel mission,' continues Marshall. 'So, inevitably, I was at the freshers' squash. The CU was one of the two foci of my Christian life, the other being Willie Still on Sunday evenings. The Evangelical Union (I appreciated the distinctive title) always had a strong pabulum of biblical/doctrinal teaching from the Philip brothers, R. A. Finlayson, Alexander Ross, Geoffrey Bromiley and others. I participated in seven church missions – Edinburgh, Stranraer, Kilbirnie, Hawick, Larbert, Johnstone and Irvine. Here you got to know fellow students far better by working together than by sharing in conferences, and, of course, there was the joy of seeing fruit to witness. There were few sympathetic university staff at that time, though Roy Campbell, who went on to a chair of economics at East Anglia (later still at Stirling) was a great help.'

While the Edinburgh CU was in trauma, the CU was almost dying out at *St Andrews* too. 'But from its ashes, like a phoenix, arose Monty Barker,' recalls Willie Still. Here again we see how resolution in the face of fading vision not only saved the day, but led to expansion and renewal. In the late eighties St Andrews CU is proportionately the strongest in Britain.

'The CU was a very ailing body' says Barker, now Senior Lecturer in Psychiatry at Bristol University. Sadly, some of its members were not the most able of students. On one occasion the minutes speak of all the committee actually being present – because they had all failed and were up for their resits together! Amid the theological uncertainties of the times, a CU president spoke of intentions to meet jointly with SCM. It did not seem to matter much to the leaders. But some saw the implications. Barker, then a second-year student, gathered a group of half a dozen or so to pray together. Among them was Katherine Fraser, daughter of Fraser of Lisuland. They prayed for God to reawaken them and give them a new spirit. They felt out on their own. But the Lord seemed to give them a burden for their own situation. Barker remembers a dark and dingy night and the decision that something must be done to stop the Union sliding further.

The upshot was that after much airing of whether to disaffiliate from IVF there was a general meeting. The vote was 19–19 with abstentions. The chairman told the meeting that he had been led to believe that the clear majority feeling was to disaffiliate. As the vote showed that this was not, in fact, the case, he gave his casting vote to the continuing cause, though he himself was going to put in his lot with the leavers. This had a very humbling effect upon the meeting and any 'triumphalist' reaction was effectively extinguished.

A new committee that included David Innes and Hugh Mathie invited Willie Still to speak on 'Is Sincerity Enough?' Twenty-three gowned students (St Andrews was a very formal place) sat in the lounge of the Baptist manse. Monty Barker recalls having to get used to Still's Aberdeen voice, 'and then, within ten minutes, he broke through, and I realized that this was a presentation of the living Word of God that I had not experienced before. It changed me for the better.' From then on things clarified in the CU, and no longer was the atmosphere one of perpetual argument. During the following year a number of Christians came up from England, some having been converted under the ministry of Dick Lucas in Sevenoaks. This mix, with some of the fruit of the new evangelical surge in the Church of England, gave a freshness to a CU that had been over-starchy. A real sense of expectancy prevailed during the 1955–6 session and people turned to the Lord. 'I was in at the resurrection of the St Andrews Union,' recalls Still, 'and for four years after that, each year I was invited they needed a bigger hall to hold the students, until there were about eighty attending their Saturday Bible study.'

A debate in the Students Union reflects what was happening: 'This house believes that the influence of the CU has increased, is increasing and ought to be diminished.'

At a mission led by Leith Samuel there was quite a turnout swelled by counter-advertising. On every swing door in every hall of residence appeared an eye-catching poster on a large shiny black card: 'No hawkers, no circulars, no evangelists.'

What was more, the opposition did its best to get under the evangelist's skin. On the first night a drunken student was deposited on his floor at 1.00 a.m. On the second night his sheets were stapled half way down so that his feet tore a great hole. And so it went on. The mission was remarkable for producing a religiously motivated group who formed themselves into an anti-mission committee. The son of one of Scotland's famous preachers launched into a harangue at question time, with a personally slanted attack on Leith Samuel's theology. Many were unsympathetic to the way Samuel replied. After the mission Samuel sent some literature to some interested students. The anti-mission committee would go down to the porter's lodge and note what post had come in from Southampton. The individual concerned would be invited to tea and had to go through a kind of third-degree questioning!

The last mission meeting had been entitled 'The Cost of Discipleship', as the leaders did not want any easy or spurious interest. Only two were converted during the week. The mission itself had certainly left them in no doubt that there was a cost involved. On the last night one man, sporting a smart waistcoat, asked a seemingly jocular question. In the prevailing atmosphere everyone thought he was having a go at the speaker, and there was a great roar of laughter. He was, however, the only one to come to faith that night and is now a university chaplain. The other man is a member at a leading evangelical church. The longer-term effect of the mission was tremendous, with about twenty professing conversion in the following months. Numbers in the CU rose above the 100 mark.

A welcome new arrival at St Andrews in 1956 was John Paterson, who came from Cambridge to lecture in geography and gave an extra dimension to the CU's life. His home proved to be a venue where non-Christians could be confidently taken. At Cambridge there had been regular opportunity to take college Bible studies, 'and my wife had many hard things to say about the CICCU attitude to marriage and my constant absences in the evenings,' says Professor Paterson. 'In St Andrews we developed a quite different lifestyle based on the home. For thirteen years on a Sunday evening after church we had open house, and I gave a Bible reading as part of a varied programme of other events.'

In the later fifties, as the tensions subsided, with leaders like Ian Fisher (a future travelling secretary and Church of Scotland minister) and Howard Marshall (who moved on later to Cambridge and was to take a leading role in the Theological Students Fellowship) there was progress in the whole of Scot-

148

land. During his period as student representative Monty Barker travelled a lot around the CUs and his friends were the presidents of the other CUs. A corporateness and identity were recovered and a new generation of unity in heart and mind emerged. Barker gave regular talks to CU leaders to provide the Scottish perspective and acquaint them with their own heritage. For example, he stressed the 'praying society movement' in Scots universities of an earlier century. William Chalmers Burns, an Aberdeen student of the 1830s, and a missionary to China, had first engaged in remarkably fruitful evangelism in Scotland. He seems to have been the first to stress the IVF principle that students should be the people to evangelize students. 'It's not overseas you ought to be going,' he said once to some, 'but here with students.' The talk on Burns fired students around Scotland and they began to see the present work as a sequel to the praying societies in Scots universities and the later-nineteenth-century missionary momentum. The existence and influence of IVF provided a rallying-point and a continuity of clear evangelical witness at a crucial time when it could have been lost. As Still says, 'It helped to restore to Scotland its ancient Reformed faith.'

The existence of the IVF family also afforded opportunities for integration into a wider evangelical world. Very often the main speakers at the Scots conference (moved to Largs to take in the numbers) were from England, including Ken Prior and Major Batt. But the percentage of Scots speakers rose as the new generation was represented in people such as the Philip brothers and Eric Alexander, whose ministry to students was to spread well beyond Scotland. At the annual Scots conference of 1956 (the thirty-second), George Philip, who was then assistant minister of Springburn Hill, Glasgow, gave the conference addresses and Alan Stibbs the Bible readings. John A. Balchin, Scots travelling secretary from 1955 to 1959, led the prayer sessions.

The presence and influence of senior IVF staff at these conferences were welcome and helped to stretch student horizons. 'Oliver Barclay used to meet the Scots presidents at the conference. We got to learn his technique. He would quietly sidle up to a new leader and say, "We ought to have a chat – how about after lunch?" So the saying arose among us, "Have you had your Oliver yet?" A man would feel very let down if his turn somehow did not come round. We all prized the quiet wisdom of "O.R.B." and the way we were sorted out. There was a constant listening by and a learning from IVF staff,' says Monty Barker. The 'laid-back', cool, personal style of Oliver Barclay nevertheless went along with a firm and definite influence which was communicated through countless informal contacts. This was a strong factor in keeping a family feeling and in cultivating a biblical perspective among student leaders throughout the four countries. As the years brought soaring numbers that kind of maturing stamp on others became less possible.

English travelling secretaries such as Michael Griffiths also did a lot of work in Scotland. Meg Foote, the women's secretary for many years, was a regular at the Scots conference. Amy Fung, an overseas student at St Andrews, has special reason to remember her attendance during Easter 1962. 'Miss Meg Foote spent two evenings explaining John 3:1–21 and John 15 to me in her room . . . After the first evening I realized what it meant to become a Christian . . . and I confessed my sin and accepted the Lord to be my Saviour that night. . . . For the rest of my time at university I prayed specifically for the Lord's work in the Far East.' She is now at the Graduate School of Theology, Hong Kong.

Chapter Fifteen

'THE WHOLE UNIVERSITY WAS STIRRED'

Following the Barnhouse missions at Cambridge came those of John Stott in 1952 and 1958. In between was the visit of Billy Graham in 1955. The justification for regular missions, 'the special effort' as they were sometimes (disparagingly) called, lay in the concern to reach new, untouched people with the gospel through teaching evangelism. Mission is for sowing, even ploughing, more than it is for reaping, though there have almost invariably been genuine conversions during missions, as we have seen. Before we take a look in depth at the significance of the 1952 Cambridge mission, we may remind ourselves that God's Word works salvation in the ordinary context of CU witness.

Tony Lewis came up to Cambridge to read medicine. His best friend from school, Stewart Gorduin, got him to go and hear John Eddison, a pre-war CICCU president, preach on Jesus' words 'I am the Way'. Tony had little knowledge of religion. But he was converted that night. He began to experience the thrills of attending the prayer meetings at Emmanuel Chapel with over 200 present. He remembers the way they encouraged each other to learn the Bible off by heart. He and a friend committed Ephesians 1–2 to memory, a verse a day. By now David Sheppard was showing exceptional gifts of caring for new converts; they had weekly Bible studies with him. Once, when the university team was on a cricket tour playing Gloucestershire, he gave his testimony at Bristol in a meeting at which David preached. He vividly recalls his first hearing of a young preacher called Dick Lucas who arrived at a CICCU meeting armed with a pile of Bibles, to ensure that everyone had a copy to follow the passage. It proved to be an exhilarating proclamation of the person and work of Christ from Hebrews 1.

Summing up his CICCU days (he is now a consultant in South Wales), Tony sees the pros and cons. 'They were foundation years when we learned doctrine, but were in danger of a lot of head knowledge and perhaps little reality of a heart-warming, experimental knowledge of God. The stress on evangelism and the need to resist worldliness was correct, but things were not easy for a babe in Christ with no Christian background. We were in danger of a whirl of CU activism and it could cover backslidings and conflicts – spiritual ones and ones relating to my medical training. It wasn't until I was qualified in London that I learned the stabilizing doctrines of grace.'

If anything produced a 'whirl of CU activism' it was a mission. If the whole thing was tense and poorly led it could be exhausting and even counter-productive. It could also be a powerful demonstration of what preaching and witness are all about. The 1952 triennial mission in Cambridge is such an instance. In that year John Stott came back to his old university as mission leader. During 1952 the king had died and there were hopes astir for a new Elizabethan age. But the signs were not too promising. The Korean War dragged on and the old Empire was disintegrating. Even student wit reflected it. George May, the president of CICCU, was sometimes referred to as George Mau Mau, president of the Kikuyu. But there were more ominous clouds that later student generations would have little to joke over. In 1952 Britain exploded its own atomic bomb and the USA its first hydrogen bomb. The keel of the first nuclear submarine was laid. Also, though it was unnoticed, a 'contraceptive tablet' (the word 'pill' came later) was made. It was to have as great an impact on future student morality as anything.

These and other issues were to catch up with Stott in years ahead, when he became more engrossed with ethical questions, developed a nuclear pacifist stance, travelled the new Commonwealth as university missioner and became an honorary chaplain to the Queen. In 1952 he was not well known outside evangelical Anglican and CICCU circles, though there, his exceptional expository gifts were beginning to excite. The major thrust of the mission, with up to 1,200 attending the final night, took the university by surprise. Students began to realize that here was someone from their own stable whose credentials, as the world counts such things, were impeccable. If Barnhouse had provoked people into giving him a hearing, this missioner quite simply impressed people into it. The compelling, scholarly and rational marshalling of biblical evidence and arguments had one end in view – the warm commendation of the person and work of Christ, the Saviour of the sinful. Critical students found there was not much room for caricature, so they had to face up to the nub of things. They might still reject the message, but it was difficult to mock the messenger and make that the excuse.

In his letter to fellow missioners at the start, Stott made clear his understanding of what the Bible meant by power in evangelism. It also shows us something of his own heart as he stood as a messenger between God and human beings.

'We wrestle not against flesh and blood, but against principalities and powers. It is for this reason that the weapons of our warfare are not carnal. The power is his, not ours. Paul knew the place of power in ministry and we could not find a better standard for the mission than his words in 1 Corinthians 2:1–5. The content of our message is to be the Word of God, which is the power of God, not the wisdom of men – and that Word of God is the Word of the cross, which is the power of God (1 Corinthians 1:15). Further, our method will not be to rely on enticing words of man's wisdom but on the Spirit's powerful demonstration of words spoken in human weakness (1 Corinthians 2:4). May the Lord Jesus, whom we shall be uplifting, keep us humble and broken, full of faith and the Holy Spirit.'

The meetings themselves, recalls Stott, were 'somewhat formal services, as we sang hymns, said prayers and wore robes.' But formality certainly did not spell deadness. 'We were all gripped on the first night by a wonderful exposition answering the question "Who was Jesus Christ?",' record the mission committee minutes. 'The clarity and logical beauty of Mr Stott's presentation, coupled with the deep spiritual impact of the theme, must have shown all present the reasonableness of Christ's demands upon us. One man who went on the first Sunday had felt he would be unable to go again but he was so struck by the first sermon that he cancelled all his evening arrangements during the following week. The progressive teaching the mission gave was a great help to CICCU members, as well as being a means of bringing light to darkened minds.'

By the Saturday night 'there was most encouraging news all round. Trinity has the most exciting news of complete heathen being converted quite independently of CICCU members and a real work of God seems to be in progress.' 'The whole university was stirred,' said a rejoicing Basil Atkinson. 'I shall never forget on the last night of the mission seeing a queue standing four deep up the whole nave of Great St Mary's, waiting to talk to the missioner.' 'I judge it to be the highest point of those nine wonderful years (1946–55) – the nearest to revival that we have yet reached,' he was to write in later years.

Now what about the 'CU whirl of activity' surrounding all this? A key to the success of CICCU missions was mobilization on all fronts by the students themselves. The main mission addresses were backed up by scores of smaller meetings and squashes. Spare a thought for the amateur caterers! College representatives and especially Ridley Hall theologs were called to serve tables. Representatives such as Gordon Bridger, S. M. Houghton and John Dart, and Ridley students such as Keith Weston and Michael Griffiths, must have wished they had the capacity miraculously to multiply loaves, or at least, sandwiches. These lads and a few lasses were transformed into bread-cutters (any sliced bread then?), margarine-spreaders and tea-pourers. During the week it must have felt like feeding the five thousand. 88 lbs of margarine and 80 lbs of sugar were ordered from one source, 60 lbs and 50 lbs from another. One man with a keen eye for a bargain noticed that tomatoes in the market were 8d (3p), whereas the shops were asking a shilling (5p) – so to the market they went for 80 lbs. 1,800 cakes were supplied by the Dorothy Café and 3,700 by Matthews Bakery (they were cheaper too!). As the money, for it all came in from various voluntary sources, the mission committee found a Bible text that said it all: 'For the stuff they had was sufficient for all the work to make it, and too much' (Exodus 36:7, AV).

The energies of all these masculine Marthas were directed to servicing two kinds of subsidiary meetings. First, faculty meetings, and secondly, college squashes, sports and old school squashes. The latter kind had been a regular feature of CICCU contact-making, the former less so. Their emergence in 1952 as a major back-up to the central teaching evangelism is worth noting. No less than seven of the speakers at these meetings were to become professors. How new this was! We were on the edge of a mini-breakthrough of evangelicals into the academic

154

world, decisively reversing the trend of half a century. It was by no means a denial of Stott's rejection of 'carnal wisdom'. It marked rather the first fruits of a new stress on academic excellence as a means of serving the Lordship of Christ. It was the spirit of the Kingham Hill conference[1] on a wider front. The main missioner was himself an example in the area of theology. Of the others, Alan Stuart was the oldest. Then came Norman Anderson and several younger men, Donald Wiseman, Douglas Spanner, John Paterson, Robert Boyd and Jim Houston. They addressed such subjects as 'The Natural Sciences and Supernatural Belief', 'Science, Evolution and the Christian Faith' and 'Faith, Facts and Physics'.

When John Paterson had been appointed to an assistant lectureship in Cambridge in 1950 he had been congratulated by Lloyd-Jones, with the accompanying comment, 'Far too many of our Oxbridge men have been getting "thirds".' But things were changing. Paterson identifies one of the greatest changes of his working lifetime to be this growth of senior academic support for the work of the CUs, contrasting Cambridge in 1950 with the later situation at, for example, Aberdeen, where as many as two dozen staff were disposed to support the CU. 'These days, each year's crop of graduates from CUs across the country yields some new academics committed to a biblical faith.' The 1952 mission marks the first block evidence for this.

The reproach was being rolled away a bit, and evangelicals were learning again that it is a good and godly thing to love the Lord God with all their mind. But students are not just (indeed, often they are just not) 'thinkers'. Furthermore, like Shylock, they share the ordinary feelings of humanity. Some were plain lonely, and few more friendly forums could be arranged than sports or old school squashes. The young Christians of the thirties and forties had as their role-model Christian sportsmen, who may or may not have got 'thirds' but who loved to share their faith with other 'toughs'. John Paterson was someone who could cross the academic/sporting divide and, along with Roland Lamb, led the boat club meetings. Cricket star David Sheppard joined with battle-scarred Godfrey Buxton at squashes for hockey, rugger and soccer clubs. Old school ties could be reassuring when one was newly adrift on the

[1]See above, p. 83.

155

Cambridge scene and a bit intimidated by Cambridge mores. John Collins spoke to Old Haileyburians; it was that old school tie that was to give him one of the most fruitful openings of his ministry, as we shall see. Tony Lewis organized the squash for ex-Repton people at which Buxton spoke. 'No less than five other school prefects who were at Repton with me were converted while at university. Memories crowd in of our return visit to Repton with Cambridge University Wanderers, a hockey side, followed later by John Stott preaching in the school chapel on Revelation 3:20.'

This may be the point to acknowledge what 'Bash' was about. These were still the days of public-school dominance at Cambridge, though it was beginning to give way as the equality of educational opportunity spread. 'It is important to remember', says John Pollock, 'that among non-Christians, right up to the mid-1950s, there was a social barrier between public- and non-public-school undergraduates. Humanly speaking few public-school men would have been won had it not been for Bash campers. Also he gave Oxford and Cambridge converts a good grounding as senior campers and then as officers.' He was motivated not by snobbery, but by strategy. One of the factors that accounted for the fruitfulness of gospel witness among ex-public-school boys was that they had had good grounding in the law of God, which 'was put in charge to lead (them) to Christ' when they heard the good news of sins forgiven.

Over at Oxford, there was an Anglican evangelical resurgence on a similar scale. Jim Packer, who really emerged at that time, was engaged in doctoral research, quietly thinking through the position he later wrote and preached with such authority. These were days when many of those converted later entered the Anglican ministry and, tipping the balance of ordinands in an evangelical direction, was one of the contributory factors to the 'fundamentalist' debate. Geoffrey Hart, converted in May 1949, and ordained in 1954, captures the atmosphere of OICCU witness in these years.

'The Sunday evening sermon was the high point of each week in term and was held at 8.15 p.m. in All Saints Church (St Martin's), on the corner of the Turl and the High. This was only a few yards from my own college, Exeter, and after dinner in hall the OICCU men could be seen waiting for or meeting friends they had invited to go with them. On one occasion

J. R. S. Taylor, the evangelical Bishop of Sodor and Man, was in competition with Geoffrey Fisher, then Archbishop, who was preaching the university sermon on the same Sunday evening at the University Church. Taylor graciously told us on the Saturday evening to pray for them both, but to bring their friends to the OICCU sermon. Fisher had been his 'fag' when they were at school together. The service was always brief, with Anglican collects very often, a lesson read by an OICCU man (rarely by a woman), and then a straightforward and unashamedly evangelistic sermon. More often than not there was an appeal at the end to people to make a commitment to Christ, but it was rare for there to be any kind of after-meeting. It was expected that the OICCU men would talk to their friends afterwards and do their best, under God, to lead them to Christ. It certainly happened and there was a steady trickle of conversions throughout my time. . . . An unforgettable visit was from Donald Grey Barnhouse, who astounded us all with his rich American accent, and his uncompromising Calvinism. I remember his powerful illustration of the fact that all men are equally guilty before God – the murderer in the condemned cell, the respectable citizen, the professor of ethics, culminating with "The Right Reverend Lost Soul, DD, by the laying on of hands".

'All in all there was something infectiously joyful about our Christian faith, though I suppose it was a trifle glib and superficial. But we had found Christ and were eager to introduce others to him. There cannot be much wrong with that. We took our faith seriously. Little was said, but most of us were teetotal and non-smokers, and going to a cinema or a theatre was almost unknown, except for Gilbert and Sullivan. Our college group' (Hart was co-representative with Michael Green) 'was large by Oxford standards. Very often our college Bible study was either a sharing devotional "best thoughts" or even a "pooling of ignorance" rather than a serious attempt to open the Scriptures. But the Saturday night Bible reading was uncompromising stuff and laid the foundations of Bible teaching, which has been the bedrock for me ever since.'

These years saw an unusual OICCU mission led jointly by the Bishop of Barking (Hugh Gough) and Dr Lloyd-Jones. Though it was something of a chalk-and-cheese mixture, it speaks volumes for the spirit of co-operation based on evangelical identity that was the feature of these days, and for which the CUs provided the best working model.

The OICCU executive committee of 1951–2 met thirty-five years later for a holiday together. 'Thank God', says one of them, Jill Dann, 'that none of that "exec." has fallen away.' The president, Michael Farrer, is vicar of St Paul's, Cambridge, his wife Annette also being an OICCU member. David Wheaton became principal of Oak Hill Theological College. Christopher Turner, the vice-president, had the notoriety of being the heaviest man in the Oxford boat that sank! His wife, Lucie, and Rosemary Storr were both converted in Oxford days and Rosemary married the following year's OICCU president, Michael Green, later author, evangelist and theological college principal. OICCU member Tony Dann played hockey for Oxford and England and was much in demand to speak to young people. His testimony had been the significant factor in the wartime conversion of his later OICCU contemporary John Boxhall.

'The OICCU group at Pembroke College', says Derek Wood of IVP, 'doubled in size in the first term of the 1952 session. A young fiery Irishman called Alec Motyer (the third of a triumvirate of future principals!) came to speak at the college freshers' meeting in 1952. At least six of that small group are now in the ordained ministry,' three of them converted that year.

It was the friendliness, cheerfulness, and prayerfulness of this group, who showed that there was reality and not just religion in their lives, that won the day, under God, as far as Tony Rees (now vicar of Cockfosters) was concerned. He tells us how it all led to his conversion. The truths he elicits show the strength of evangelical conviction in many of these future Anglican ministers.

'The OICCU taught me, through the Holy Spirit, that the atonement is at the very heart of the gospel.' The problem of the meaning of the cross had begun to puzzle Tony Rees some years before, towards the close of a three-hour Good Friday service in a South Wales church.

'The preacher happened to drop an aside that started it all. "I have often found", observed John Bunyan, "that a word spoken by the by has done more good than all my carefully prepared discourse." You may not consider the remark very startling or new but all he said was, "Christ died there for our sins." I must have repeated this phrase many times in the recitation of the Creed but it had never hit home to me before. Even so, the remark came not with peace but with confusion. What on earth was the connection between my sins and his death? I just could not see the relevance.

'It was a whole three years later that the question was answered in a very different church 200 miles away – St Martin's in the High, Oxford. The answer came as I was taken along by a Christian friend week by week and eventually I saw it all. Christ died for my sins in the sense that he bore the penalty for my sins in a judicial death under the law of God. What should have happened to me happened instead to him. He took my place not only as my representative but also as my sinbearer and substitute. Since he has borne the curse, why should I bear it a moment longer? So a burden rolled off my back which has never since returned, though other burdens have come not infrequently. Old habits die hard and I was not changed overnight. Looking back I see so much imperfection and sinfulness for which I need to apologize. But in the perspective of time I can see that in the year 1952 the whole direction of my life was changed, transformed not by my resolution but by God's grace in Christ. I have never needed the arguments of the theologians to convince me that the Bible was the Word of God. As far as I was concerned it authenticated itself.' In like manner his new desire to meet with others who shared his faith 'was not self-moved. It all found its origin in that great dynamic of saving truth: "The Son of God, who loved me, and gave himself for me." '

These were the keynote elements of evangelical life – the sinner's faith in the cross of Christ, the believer's love for the Word of God, and a warm recognition of Spirit-given, brotherly unity in those truths. In the early fifties they seemed to possess exceptional power to erase the boundaries of the day and the secondary traditions of earlier days. It was summed up in the title and content of the 1954 mission led by Stott – 'Christianity is Christ' – which was an exposition of basic Christianity. It was at that time that Tom Walker, later a travelling secretary, found Christ as Saviour from sin. The first meeting of term had made him face up to it. 'I had particularly hated the piercing, direct preaching of Maurice Wood in that first sermon.' He had gone expecting it to be the university sermon, probably respectably delivered in Latin!

'It turned out to be a most penetrating exposition guaranteed to pierce the armour of a self-righteous sinner.' He faced the pain of self-discovery. When, at the time of the mission, he found abounding and overflowing joy in the discovery that Christ was risen, alive and had forgiven his sins he dashed upstairs to tell a friend. 'My friend's reply was cool and calculated. "Now let's go out and buy you a proper Bible with print large enough to read, and an alarm clock." The discipline of keeping communion with God in order to grow into his love had begun.'[2]

During that same mission Katharine Makower was converted (her future husband Peter having been converted at the 1952 mission at Cambridge) 'I feel very conscious', she said, 'of the great debt I owe the spiritual giants of the two or three generations ahead of me, and to their work in the OICCU and CICCU and elsewhere, and feel we have much to learn from them.' It was this awareness of the unfolding heritage of evangelical witness that led to her book *Follow my Leader*, the story of the triumphs and tensions of Murray Webb-Peploe, a key person in the life of the CICCU after 1919 and one of the members of the first conference that year. Norman Grubb, in his foreword to the book, described the passion of Murray's life to be 'wholly and totally the bringing of Christ to all those "without God and having no hope" '. It serves as a reminder of the priority that it is our calling to follow still and which seemed to form the consensus of conviction in the 'fundamental fifties'.

The effect of this priority we shall illustrate by calling in at the Southampton CU. In Southampton a situation developed which illustrates perfectly the impact of conversion to Christ upon the evangelical ministry of the church. Harold Rowdon of London Bible College tells of his student friend John Williams, a sportsman and college character in the Southampton of the early fifties. After becoming a Christian he stood out as one who maintained his links with student life in general at a time when most of the CU had little time (even if they had the interest) to become involved. After teaching chemistry at Makerere University, Uganda, he returned home, trained for the ministry at Ridley and became curate at the Round Church, Cambridge. He was later appointed vicar of Highfield Parish Church, Southampton. Up to that time there was no

[2]Tom Walker, *Renew us by your Spirit*, pp. 61f.

clear evangelical Anglican ministry in Southampton, and Anglican members of the CU attended Above Bar Church. Fired by that example of what an evangelical church can be, Rosemary Aldis, a daughter of Arnold and Dorothy Aldis, and a CU member (now with OMF in south-east Asia), coveted the same for her own tradition. She made representations to the bishop. The living of Highfields, Southampton, is in the bishop's gift – hence the later appointment of John Williams. Gradually over the years he led that church into evangelical convictions and ways, and students in the city have another church to which to take non-Christian friends. What a fascinating picture would emerge if we could pick up the strands and follow all such stories of college, conversion, call, and church across the face of our land.

Chapter Sixteen

LONDON LIFE

As the newly appointed resident assistant surgeon at University College Hospital, London, was about to enter the refectory for lunch on his first day, he was enthusiastically set upon by a group of Christian medical students. One of them slapped him on the back and shouted 'Hallelujah!' At last they had some-where to meet! A foundation decree of the hospital prevented any religious meeting-place on the premises. For some time they had specifically prayed for a Christian senior resident to be appointed so that they could meet in his flat. Thus the 'Hallelujah' when Denis Pells Cocks got his post. From 1950 to 1954 his flat was an open meeting-place for fellowship and evangelism. The doctor, too, was richly blessed in his own Christian life through such contact. At their farewell party before he left for a consultancy in South Wales, he and his wife were presented with a signed copy of the IVF's major publishing achievement to date, *The New Bible Commentary*, a fruit of the 1941 Kingham Hill conference. They were also piped out of the hospital by a Scottish medical student. He had been permitted to practice for the occasion in a telephone booth – and then only when others were out of earshot at lunch!

All over London in the 1950s such cells of life were propa-gated and multiplied as more Christians sought to hold out the word of life among their contemporaries. Take, for instance, the conversion of medical student Roy Stowe, now a general practitioner in the south of England. He and another non-Christian friend inhabited the only large double bedroom in a University College hostel, and Christians coveted that room as a meeting-place in one of their recurring attempts to get round the restrictions. Stowe had already been persuaded to attend All Souls by fellow student, Graham Melville-Thomas (today a consultant psychiatrist in South Wales). Graham's gentle, 'non-pushy' replies to his growing questions, as he came under the penetrating preaching of Stott, had gained his confidence. Stowe soon agreed to CU people using his spacious bedroom for an evangelistic meeting taken by Leith Samuel. Afterwards he was handed a copy of Stott's *Becoming a Christian* and, coming across it months later, decided 'to read the thing'. He got to page 13. It stressed the need to accept Christ personally.

'That's what's wrong, then,' he thought. 'I've never done that.' There and then he knelt and did so. One of the immediate results was that he found he no longer hated Stott's probing sermons, but began to lap up the Bible's truths. Quite soon afterwards he approached Stott to talk to him about his brother, a student at Cambridge. It was just after Stott had returned from the mission there in 1952. 'I'm concerned about my brother,' he began to say – only to see the rector throw back his head and laugh. His brother had himself just become a Christian at the mission and had started to express similar concern about Roy!

Stott followed up his 1952 CICCU mission with a London one in 1953 entitled 'That Ye Might Have Life'. It opened and closed with full churches at All Souls on consecutive Sundays. In between, each college had its own missioner. John Collins' time at University College was so blessed of God that it was continued the following week because of the great interest shown.

In March 1954 this was followed by a quite remarkable event. Billy Graham had commenced his series at Harringay and it was difficult not to be aware that something special was happening in the life of London: week after week of capacity crowds and crammed Underground trains full of chorus-singing Christians. LIFCU persuaded Billy to speak to a student audience. The University College gymnasium was booked. We shall let 'Jeremy's Diary' in the University students' newspaper tell the story.

'BILLY SQUEEZES THEM IN – AND MORE

'Enthusiasm was high; enterprising souls scaled the wall bars within the Gym. Others assaulted the windows from without.

An air of expectancy mingled with a little irony prevailed until Dr Graham arose to speak. Few visitors to University College have given rise to so much speculation as Billy Graham. It is commonplace, I know, to talk of his magnetic personality, but it was certainly powerful enough to empty the Union lounge and interrupt the Dionysiac ritual at the Bar, where High Priest Charlie was eloquent on the dangers of Evangelism.'

Indeed, not only the drink trade felt intimidated by Billy's presence. The following day LIFCU felt it wise to cancel a meeting due to be taken by Maurice Wood because of 'difficulties with the Students Union'. The problem was that the Union had already cancelled its previous day's meeting because of Billy's visit and it did not want LIFCU to compete again with its postponed gathering.

So there is plenty of evidence that LIFCU was alive to its opportunities. But what was happening in the lives of people – is there evidence that God was at work? We shall take three examples, one English and two West Indian students. London was especially the place where overseas students gathered, and where special attention was given to their needs.

Jane Lodge-Patch (later to work with David Sheppard at the Mayflower Settlement in East London and now Mrs David Hewitt) came to Bedford College in 1948 to read sociology. Her brother Ian had been converted at Cambridge some years before and then moved to continue medicine in London. During her school holidays (she was six years his junior) he took her to hear Colin Kerr, John Stott and Lloyd-Jones. In her first week as a student she heard Dr Muriel Crouch at Bedford College. 'She gave a clear-cut message of the choice that lies before us – God's way leading to eternal life and our own way leading to hell. I was left in no doubt about the issues for me.' Then for three consecutive Sundays she heard 'the Doctor' bring home the words of Christ, 'Come unto me, all ye who are weary and heavy laden, and I will give you rest' (Matthew 11:28, AV).

That rest, when it came, came by surprise. 'In our hall of residence there were two Indian sisters. We discussed religion for hours. One was an atheist. We sat up late one night awaiting the announcement of Princess Elizabeth's first child. "If there is such a person as God", said one of the Indians, "he could not possibly be interested in us mortals." This ran totally contrary to all I had been warming to in the past weeks. As I returned to my room I had a strong sense that Christ was at the door of my life; it was now or never. I asked him to take over my life and the next day sensed a new hunger for the Bible.'

There followed, as she grew up in the nursery of the CU, the ups and downs of an eager Christian life – the rebuffs, the pride, the disappointments, the energies, the passing romance or two. Rebuff came quickly from her psychiatrist father. 'Observing the change in me, he commented, "Oh, you've seen the light too, have you? Never mind, you'll soon grow out of it." ' But there can be priggish evangelical responses, too, and she became dismissive of all the other religious societies.

But she was not afraid to relate to others of a different stamp. Indeed, she put great energy into tackling even her seniors. Impressed by Leith Samuel's little booklet called *The Impossibility of Agnosticism* she took along some copies to a tutorial meeting with the philosopher O. R. Macgregor. He sportingly agreed to read it and discuss it. One of his criticisms she passed on to the author, who incorporated the gist into a revised edition. She had less success when she invited her social studies professor, Barbara Wootton, no less, to a mission meeting. 'Frightfully sorry . . .' She discovered that students, too, could be almost as difficult to get along to an evangelistic meeting. A notable exception was the splendid job that Meg Foote, the travelling secretary, did in gathering students together for the smaller evangelistic Bible studies in hall.

One of her other special enjoyments of CU life in London had been Freddie Crittenden's Bible studies for overseas students 'in a plushy flat off Wigmore Street.' It had begun to dawn on people soon after the war that the combination of evangelical student groups in London colleges and evangelical churches strategically placed in the city provided natural 'welcome' centres for the increasing numbers of overseas students. What began as concern and hospitality for the 'stranger in our midst' became a well-organized network of contact for Christ's sake. Norah Nixon and J. O. Fraser's widow were the first to arrange hospitality, followed by Freddie Crittenden.

Then the International Friendship Campaigns got into gear. By 1952 the IVF and the Evangelical Alliance opened the Alliance Club, an international hostel in Bedford Place. Of the fifty residents, half were members of the CUs and the other half were overseas students. The numerous welcome links are best shown in operation by letting two overseas students tell their own story.

Faith Linton (née Nation) came to University College from Jamaica in 1951 to read French. 'I benefited enormously from the IVF's special interest in overseas students. Almost immediately I was befriended by Christian students. Not long before leaving for England I read the Acts of the Apostles and was struck by the difference between my experience and practice of Christianity and that of the New Testament Christians. I assumed that the passage of time accounted for the degenerative process. It must have been in my first term that I wrote home to tell my parents in Jamaica that I had met people who were "just like the New Testament Christians" whom I had longed to be like.' Her friend Jean Peck accompanied her to every Friday meeting. The messages were on the cross. 'It was a spiritual and intellectual diet that exactly suited my hunger. I was fascinated by the depth of the teaching.' Phyllis Stevens introduced her to the ministry of Dr Lloyd-Jones. 'My whole being was caught up in a process of enlightened and radical restructuring of thought and values. I entered into a deep assurance of my relationship to God in Christ . . . it all seemed too good to be true.

'I was also subjected to a glorious bombardment on many other LIFCU fronts. We were entertained graciously in the homes of the Clarence Fosters, the Buxtons, Mrs Menzies, Miss Jonas. Often there were Muslims and Hindus there and on each occasion the gospel was wisely presented. I went to the IVF houseparty in Keswick. Phyllis even persuaded me to attend the Puritan Conferences. I can still hear and see Leith Samuel after more than thirty years – so clear and dynamic; John Stott who, it was said, covered in thirty minutes what Martyn Lloyd-Jones took fifty minutes to expound; vigorously and delightfully unusual individuals like Graham Scroggie and Douglas Johnson, and men like Alan Stibbs, Ernest Kevan and Jim Packer whose superior gifts were totally consecrated to God. I remember with especial warmth Meg Foote who offered me friendship though she was counsellor to thousands. Above all, we were thoroughly grounded in the fundamentals of the faith. Experienced Christians and abundant literature provided opportunities to investigate and find answers, so that we learned to contend for the faith, to defend as well as present what we believed. It was a life-changing experience.'

Back home in Jamaica, Faith had a twin sister – Joyce by name. With something of the rebel in her, Joyce found her heart sinking as the letters came, with their summaries of the Sunday morning sermons at Westminster Chapel. To her, religion was a grim multiplicity of rules. She dreaded going to England to join her sister.

When she did get to London in 1953 she was amazed, relieved and interested to observe that her sister had a new quality about her life. That term she listened to John Collins. 'What I heard stripped me further of my defences. I was like a diver poised at the water's edge. All my life seemed to lead up to this moment.'

'I want to be a Christian,' she told the missioner. ' "I have been sitting on the fence too long, but . . .". But I was still afraid . . . I put my problem in these words: "I want to be a Christian but I do not want to do anything that is in bad taste." . . . "Do you think", he replied, "that God would ask you to do anything that was in bad taste?" I was well answered. The idea was incongruous. So it was possible, I realized, to be myself, to keep my tastes and preferences and to be a Christian. God was not asking me to do violence to myself; He was not going to force me into an alien mould. Another hurdle was removed. . . . God was not going to force me into another mould but He began to change me from the inside. . . . What I had strained at before became clear and simple because I knew it in my own experience.'[1]

She still coveted her independence. She was wary of conformism with its 'tentacles of restrictiveness and railroads of prescription'. She did not fit in easily with CU contemporaries, who were much younger. But she wanted the reality and soundness of a personal relationship with God, which she saw in others, inside herself. 'Though it was costly, nothing else would do. I also began to understand what the cross means, I came to appreciate the reality of evil, a powerful, personal evil pitted against God. . . . And now I began to understand what the "song and dance" of Easter is all about. I did not have to force myself into the song of triumph, the sense of triumph was beginning to burst out of my own heart. . . . I saw the unity of the Bible converging upon and revolving round the person

<hr />

[1]Joyce Gladwell, *Brown Face, Big Master*, p. 73.

of Jesus Christ. This was the most exhilarating experience of my time at university.'[2]

She began to see why her sister had summarized those sermons. 'We made our way to Westminster Chapel. . . . The joy and eagerness with which we looked forward to these Sunday morning services were never disappointed. . . . The congregation abounded in young men, many of them students, so that the singing swelled heartily. . . . We listened with fixed attention while the Doctor took a single verse of Scripture and opened out a panoramic view of the spiritual world. He showed us the eternal issues that put our own world in perspective; God, working out His purposes that go beyond the scope of history, yet involved in history – a caring, knowing, loving God. We learnt of His anger and we were sobered but not resentful, and we could see where suffering has its place.'[3]

One of the marvellous providences of these years was the way the ministry of IVF and churches at home helped on the next phase of gospel advance in Africa. Tony Wilmot and Honor Ward write of the young men, converted in Africa through the developing school and college witness there, who came to university here 'and had their faith significantly matured in Britain through IVF experience'. Staying at the Alliance Club in its early years were, for example, Festo Kivengere of Uganda and Felix Konotey-Ahulu of Ghana. 'CUs in Britain, and in at least one case a Christian British landlady, made a great contribution; as the years went by we began to get people such as Felix who had developed immeasurably spiritually while in the UK taking his medical degree. . . . Such brought with them a clear witness and wide experience of what Christian work in a university could mean. Their arrival marked the end of one preparatory era and the beginning of another and much better one, because they were witnessing as Ghanaians and not as expatriates.'

This, of course, was not just a London ministry. One example from Southampton could be multiplied from many cities. John Agamah was a member of the Southampton CU at this time. The CU there owed a tremendous debt to the Taverner family, who held open home, Sunday after Sunday, for tea and Bible study. When John returned to Ghana he repeated the pattern, and now Ghanaian students speak of his home Sunday after-

[2]*Ibid.*, pp. 75–76.   [3]*Ibid.*, p. 77.

169

noon Bible study tea parties, run on the Southampton pattern. Names abound from other African countries too. Central to it all in London was Freddie Crittenden whose ministry was two-way. He loved Africans and could tease them in a way that no-one else dared, and they loved him. He drew them. He also sent British people away with a vision for Africa and he did a great deal in getting them to go to schools and universities there.

Another link forged between overseas students, the IVF and the London preachers was when the latter preached abroad. Though some overseas students shared their Sunday between All Souls and Westminster Chapel, most became committed to one or the other. Few can have had the 'pull both ways' that Robin Wells had when he came from South Africa to London. While a student in South Africa, IVP books, especially by 'the Doctor', meant much to him. When Lloyd-Jones preached there in 1958, Wells heard him at all four of the local meetings and then drove him a couple of hundred miles to the next engagement. So it is not surprising that, when they came to London (by then Wells was married) they should make the Chapel their home. But the decision was not a straightforward one. He had chaired the mission committee in Johannesburg University, when John Stott was the missioner. Stott saw Wells off on the boat train to Capetown, returned by air, and met him on arrival at Waterloo! And All Souls made them very welcome. 'But in the end our free-church background, our increasing interest in Reformed teaching and the particular appeal of "the Doctor's" ministry drew us to the Chapel. When I was sweating it out past midnight at Imperial College night after night, my treat of the week was to take Friday night off from my laboratory work and come to the Romans expositions. I can still remember the oasis-like experience of sitting in the pews waiting for the meeting to begin.'

What impact did this ministry have on students in general? Wells elicits three things. First, its intellectual rigour and honesty, and the preacher's conscientious concern to wring out of the text the true meaning, was deeply satisfying to young people with quick and lively minds. Objections and difficulties were confronted without flinching. Secondly, surrounded as he was with so many young people with the light of newly discovered truths in their eyes, and beset by the temptation to become bigots, his concern was to maintain a balance. He gave many examples of people whose ministries had withered because they had become unbalanced, not only in undue emphasis on certain specific truths, but in an emphasis on doctrine at the expense of practical and experimental things or to the exclusion of emotional depth and passion.

This leads to a third emphasis which had much bearing on the theological situation as it was developing in LIFCU and the evangelical world at the time. Robin Wells came to London in 1959 and in some ways his own personal pilgrimage mirrors the kind of tensions that were around. With the rediscovery of older Calvinistic and Puritan principles, there had been a strong reaction against some of the methods of evangelism then current in mass campaigns. Lloyd-Jones himself expressed strong reservations in this area. But one unlooked-for effect was that it led many to be suspicious of evangelism itself. For a while, many CUs felt paralysed and unable to proceed. The reaction also falsely inhibited many of the young preachers, Robin Wells included. 'Having come from a background where all sorts of means were used unquestioningly in evangelism, without any understanding of the necessity of the work of the Holy Spirit in regeneration, I went through a phase where I was so afraid of any undue human role, whether in oratory, or in other ways, that I became severe and inhibited in preaching. It took a long time to work that over-reaction through and recover from it.' Yet many times he had heard 'the Doctor' say something which he only later came to absorb and apply to his own problem here. He used to stress that a person must be himself and that a person must be 'free'. He would especially stress this when an overemphasis on God's sovereignty left people leaden and lacking in any evangelistic 'go'. And anyone attending his Sunday night preaching services could not fail to see his own freedom to be impassioned and urgent in evangelism. Yet so many seemed to miss that and over-react. 'As one who had to go through the healthy but painful process of rethinking everything I said, every practice I had become familiar with, in the light of fresh understanding of biblical truths, I came to see how important it was that there was freedom in the work of preaching. In the process those earlier references of the Doctor were a great help in rescuing me.'

There was strong support in the LIFCU for *The Banner of Truth* magazine when it was launched, especially in King's and Imperial Colleges. In October 1959, Jim Packer led LIFCU's pre-mission conference on the subject of 'Evangelism and the Sovereignty of God'. This put the whole church in debt to a student initiative, for IVP published the talks under that title. Packer was one of the leading critics of the prevailing tendency to rest everything on man's decision and apparently little at all on the Spirit's work in regeneration. But did that mean, then, that he did not believe in evangelism, as some concluded? 'The aim of the discourse is to dispel the suspicion (current, it seems, in some quarters) that faith in the absolute sovereignty of God hinders a full recognition and acceptance of evangelistic responsibility. . . . Always and everywhere the servants of Christ are under orders to evangelize, and I hope that what I shall say now will act as an incentive to this task.'[4] He did so in bracing contemporary idiom and his answer helped many to see the way through to a more theological base for evangelistic action. Many a subsequent student leader seemed to get the balance right much more quickly. Lindsay Brown, IFES Europe Director, with an outstanding gift for conveying the evangelistic task, recalls his early OICCU days in the 1970s. 'My basic theological formation took place in Oxford. By the end of my first term I was convinced of the sovereignty of God, and that as a general rule, John Calvin's interpretation of Scripture was the right one; I had become a Calvinist without losing a concern for evangelism or missionary awareness.'

As this debate retreated from the forefront of interest in the sixties, another arose to take its place. It was to test and tear evangelical relationships more obviously than the Calvinist/Arminian tensions. It was to be both stimulus and distraction in church and student worlds. It majored, not on doctrine, but on 'experiences', and came from the rapidly growing charismatic wing. Students, instead of endlessly debating predestination in late-night discussions, began, just as endlessly, to debate spiritual gifts instead. Some, who had been rightly stirred to read and think more theologically by the Reformed perspective, were in danger of barren biblicism. Others, put off by the sometimes apparent, sometimes real, lack of joy and vitality of such contemporaries, oriented towards feelings and went high on charismatic concerns. A pendulum swing is once more in evidence.

Rightly handled, such a swing is often the way that the faith

[4] J. I. Packer, *Evangelism and the Sovereignty of God*, pp. 8–9.

172

has been kept from veering too far off course in one direction or another. But from now on the new forces of the 'swinging sixties', breaking free from authority of all kinds, were also to push the pendulum. The real challenge to the CUs was to come from powerful cultural forces that could have taken that swing well beyond the self-righting mechanism of Scripture's balances. The CUs were to need great love and biblical wisdom if they were to continue to steer a straight course. Our penultimate chapter entitled 'When the World Changed' analyses some of the tugs and tendencies.

Chapter Seventeen

TRAVELLERS' TALES

Hugh Evan Hopkins turned up the old log books of his travels for IVF in 1938–9. 'How small, isolated and generally ineffective were the university CUs in my travelling days compared with today. But at least they kept the lamp of faith burning, however dimly. A number of those whose names I recorded in my log have gone on to make their mark in church and country and overseas, and none of the dimly burning CU lamps have gone out. Indeed, the story of the IVF is the story of faithfulness rewarded by greater influence and wider responsibilities.'

In those far-off days, and for ten years or so after the war, the visit of a traveller was a real event in the smaller CUs. 'One saved up hard questions and hard cases for the welcome arrival of help.' With few reliable books, not many CU-conscious ministers, and few sympathetic seniors, the rare and roving travelling secretary was often the reason why a lamp still burned on into the next term. They were tramps for God, who lived out of suitcases and slept in some strange places. Their labours were phenomenal. By the late forties there were six travellers and three at the office who could sometimes add weight to the scrum. Leith Samuel's role as university missioner continued till 1952.

When Leith was called to Above Bar Church, Southampton, his travelling days were done – full time with IVF, that is. In Roland Lamb God graciously gave to the work once more someone gifted to sustain its main trust, that of evangelism. The two men first met at Swanwick in 1952. 'Over coffee together Leith told me he had felt the time had come for him to settle down now that he and Mollie his wife had started a family. "Of course," says he, "you're not married, or are you?" "Well . . . yes . . . I am, and with three young children under four." Stunned silence. And then: 'Man, you must be mad!'

Roland Lamb had not had any connection with a university since graduating, before the war, from Jesus College, Cambridge. He had been converted at a Bash camp. 'Though I remained fully assured of my own salvation, training for the Methodist ministry rocked me to the foundations, largely through lack of previous sound teaching at any real depth. I lost faith in the Bible, but discovered no alternative gospel that worked. During my four years as an RAF chaplain, however, I did see conversions whenever I preached the biblical gospel. I remained in that wilderness for seven years.' Then from 1949 to 1952 he began to see conversions again as the Lord dealt graciously and traumatically with him. The traumas came as the leaders of two successive local churches decisively rejected his evangelistic ministry.

At a Methodist convention, Roland told his story to Fred Mitchell, a co-speaker who was Home Director of the CIM. ' "The IVF needs an evangelist," thought Fred, and he suddenly asked me if I'd consider becoming an IVF travelling secretary. I just laughed at the impossibility of it.' But in a fortnight he had been appointed.

In good Wesleyan tradition, the country became his parish. For a while during that period there were only two male travellers covering the whole UK – thirty universities and as many colleges as survival permitted. The other was John Weston, who had recently returned from six months in the older New England universities, looking out and encouraging evangelicals to establish a campus witness. Weston's role was basically to help CU leadership. Lamb had a more evangelistic brief. There were long stretches away from home; the single travellers could be away for fourteen- or twenty-one-day forays. This is the point to thank God for the wives of the field workers. After the first year Lamb approached a young convert of their previous church. Would she be willing to live with the family and help his wife Jill with the children during his absences? She was told that the Lord would have to provide the wherewithal. 'On my return to London D.J. called me into his office to tell me an anonymous friend of IVF was so concerned for my wife that he had offered to pay for us to have a girl to help, if we could find one. Even D.J. was taken aback when I said I had just approached one who would be willing to do exactly that. Soon after, one of the Lord's faithful stewards provided us with a lovely house.

'How I found time to travel, prepare messages, keep up correspondence and spend time with the family I can't imagine. I see from a random dip into my Filofax' (the now trendy personal planner had a full life with IVF before the yuppies were born!) 'that on one three-day visit to Leeds University I spoke seven times and noted two definite conversions and brief details of personal talks with sixteen other students.'

At one weekend in the midlands the Lord blessed again. Lamb was surprised; he had been asked to give them a subject six months before, so he had given one he had been due to speak on that very week, which, in the event, proved rather flat. He almost changed his theme, but this time the Lord was present in power in the preaching of it and several professed conversion that night. Not only so, for on the Monday he spent the whole day in personal work. 'Just what has been going on?' he asked the president, for he wondered what lay behind the spiritual stir. The student leader traced the cause back to a missionary weekend a month before. He had asked the speaker, a Sudan United Mission worker, how he thought the weekend had gone. 'Oh, I'll drop you a line about that when I get home.' His letter rocked them. 'You might as well shut down the CU, for all it's doing' was, in effect, its conclusion. The president promptly summoned the committee. They had to admit the missionary was right. There was only one thing to do. Not shut down, but pray. And that they had done urgently ever since. Then the visitor knew why he had stepped into the path of the Spirit.

During his IVF days Lamb grew close to two men whose futures were to show very different responses to the kind of anti-evangelical ecclesiastical attitudes that Lamb had himself experienced. Elwyn Davies was on the staff as Welsh traveller. Roland's next move was to Aberystwyth for six years as a Methodist minister. 'For five years we had the privilege of acting as host church to the Evangelical Movement of Wales conference, and the ministry I was thereby able to enjoy left an indelible impression on me and my future ministry.' Elwyn Davies, and Roland Lamb himself, were eventually to play leading roles in the secession movement of the sixties when many evangelicals left their denominations. They sought closer ties with like-minded evangelicals in an attempt to preserve and express biblical truth which they saw the mainline churches abandoning. Lamb became General Secretary of the British Evangelical Council.

The second man, Donald English, also a traveller from 1955 to 1958, was a Methodist. His future was to take a different course regarding the denominational issue, as he stayed in his denomination while maintaining his evangelical commitment, in the hope of advancing the cause of biblical truth within the system. He became President of the Methodist Conference, and a regular contributor to Radio 4's 'Thought for the Day'.

His travelling days coincided with strong attacks by many church leaders on evangelicals and 'fundamentalism', climaxing in the hailstorm over Billy Graham's Cambridge University mission of 1955. Douglas Johnson entitled the annual report of 1955–6 'In Such a Conflict'. In the year when Tyndale House was extensively enlarged and a research grants scheme for biblical scholars inaugurated, he turned to Tyndale's words:

' "Amid the general darkness that prevails, amid such tumults in the world, in such a conflict of human opinions, to what refuge shall we flee sooner than to that sacred anchorage of evangelical doctrine?" In our day those who hold to evangelical doctrine are again forced to do battle for the truth. In the interests of "being positive", many are tempted to avoid controversy at all costs, a comforting practice, which often, however, betrays the truth. Lip service is often still paid to Bible, Apostle and Reformer; yet frequently only the semblance of authority is accorded to the heart of the gospel.'

'In the fifties we evangelicals were very much more in the situation of fighting with our backs to the wall,' recalls Donald English. 'The "fundamentalist witch-hunt" was on. We had very few established evangelical scholars then. Those we had, like Alan Stibbs and the young Jim Packer, were also expected to spend their days travelling the country, speaking at meetings. How they got any writing done is a mystery to me. The theological scene was almost totally alien to us, apart from the evangelical Anglican colleges. I think our sense of having to defend what was under severe attack probably widened the gap between us and other Christians in order to ensure clarity about our own position. And we may, in our suspicion of the social gospel, have neglected social and political issues. On the other hand, we were quite clear that we were really in the business of bringing spiritual babes to birth and then handling them in the earlier stages of their lives. I cannot imagine life without those three crucial years and I cannot thank God enough for what I learned through IVF.'

Also happily wandering the country in the mid-fifties was Michael Griffiths, the present Principal of London Bible College. He witnessed the 'fundamentalist witch-hunt' at first hand in Durham. A few months before John Stott began a mission there it got the full treatment. It is doubtful if we appreciate how much we owe this generation of evangelicals for refusing to be blown off course. The then Bishop of Durham launched a public attack in the diocesan magazine on the Friday. Then the mission was attacked in the cathedral on the Sunday by a canon, and on the Sunday night John Stott launched the mission. Ecclesiastical scorn had one spin-off: it gave an opportunity to clear up misconceptions about 'the fundamentals'.

The pressure on a missioner in such circumstances can be enormous. Does he 'answer' the critics or does he go straight ahead with his direct task? On that first night, says Griffiths, Stott preached a masterly sermon on the examplary nature of the death of Christ from 1 Peter 2:21. But he went on to explain that Peter did not stop there, and so neither would he. He then expounded the verses that followed. There the death of Christ as a substitute for sinners is plainly taught. Not for the first time this gospel doctrine had been publicly assailed. It was not allowed to go undefended in this mission. Writing more than thirty years later, Stott says in his book *The Cross of Christ*, 'The fact that (the centrality of the cross) is not always everywhere acknowledged is in itself a sufficient justification for preserving a distinctive evangelical testimony.' Its centrality 'has certainly been a vital factor in the history of what is now the Universities and Colleges Christian Fellowship.'[1]

That distinctive testimony involves both defence and proclamation, and under the pressures at Durham, the assistant missioners sensed that the preacher was perhaps more aware of those he was trying to answer than of the needs of those being invited to hear the gospel message. 'John, don't be so conscious of the opposition of these theologians. Preach!' And

[1]John Stott, *The Cross of Christ*, p. 7.

so he did, including a magnificent message on Revelation 3. It is interesting that in Durham in 1979 the CU went into the cathedral for the closing meeting of the mission, such was the change in the attitude to what the CU stood for. But what a constant ebb and flow there is in this battle for a biblical mind. For at Durham the reverse has re-emerged.

Leith Samuel was no stranger to the jibe 'fundamentalist'. But he showed how explanation can turn it back on the user. In one mission at Loughborough he was invited to lunch with the principal beforehand. Then the invitation was cancelled. A message was sent directing Leith to meet him in the cloisters. 'I hear you are a fundamentalist – so the chaplain tells me.'

'What do you mean by that, sir?'

'Well, I don't exactly know.'

'If by "fundamentalism" you mean someone who believes the fundamentals such as you have in the Creed' (and here Leith enumerated some), 'then I'm one.'

'Good man!' was the surprise response. He had obviously been afraid that some awful extremist was about to descend on his campus and cause trouble. It turned out that many of the senior staff appeared with the principal at the meetings each evening.

The best way to defend the fundamentals of Scripture is to proclaim its saving message. One of the ways God honours this is to save people who later become scholarly advocates of the reliability of Scripture! James Packer's 'Fundamentalism' and the Word of God was the right book at the right time when it came out in 1958. Over the years other students had been and were being converted who would add their expertise to the defence. Two Liverpool men, for example, owed much to the preaching of Leith Samuel – Colin Brown, editor of The New International Dictionary of Theology, and Kenneth Kitchen. The latter heard Leith during his early weeks at Liverpool.

'I went up in 1951 to read Egyptology with biblical Hebrew (to be studied under a certain W. J. Martin). How biblical I wasn't on my arrival you may judge from the fact that I had been studying Hebrew for a week before it dawned on me that this was, of course, the language of the Old Testament! I lived in Derby Hall where there were several CU members and I was taken along to meetings. My sharpest memory is of listening to Leith Samuel, twice, and then of working through his booklet Ready. His theme had been a challenge; at university people looked eagerly to further development of mind (academic achievement) and body (sports, etc.). But what of the spirit and spiritual dimension of life? The booklet spoke dramatically of a person having (so to speak) no hope – but certainty, certainty if entrusted to Christ Jesus and his redeeming work. So, on the basis of John 6:37, "All that the Father gives me will come to me, and whoever comes to me I will never drive away," I committed myself to him that week. I went on to be a regular CU member. This new dimension in life had its academic effects too. For him, I determined to be the best I could be in my work, and the whole marvellous world of ancient Near Eastern background to the Old Testament opened out before my mind's eye in all its rich promise. Having to read both pharaonic Egyptian and biblical Hebrew side by side was an education in itself – and seeing how very similarly both languages were articulated in their literary products, it soon dawned on me how erroneous, on purely academic grounds, the usual shibboleths of Old Testament study (JEPD etc.) really were (and are). "Fundamentalism"? I had no need of that hypothesis!'

When research opened out he prayed ardently about choosing the right topic, and professional advice and his own inclinations settled on the western Asiatic loan-words in Egyptian. A year later he obtained a lectureship, and the sheer weight of teaching at Liverpool saw the thesis shelved. But the study of most of the other languages of the ancient Near East reinforced still further his academically based scepticism of the subjective procedures of a large amount of Old Testament 'scholarship'. Over the years the fruits of his own work have been *Ancient Orient and Old Testament*, *Pentateuchal Criticism and Interpretation*, and *The Bible in its World*. 'In a sense all these stem from the 'enlightenment" granted me back in late 1951. Under God my feelings of gratitude to his instruments, the Liverpool CU and Leith Samuel, remain cherished always. There have been tough times, sometimes bitterness and in some directions disillusionment; but the basic answer has always remained – cling firmly to our beloved Lord despite all, and keep life's ship headed firmly into and through the storms.'

Overt hostility can, of course, be healthy, especially when it is a response by non-Christians to the rising visibility of a Christian presence and leads on to the active engagement of proclamation. Michael Griffiths was in at the death throes of one student society opposed to the CU. In Reading in 1955–6 the CU numbered a tenth of the student body, drawing in over a hundred members, and there were many added to the faith. People sat up and took notice. A group of atheists founded the 'Hell Fire Club' as a counter. They discovered that though it might be easy perhaps to say that you were agnostic, it was a different proposition to maintain an aggressive and intellectual 'There is no God' stance. The meeting that saw the club wind up went through till early morning with Christian students and the travelling secretary present to the last. It folded up because it could not maintain its position in such discussions. A decade later, however, the aggressive stance of humanism was to become much more assured, and they would not yield ground.

One of the great thrills for the traveller who has his own eyes on the mission field is to visit CUs that have men and women praying for and preparing to go overseas. There was much to depress in this, for this perspective was not present everywhere. But Griffiths loved to go to Newcastle CU, for example. It was a blessing to be among them. The committee was a tonic to be with, and encouragement in sharing a world vision was a two-way affair. One fellow gave up his position in a family steel firm to serve the Lord overseas. The fifties as a whole provided strong leadership from the front. John White was the first of five consecutive IVF student chairmen who were to go to different parts of the world. J. D. C. (Jock) Anderson (who went as a medical missionary to Sind, Afghanistan, and has latterly been at the International Centre for Eye Health, London, and so maintained contacts with overseas doctors and nurses), John Bendor-Samuel, Michael Griffiths and Nigel Sylvester complete that roll. John Callow of Wycliffe Bible Translators is just one example of a student converted at university (the Stott mission of 1952) who followed such leaders on to the field.

Griffiths recalls some of the senior people who made the CU context a training-ground for this kind of spirit. 'George Ingram had been a missionary in India and was often invited to Swanwick because of his capacity to convey the urgency of the Great Commission. Armed with a list of "exec." members he would go round them with the message, "If the leaders didn't lead to the mission field, then others wouldn't follow." He would ask three questions: "Are you saved?", "Are you filled with the Holy Spirit?", "Are you going to the mission field?" Those who had never faced the matter were asked, "Why not?" Professor Short also constantly kept this before the student gaze. He had immense interest in Africa and Asia, and concern to see students go. It was refreshing to have this missionary zest in the professorial leadership of the day.'

Side by side with Griffiths' enormous vitality and serious application to the work went a *joie de vivre* that students loved. He much enjoyed working with Major Batt. He recalls a mission at Cirencester Agricultural College. The students there at that time were very county, upper-crusty, driving their own Triumph sports cars and many of them training to run their own family estates. Bill Batt was at home with this flat-capped gentry crowd. The mission created a stir. Griffiths recalls sitting in the principal's room, which had been temporarily allocated to him, preparing for a meeting. The room was situated over a kind of archway with a corridor below, through which the students came and went. He heard two passing students engaged in an argument – one claiming to be a Christian and the other saying that he didn't think he was. Taking the booklet *Becoming a Christian*, the hidden observer silently flicked it out of the window and watched it pirouette through the air and land at their feet. They were puzzled to say the least, but walked off reading some of the answers to their argument.

A word about hospitality. The travellers were at the mercy of students, but there were some outstanding hosts and host-esses who were especially important to the women. Marjorie Telford, who was converted as a student and travelled from 1956 to 1959, owed much to friends all over the country, such as Miss Finlay in Aberdeen. There were hard times too. She found it so cold in one conference that she slept with gloves on. The women of that era found it more difficult than the men to leave every little personal preference aside and 'muck in', when, for example, they slept in church or town hall during church campaigns. 'Some cities we found very dirty and clothes meant for several days could become dirty in a morning in smog-bound Britain. However, drip dry was just coming in in my day and I remember when Don English was given a natty nylon shirt – one of the first, I think.' Griffiths speaks of the time he stayed at Camp Hall, Hull. This was a former army camp of corrugated iron huts in a field. He was taken to his bed late one night to discover no light (cut off), no water (cut off) and no bedding – just a mattress.

A postscript appeared at the end of a long list of helpful suggestions to new travelling secretaries: 'When you are feeling depressed, dejected, completely spent (and desirous of dying!) note carefully how God himself dealt with Elijah (1 Kings 19:3–8): *adequate sleep and some good food!*'

Some of the travellers, especially those with ministerial experience behind them, were at their best leading student teams in local church campaigns. The first ever had been at Birmingham in 1934, when Ronald Inchley, then the local midlands representative, organized hospitality for eighty students serving five churches, and feared that his hair would go white with the worry. That team was led by Hugh Gough, but all subsequent ones up to 1954 were led by L. F. E. Wilkinson, whose main goal was to bring the gospel to industrial areas.

Leith Samuel and Roland Lamb were spirited campaign leaders. At Derby, Leith and the team asked permission to speak at the Rolls Royce factory. They were invited to a meal with the directors, and told to contact the conveners if they wanted a factory-floor meeting. There were both night and day conveners. It looked as if they had got their heads together. 'It's not fair to visit the day shift only, so . . .', obviously thinking that there would be no offers for a 1.30 a.m. meeting from raw students, they put this as a condition of a daytime one! The team were, of course, delighted with the conditions. At the scheduled 'Workers' Playtime' spot at 1.30 a.m. the stage curtains swept back to reveal Leith and some of the team, game to give testimony to Christ. Leith laboured hard to get his team to relate appropriately to the locality, gathering as they did from different areas. He took them all through the Derby Pottery works to help them find relevant local illustrations, a typical example of his attention to detail.

Roland Lamb's very first commitment as a staff worker was at the Bootle mission. 'It was an unforgettable experience; we all but gave up half-way through the week. But then the Lord clearly indicated he was going to bless. We prayed "the prayer of faith" together, and carried on, though we saw no outward evidence of blessing till the very last night, when twenty-one folk professed conversion.

Later, in the Potteries, he led a dozen teams with 165 students. 'One night, two students were "fishing" at a bus stop, inviting folk in to the service. One man approached in this way said he would have come, but he was going to meet his wife and couldn't. "If that's so," they responded, "if you really think we've got something you need, don't worry about not coming to the meeting, come at 9.00 p.m. and have a talk with our team leader." "OK, I will," came the unexpected reply. And so he did, and in five minutes was literally weeping his way back to God.

'He went back home to tell his wife. She told him to go to bed – he'd feel better in the morning! But she awoke to find him offering her a cup of tea before going out to work. She was astonished. He had never even thought of doing such a thing before. Two nights later, at the end of the evening meeting, she also professed her faith in Christ. Some months on, when visiting Keele University, I called to see them. They had read through the four gospels together by then, and plied me with questions arising from them for well over two hours, along with very practical questions as to how to witness to others at work. It was then that he told me he had an uncle in the Salvation Army who had been praying for him for years.'

At a campaign in a Methodist church a young wife was present while her husband sat in with the children. But no great impression seemed to have been made. The next evening the roles were reversed, but while her husband was at the service his wife came under overwhelming conviction of sin. She lay awake all night until, as the dawn was breaking, she suddenly heard a cock crow in the distance and immediately the thought came to her, 'If Christ could forgive Peter he certainly will me!' Almost at once she fell into a deep sleep, and when she awoke again it was with a sense of peace that she really had been forgiven. And so it has proved to this day.

These campaigns varied much in impact, and our sample is all too confined; but year in, year out, it did the students immense good to see the power of the gospel at work in church situations through preaching and through Christians getting alongside folk. Up to the early sixties was an era when the nation outside the churches had not become so hardened to the gospel and opportunities abounded because complete outsiders would more readily come in to hear the gospel preached.

In the goodness of God, right from the earliest years of the Fellowship, there have been senior academic staff who have voluntarily given their ministry to the student world. One or two have been virtual part-time travelling secretaries. At first the Herculean labours of Rendle Short stood out alone. He was familiarly known in London hospital circles as 'our honorary senior trav. sec.'. Then came a few to stand with him, such as surgeons Arnold Aldis and, after the war, Bill Capper of Bristol. The back-up these gave to the very few full-timers cannot be exaggerated. Aldis, especially, spoke massively all over the UK. He must have been the most used speaker of the evangelistic/apologetic type in the forties and fifties. 'It was a happy day for the IVF when he arrived as a student at University College and made it evident that he intended, with his whole heart, to walk in the faith of his fathers', said the annual report of 1956. On many a Sunday night he travelled back by overnight train to Cardiff from as far afield as Glasgow or Cambridge, snatching sleep before operating again at 9.00 a.m. on Monday morning. One night he had returned on a crowded wartime train and had to stand in the corridor all the way. 'How did you manage to get any sleep?' his wife asked. 'Oh, I slept standing up,' came the matter-of-fact reply.

Time and again, after a freshers' squash led by Aldis, CUs would feel that the clearest possible presentation of the faith to a modern student had gone out. His method was a mixture of apologetic and exposition, given with an ease of style that was never difficult to listen to. In fact, he never used notes. He read and knew his Bible well, but he found that the best way to prepare a talk in the midst of a busy life was to go for a long walk and work it out before the Lord. He would then deliver it word perfect. Oliver Barclay well recalls hearing him speak at Cambridge on the passage from James's letter, 'What is your life? You are a mist that appears for a little while . . .' (4:14). It spoke directly to the non-Christians present.

Bill Capper travelled less than Aldis and spoke more to medics. His delivery was blunt, almost boisterous, and he was a great encourager. The comment of an SCM staff member in the fifties is illuminating: 'Of course, Aldis and Capper and other university staff are so valuable to you – probably worth more than an extra travelling secretary each.' We have already noted how more and more people in senior positions were only too glad to share their trust in the Saviour and to welcome opportunities to undergird the biblical witness of the growing CUs. It is a telling fact that the SCM's conviction that the old biblical gospel had nothing to say to the modern university world found its own ranks of academic supporters with no gospel to preach and little or no appetite to travel and share their doubts. There is place here for humble gratitude to God that the previous generation's hard-pressed determination to stick to what the Bible said had now borne fruit among the very people that so many maintained it could not possibly reach. It is most instructive to see the way sociologist Steve Bruce marvels at the continuing resonance of the biblical message, as opposed to dated liberalism, in the modern university world of the eighties.[2] God grant that we do not move away from our own foundations.

[2]Steve Bruce, *Firm in the Faith*.

Chapter Eighteen

TCCF, TCCU, AND TEARS

Had we looked up the CU secretary of Loughborough College on the day of the CU's annual meeting we might have found it difficult to believe what we saw. It had somehow become the tradition for the secretary, before presenting his annual report, to run backwards around the athletics track holding aloft an open umbrella. Was this a hidden formula for success?! Between 1951 and 1954 the CU, under the leadership of men like Arthur Pont and Bill Brooks, grew from ten to almost 120. That must be difficult to parallel. Quaint secretarial antics apart, the CU was noted for its disciplined demeanour. 'How well we students dressed for the weekly teaching meetings held in the famous Athletics Stadium Pavilion!' says John Todd, now a lecturer there. 'Not to dress in blazer and tie would have been revolutionary and only a few art school types would dare to come in without a coat.' The CU had come a long way since Dr (Sir) Eric Richardson had spoken at its inaugural meeting back in 1944 on 'The Faith of an Engineer'.

Since those days, witness in the training colleges (the Training Colleges Christian Union, TCCU) and the technical colleges (the Technical Colleges Christian Fellowship, TCCF) had advanced rapidly. There was a considerable number of Christian lecturers in these colleges, the continually increasing number of Christian graduates coming through university CUs tending to penetrate here more quickly than they did on university staffs. The colleges work developed its own national student leadership, each branch with a great sense of mission to the colleges of its own type and ethos, and developing, too, a sense of family through their own conferences.

Loughborough was the strongest of the college CUs, from which many of the national leaders came. It was during the upward surge of the early fifties that Leith Samuel led the 'You're a fundamentalist, aren't you?' mission. Among those who professed conversion that week was a fellow just out of hospital. He had built his own small aeroplane and flown up to college. But he had a disagreement with some telegraph wires and crashed. 'Why on earth am I still alive?' he kept asking himself. He came to the mission and heard God's good news clearly for the first time in his life. He turned to Christ with the excited confidence: 'This is why I was spared.' Paul Simpson found his way eventually to the north-west frontier as a missionary. He and his wife are now deeply involved in ministry among Asians in Britain.

The turn-out for the John Stott mission in 1958 was remarkable, with about half the college attending the series. The Munich air disaster, which occurred that week, had sobered students – particularly as Loughborough, then as now, had many aspiring sportsmen in training. The engineering department turned out in strength to hear John Laing. It was not uncommon for the Loughborough contingent at the IVF Keswick camp to number up to fifty strong.

There was a big demand for their services in the local churches too. In one term over seventy teams of at least three students each were involved. By 1963 the CU had taken four church missions, using wholly its own personnel. Over twenty students would form these teams. This had the effect of making students seriously consider their future before the Lord. Out of a college mainly comprising engineers and teachers Loughborough saw fifteen men enter the home ministry and a similar number become missionaries over a period of ten years or so. Missionary interest was high. A number of graduates of the fifties formed a Loughborough College Missionary Fellowship. This group still supports fully one of the CU members now serving in India. There was a genuine commitment to evangelism. John Todd gives one instance that remains in his memory.

'A dear man went to be with the Lord a few weeks ago, after years of faithful service. As a student he was taken on a CU bus to a showing of *Souls in Conflict* (a Billy Graham film) in Leicester. He happened to sit next to Tom Farrell, the Olympic runner, in the cinema. At the appeal Tom got up to go to the front. The lad next to him said to himself, "If it's good enough for him, it's good enough for me." And he went forward – to be told more of the way of salvation by Tom, who in fact had moved forward to do counselling duties.' Michael Marwood, another first-team athlete, now in prison welfare work, got to his first CU meeting, not by bus, but on the back of Arthur Pont's motorbike. 'The warmth of welcome made me feel accepted at once – I did not have to earn acceptance as in all my relations with other people. From then my faith deepened and I had a purpose in life and a new attitude. It influenced me to move from interest merely in machines to involvement with people.' It is noticeable how many Christians with a technical training have also revealed strong pastoral qualities.

In 1966 there was an amalgamation of colleges in Loughborough when it attained university status. This took it out of the TCCU and TCCF, along with other colleges that changed status then. But the overall work was well established by that time. During the fifties the TCCU conference began to pull in people and would one day have as big a turn-out as the universities' conference. By the early seventies the work in the colleges had so increased as to become nearly half of the total as CUs multiplied in colleges of all kinds. This led in 1974 to the change of name from Inter-Varsity Fellowship to Universities and Colleges Christian Fellowship.

As the work spread, art school students seemed to be the most impervious to the gospel. It was difficult to get this gifted but needy community to take the gospel seriously. The few Christians in art colleges were always under pressure and, certainly until the later sixties, the main emphasis was on helping them to survive. Yet during the years of student protest, when art colleges showed acute unrest, things began to change. We shall follow this transitional period through the eyes of Maeve Edwards, the first full-time worker in the field.

Her time as an art student at the turn of the decade shows that it was possible to survive as a Christian in such a milieu. But it also shows that the presence of TCCF was crucial in this when one's home church offered no help. At Swanwick she discovered *In Understanding be Men* and read it all the way home in the train. It was a revelation for their little art college group when they discovered the Bristol University CU. Attendance there 'meant blessed Saturday nights of superb teaching that had never come our way before'.

Grateful for the help she had received, Maeve began to plough something back into TCCF when, in September 1964, she joined the staff, with responsibility for co-ordinating what existed in art colleges and pioneering in areas where there was nothing at all. She was the only woman on the TCCF staff, and so added visits to women's agricultural colleges – 'quite a challenge, as I knew I was scared of cows and horses, and on being shown around one college by the principal, discovered I was scared of pigs too!' Art schools did not provide quite the same kind of alarms, but her pioneering took its toll, and she did not run to her full term of three years. Here was a tough assignment over a huge area, but it was tackled at exactly the right time and so laid foundations for what came later.

'Reading my diaries of twenty years ago, I ended up in tears. I'm surprised I'm so affected by it still, but thankfully recall a chance meeting last year when someone introduced herself to me and said what an encouragement I had been to her in art school days, when my only memory was her tears.' More often than not her role was the constant hard slog of meeting one or two new people over coffee. Her comments reflect the inertia. 'A defeated, sad little group', 'very depressed', 'disheartened', 'mixed up and not quite sure where they stand', 'the chairman turned out to be a Roman Catholic and the secretary a Quaker', 'they got the day wrong', 'my student contact didn't turn up though the liberal studies lecturer bought some books for the library.'

'The arts students fell into two groups, the Reformed and those whom I describe as "woolly" "waffly", "frilly" and "vague". It is hardly surprising that the latter were an easy prey for philosophy lecturers where Zen Buddhism was actively promoted as part of the "You must experience everything" curriculum. In an endeavour to meet this, the first leaflet for art students was produced by us and led to some fierce discussion amongst the woolly groups, whilst the Reformed group really didn't think it said anything much. At Corsham – Bath Academy – there was a particularly religious waffly group, and so I would wonder where the "sound" students were on my visits, until I discovered that a certain D. M. Lloyd-Jones was preaching at the local Bible rally, coinciding with my visit!

'Unusual among the art students was a lone, faithful girl at Ravensbourne who organized and ran a programme on her own each term. My meeting there started with twenty or so, with me seated on the model's dais – and rose to fifty or sixty, most having joined in to mock. It was very hard going . . .' On a later visit only six turned up for a Bible study including 'X, a model, willing to be convinced on my last visit, and Y, his entire jumper covered with rows of milk bottle tops like medals. He was delighted that I'd remembered him and noted his new hairstyle. He comes now to every meeting but always asks the same questions. . . . At the close A saw me to the door, and we were greeted by several of the rowdiest of last time's hecklers and a volume of swearing from one group – because they'd forgotten to come to the meeting!'

One splendid group was at Brixton where there were good contacts on the staff and where Maeve visited for a week each year speaking daily to all the liberal studies classes. Small struggling groups met in all the large London art colleges, but the most profitable way to meet was as a combined Bible study group. This had been pioneered by Don Harding while a student at the Royal College of Art a few years previously. 'Squashed into my tiny bedsit it was a delight to hear those who were clear about the gospel gently teach the muddled as well as to talk about art far into the night. Those who shared the house always commented on the odd assorted garments heaped outside my room on those evenings; in the 1960s, knee-high lime-green suede boots belonging to one of the men were more than astonishing. However, the group soon became more arty and less biblical in its thinking.

'Parallel to all this was the growing charismatic debate and pouring oil on to troubled and split CUs. . . . But my main recollection is of holding weak hands and making firm feeble knees . . . until my own knees became somewhat feeble . . .'

It was just when Maeve began to fade off the canvas that the Christian art world was on the edge of a remarkable work of restoration, and she had herself been in at the start. A friend and co-worker of Francis Schaeffer, Professor Hans Rookmaaker, Professor of the History of Art at the Free University, Amsterdam, began to influence the art students at the same time as Schaeffer began to get a more general hearing. The only conversions that Maeve Edwards noted in her time with TCCF were of three students from Birmingham at the first art students' conference. Rookmaaker's introduction to the art students was on tape at this conference. His real personal impact was to come later. None of the students read Dutch and the most Maeve could do was to show them the pictures in his book. 'His first appearance, looking much like Harold Wilson,' says Maeve, 'was in my flat. We decided to give him an English tea and, along with the cucumber sandwiches and cakes offered him an assortment of spreads to go on the hot buttered crumpets. I recall our mutual bafflement over endeavouring to define a crumpet and then dismay as he chose sugar to spread on it . . . and subsequently on himself, his shirt and the carpet.'

The spread of his influence was to be more constructive. IVP's publication of his profound work *Modern Art and the Death of a Culture* in 1970 was of immense help not only to the Reformed but to some of the 'woolly, waffly, frilly and vague', giving them much more confidence as Christians and a more positive role as Christians in their own world. Maeve's tears had not all been in vain.

In the 1960s twenty-one new universities were established, some, like Loughborough, becoming universities through change of status. The first new campus after the war was that of the University College of North Staffordshire in 1950. This became the University of Keele in 1962. We shall therefore take Keele as our example of the challenge to IVF of this expansion. Could CUs get going in the highly secularized environments? How would they react to the influence of chaplains who wanted all Christians societies to get together? Would evangelicals continue to see that it was just as important to nail their witness to the biblical mast? The story of Keele presents some of the challenge and the response which the new university CUs of the sixties would each have to face.

When North Staffs started it was housed partly in the ancestral home of a Staffordshire family and partly in Nissen huts of a recent army camp. Two essential requirements for students were gowns and gumboots. Roads were still a dream of the future.

An inaugural meeting of sorts was taken by a combined team from OICCU and CICCU – a tremendous example of the older CUs instantly seizing the initiative. Probably the original contact with Christians on the campus had been an earlier visit by the IVF midlands representative Derek Burke. Soon a regular nucleus existed. As the new institution sought to gain its identity, strong attitudes of various kinds arose on the campus, prophetic perhaps of later new campus problems. In 1952 came a crisis, with rumours abroad in the Potteries that the new college was a hotbed of Marxism. So much was this so, that each society had to have a member of staff on its committee. In 1956 Leith Samuel, always game for a new adventure, took the first mission. There was a buzz of interest through a debate that week. Just about everyone stayed until the end and one African student, later an MP in Nigeria, spoke most movingly of the work of God in his home town.

One of the problems of an isolated and self-contained campus was that couples began to pair off within weeks of arriving, again a trendy pointer to the changing sexual mores that were to affect student society much more radically. This preoccupation with partners was soon imitated to some degree by CU people and they were giving little moral and spiritual leadership. At one special weekend Michael Griffiths and his fiancée Valerie were invited. 'It was particularly interesting', observed one student, 'that neither Mike nor Val allowed their engagement to hinder their Christian witness or personal work and Mike gave very helpful advice.'

The arrival of Professors David Ingram and Donald MacKay on the staff did much to transform the quality of life and confidence of witness among the students. Their background presence provided shelter for a battered CU and enabled growth to occur. They witnessed positively in campus meetings and regularly held open house on vital subjects. Professor Ingram gave a talk on 'Order and Purpose in the Universe' (a talk that was to grip many audiences in campuses up and down the country) at the time when he was lecturing to Keele students on astronomy. The whole thing was a great success.

The 'open house' evenings for discussion saw many profitable confrontations in an atmosphere of pleasant informality and warm hospitality. One memorable occasion in 1965 saw 120 students 'infesting most of the rooms of Professor Ingram's home', which was 'wired with extension speakers for the occasion', listening to a debate on 'The Concept of God' between Professor MacKay and the atheist professor of philosophy, Anthony Flew. All this was accompanied by encouraging growth in the CU and a deepening of spiritual commitment in many. In answer to specific prayer by a small group meeting each day before breakfast ten students were converted.

The Christian life is a whole, and here we see how biblical belief, moral behaviour consistent with it, and a converting influence upon non-Christian friends, began to become the mark of a maturing new evangelical outpost. A sensitive and crucial issue was how faithfully could they keep the fundamentals of the faith fundamental to their life and witness. While the Students Chapel Council at Keele had been solely a co-ordinating body the CU has remained part of it, but when strong pressure was exerted in 1965 for the Council to be transformed into an executive body the CU stood firm for its distinctive doctrinal stand. Consequently an ecumenical Christian Society was formed without the CU. Cordial relationships though contradictory views were maintained throughout these discussions. Whenever this matter of co-operation came up, and it was to do so a lot as the new universities produced the need for clear policy to be established once more, it was never a question of minor differences of opinion. Taking a firm stand over biblical truth was often necessary because other religious views contradicted what was central to the faith. When essentials of the gospel are at stake it remains a matter of principle and duty for CUs to stand by their convictions and to know why they do so. If, in the process, cordial relationships can be maintained, as in this Keele incident, then much has been gained for the practice of truth as well as for its defence.

Chapter Nineteen

ADDING TO THE CHURCHES

From the beginnings of its history right up into the early 1960s the IVF, though constantly growing, continued to be compact enough to be aware of its own identity as one work under God. But the sheer variety of people converted at university over these years meant that they themselves were the seed bed of a further rich variety of Christian growth. By today that variety can bewilder, and green shoots seem to have gone off in all directions, some fruitful, some in need of pruning. In this chapter we shall give examples of CU members who were later instrumental in Calvinistic resurgence, charismatic renewal and Christian apologetics. The life of the church has been both renewed and riven. Different branches forked away from each other in the sixties. But there is often a common root from which much of this vigorous growth came – CU evangelism.

The church grows in real terms only through the Spirit's work in regeneration. So again, we stress two essentials. First, the primacy of the biblical gospel that saved these people, bringing them to spiritual life. Secondly, the student evangelistic concern that reached them with that life-giving gospel. People in later life tend to drive at different speeds and along parallel lanes of the King's highway, and so it is well to remind ourselves that there is only one way of salvation. Humanly speaking, none of us would be on that road at all without the evangel that was preached to us and the evangelism that reached us. The rock from which we were all hewn comes down to this: that someone passed on to us the good news that Christ the Saviour receives sinful human beings. It is but the testimony of history to record that the means God was pleased to use to save so many were the CUs in the universities. It is a plain fact that when CUs see their calling as the defence and proclamation of the gospel, God truly adds to the church.

We have seen how Christians in London and Oxford were rediscovering that the roots of evangelical life lay deep in the biblical teaching of the sixteenth- and seventeenth-century Reformers. Quite independently of this, a similar providence arose in the north-eastern corner of England. Durham had been the only university outside Cambridge, Oxford and London to be represented at the 1919 conference arising out of Norman Grubb's vision of the IVF-to-be. A solitary Durham man had turned up.

The CU was well established though still not large. With its dominant cathedral, 'half church of God, half castle 'gainst the Scot', and its church-based colleges, Durham had a strong ecclesiastical atmosphere. It seemed to hang over the city like a pall of piety. But, like the mists that cover the banks of the river Wear, it was very patchy and student behaviour was as typical here as anywhere else, while evangelical students coming up to read theology were often amazed at 'the perfect indifference of our lecturers to the truth of Scripture'.

Such was the impression of Iain Murray. Iain was a Christian and his background public school. Coming up at a similar time from a working-class background and not a Christian was Don Elcoat. With a state scholarship under his undergraduate gown, he felt equal to it all. Or did he? Underneath he was full of self-doubt.

Iain settled to the CU. 'It played a far greater part in my active life at university than anything else. Rightly or wrongly the CU was our spiritual home, and while we attended church regularly and taught in Sunday School, there was no question that the CU and the speakers that came were our main source of help. Most Sunday evenings the CU's evangelistic service was crowded out and clearly did good. Of course, the CU then would probably be described as pietistic today, but witness was definite and there were, I believe, regular conversions.'

Don Elcoat was one. He had been warned about societies vying for support so he just joined the soccer team. But the kindness of the CU representative who carried his bulging cases up three flights of stairs, and an intriguing invitation to attend a 'freshers' squash', made him curious to go. 'In the event it was to change the whole direction of my life. A hard-hitting

198

talk from a geology lecturer left me wishing I could get out and hide, yet wanting to know more. I was soon attending Bible studies, keeping my end up in discussion, but inwardly in a turmoil.'

Under the shadow of the east end of the great Norman cathedral lies the smaller church of St Mary-le-Bow, where the CU held its regular evangelistic services. After attending several of these he was led to receive Christ as Saviour. Returning to his room he was 'brought through' as a friend explained the way more clearly.

It was during this period that the library of a former Methodist minister, James Shipardson, which had been locked up for many years, was sold. Those with an eye for a good bargain soon realized they were on to a spiritual goldmine. Students began to see the evangelical faith in a more historic perspective, and its early results were to give them a much deeper interest in doctrine. Jonathan Edwards, the leader in the eighteenth-century awakening in America, was especially prized by Iain. 'None of us had ever been to the Puritan Conference in London, and the resurgence of interest in the Puritans in Durham was not directly linked to what was happening elsewhere.'

By the late fifties Iain was involved in launching the Banner of Truth publishing house in London and his friend from Durham joined him in the early days of the firm. They started in Westminster Chapel 'in a room no bigger than a store cupboard'. When their lone Durham predecessor had gone to London some forty years before to share in the early stirrings of IVF, the Calvinistic heritage of the church was in almost total eclipse. As the IVF grew, members acquired a renewed sense of the importance of biblical doctrine. They wanted stronger meat. When many found it in the Puritans they naturally began to serve it up for others. Not everyone could cope with the diet. It was nutritious stuff. But some found it tough meat. It took a while to digest in the system and it upset some. In the meantime there were others turning to Christ in the CUs who did not taste the fare at all and were later to be activated by charismatic interests. We shall go back down to Cambridge to find some of them.

The tapestry of evangelical life had woven into it many colourful strands. None more so than David Watson, the ex-

Royal Horse Artillery officer who exchanged horses for academic life at Cambridge.[1] With worldwide charismatic influence ahead of him, he began student life cynical and wayward, even a bit wild in his ways. He had no religious inclinations. But in that decisive time for the uncommitted newcomer he acted on impulse and turned up at a 4.00 p.m. tea party for freshers. The speaker was John Collins, by then a curate at All Souls, London. David's cynicism was disturbed by the speaker's genuineness.

As people were leaving at the close, Collins recognized the freshman's old school tie. He quickly got a promise from him to come to breakfast next day to talk more. Around the table they talked about a lack of purpose, about the unreality of God caused by the breakdown of communication as a result of sin. The listener was surprised to find that he did not need much convincing. If God did exist and he had turned his back on him, it followed that there would be a communications breakdown. He was even prepared to admit he needed God's forgiveness.

John Collins then 'took a piece of burnt toast and placed it on his upturned left hand. "Let this hand represent you and this toast represent your sin. . . . Now let my right hand represent Jesus, who had no sin at all. There is a verse in the Bible which speaks about the cross like this: 'We all, like sheep, have gone astray, each of us has turned to his own way; and the Lord (God) had laid on him (Jesus) the iniquity of us all' " (Isaiah 53:6). As he said that John transferred the toast from his left hand to his right. "Now," he said, "where is your sin?"

'My arrogant self despised the simplicity of it all. But it was as plain as could be. "I suppose my sin is on Jesus," I replied. In my heart I was beginning to see it.' As the conversation developed David saw the cost of becoming a Christian, and the promise of Jesus in Revelation 3:20. He saw the directions that God had given him. Alone, he read John Stott's *Becoming a Christian* and realized it must be all or nothing.

Some days later he was astonished to find a note on his table from David Sheppard, promising to look him up. Almost every week he went round to Sheppard's room in Ridley. 'He helped me to know the only foundation that will stand firm against every wind of doctrine and storm of life, the foundation of

[1]For these and further details, see David Watson, *You are my God.*

Jesus Christ.' They read different passages of Scripture to meet his need: Psalm 103 (assurance), Psalms 32 and 51 (repentance), Isaiah 53 (the cross), Luke 24 and 1 Corinthians 15 (resurrection), James 1 (temptation), John 17 (prayer), Romans 12 (service), and so on.

At first he found it foreign and very difficult to relate to the CU in his college. He had nothing in common with them except the Saviour. In his developing intellectual battles in the philosophy course he found his psychology supervisor, Malcolm Jeeves (now Vice-principal of St Andrews and Professor of Psychology) a help in integrating his faith and his thinking. So, through the combination of regular Bible study, Christian fellowship and a Christian academic perspective God began to prepare him. Converted in the fifties, he seemed providentially shaped as an evangelist to fit the later sixties. His university missions caught the mood of those days when people were asking questions from well outside the base of Christian morality.

Roger Forster is not, for a change, an Anglican! He was, nonetheless, brought to Christ through the preaching of a bishop. When he got to Cambridge he had never met anything like the evangelistic enthusiasm which greeted him on arrival. He was persuaded to read for himself the first three gospels and was taken to hear Hugh Gough, by then Bishop of Barking. The meaning of the cross was explained in such relevant terms 'that I knew that I had to give myself to such a God to live in his world in his way'. As with others converted at Holy Trinity he has returned there to preach and seen other lives given to the Lord in later days. He has been called on time and again to lead university missions since the mid-sixties and is still at it, initiating also inner-city fellowships through the ministry of Ichthus.

Michael Cassidy and Ranald Macaulay were schoolboy friends in South Africa, the one ebullient, infectious and destined to preach to multitudes, the other steady, analytical, with a ministry of apologetic and ethical concerns ahead of him. Michael left school in 1955, a nominal churchgoer. Then 'members of the CICCU got their loving clutches on me within hours of my arrival'. He describes their impact on his life in his refreshing and influential book, *Bursting the Wineskins*. Their sustained, caring, zealous evangelism 'brought the glorious wonder of conversion to Christ. . . . I remember that gentle English morning in a little English bedsitter, when, with the help of my friend Robert Footner (converted the previous year at Harringay Crusade) I said "Yes" to Jesus Christ. . . . I remember the overwhelming realization at the end of that momentous day that Jesus Christ had taken up residence in my heart.' He wrote in his journal of October 1955, 'As I realized the true wonder of that promise of Revelation 3:20 things began happening with almost alarming rapidity. It was as though I was having a radio wave of joy filtered into me – a new surge of wonderful life – and above all a new and hitherto unexperienced feeling of God's presence – all this in a day.' His desire to witness was instant, constant, irrepressible. Such spiritual delights enthralled him that half the college knew quite soon. In retrospect he sees some of his witness as insensitive, and wisdom was to come later. But what he had found in Christ 'was hardly something to suppress'. Again and again excitement in God filled him. It all seemed summed up in the testimony of another first-year student of a far-off generation, whom he soon read about. Temple Gairdner, converted while at Oxford in 1892, was later to be an ambassador of the gospel in Cairo. He had written: 'The sense of newness is simply delicious. It makes new the Bible and friends and all mankind and love and spiritual things and Sunday and church and God himself. So I've found.' 'The deliciousness of that sense of newness' precisely expressed Cassidy's feelings.

He had left behind in South Africa his friend Macaulay. For the next twelve months their paths diverged entirely. Macaulay had been a nominal Anglican, but during the twelve months following school he read widely in existential literature, gave up his churchgoing and soon lost his way. In 1956 he began at Cambridge. At the first opportunity his friend invited him to the CICCU. And once more God worked. The clear, uncomplicated message of L. F. E. Wilkinson was the means of his conversion. A very lost person sought and found Christ.

Whereas Cassidy went straight into overdrive on the fast lane, Macaulay was less inclined to sheer acceleration. But he was moving. He wanted to know more about prayer and so the prayer meeting was his priority. He gave his testimony at A. G. B. Owen's factory and joined his friends at Criccieth CSSM beach mission. These forms of service are proven means of strengthening a young Christian's resistance to secular influences and give him increased cohesion with other Christians.

Yet, before long, Macaulay somehow began to feel that 'he was going down inside'.

The problem was one of intellectual consistency. He found he was having little help regarding questions he was tussling with as a student. He was reading jurisprudence (the philosophy of human law) and he was not getting Christian answers in areas that seemed to him to challenge the basis of what he believed. There was a tendency, he felt, for so many of his Christian mentors to equate Christian maturity with a deepening of personal piety. He longed for holiness himself, but found it personally stunting in that quest to be discouraged from pursuing the biblical answers to 'issues' of the day. He was groping for a principle of authority he later found in that of *sola Scriptura supra omnes* (Scripture alone above all).

Then, in 1958 the dynamo called Cassidy went off to Switzerland, to a centre called L'Abri, a work then in its infancy, where Francis Schaeffer was attempting to give biblical answers to modern dilemmas (and a centre which Macaulay now helps to direct). Cassidy was thrilled. (See *Bursting the Wineskins* for the way his path developed.) Later that year Schaeffer paid his first visit to Cambridge. It was a low-key visit. He stayed in the Garden House Hotel and met small groups. Most did not see the visit as marking anything significant. Others were suspicious of his being 'into philosophy'. Ironically for Macaulay he was introduced that year to Bash camps by the CICCU vice-president Clive Boddington. There, the fencing off from such an approach as Schaeffer represented was firm.

Nevertheless, for a handful of students such as Macaulay, that visit effected a life-directing transformation in their confidence that the Bible did confront modern man's rebelliousness and showed him where he was wrong. He was satisfied also that Schaeffer was a servant of God's kingdom and not a kingdom-builder of his own. Furthermore, many of his sceptical contemporaries were to benefit in later years from Schaeffer's writings. Clive Boddington, out in Africa and feeling acutely the pressure of humanism around him, began to read Schaeffer's *The God Who is There*. It showed him the heart and the mind of the writer and ministered deeply to his human and spiritual needs. Over in Manchester University, Jerram Barrs, puzzled by the riddle of life and seriously plagued with a sense of its meaninglessness, was converted to Christ through the help of two CU students who had a dimension of life and witness that seemed to answer his core needs. He found later that they, too, had come under the integrating influence of L'Abri.

Schaeffer came from a very different kind of American evangelical 'stable' and his language and thought forms were bewildering to the average churchgoing English evangelical. Yet his background was as careful about defending the faith as was the CICCU. The problem of acceptance lay partly in the mistrust of CICCU members about the academic approach to religion. They were still defensively fighting the tragic tendency that, in the SCM, had substituted philosophical thinking for biblical. They were rightly determined not to go down that way and lose the gains of their hard-fought stand. Had more been able to 'hear' what Schaeffer was saying about 'true truth' and the Scripture, they might have perceived more quickly that here was an ally fighting the same battle, but on a wider front. Schaeffer's perspective later excited many and helped them to see why things were happening in the world of ideas and morals and where secularism was going. It was a strong tower against the sixties avalanche. The next chapter will show that he was a prophet of his day. Much that he warned about came sweeping across the face of the land on a very wide front indeed.

It is difficult to avoid the impression that though evangelicals went into the sixties stronger than at any time this century, their capacity to meet the colossal crises of the times was vastly diminished by the problems emerging in their own ranks. Though that story is not our theme, the CUs could not but reflect the tensions and disunities. Evangelicals had now got so many on board that it became very easy to rock the boat! The single-minded goodwill in elevating the centralities of the gospel that we have seen in the CUs, and which was, in large measure, reflected in the evangelical community, came to an end as issues of ecclesiology and pneumatology came to the centre. In succeeding years UCCF has worked hard at resolving these new tensions among different evangelical groupings. For a while the air has been full of the sound of new voices. Gradually there has been a more concerted attempt by many to listen carefully to each other as the kingdom of God has shown that it always has things old and new. Many bridges have had to be rebuilt or newly built. But as we review the last twenty-five years in the next chapter, 'When the World Changed', we shall not so much assess the domestic changes as analyse the cultural shifts of mood and mind-set that hit the faith from without. They still constitute the main challenge to church and CUs, and the last chapter sketches some of the ways in which that challenge is being met.

PART FIVE
THE 1960s ONWARDS
YOUTH . . . FAITH . . . TRUTH

Chapter Twenty

WHEN THE WORLD CHANGED

It was in February 1960 that Harold Macmillan spoke in Cape-town of 'winds of change' blowing throughout Africa. A month later he was installed as Chancellor of Oxford University. He could well have applied the same image to the future of the universities in the UK. There were things blowing in the wind here, too, that were to change the whole climate of the student world. If we take 1919 as the starting-point of our story, then the next forty years to 1959 had about them a recognizable continuity both in terms of evangelical witness and of what 'the student world' conjured up in the public mind. If we take 1928 as our starting-point, the fortieth landmark from there – 1968 – brings us into a different world. By then the 'student image' was a perplexing one to many and evangelicals on campus went through a testing and exciting time. Their message was the same, but how far should their image change in days of change? What were the biblical fixities that were God's constants and therefore ours, and what were the fluidities of culture and tradition? It was a matter of 'baby' and 'bathwater'. The 'baby' – truth unchanged, unchanging – was to be preserved at all costs. But 'bathwater', after all, needs to be changed. Obviously, Christian students needed to be fresh and relevant in their witness to abiding truths if they were to capture the ear of 'the restless ones' that made up their generation. It would, therefore, need mature perspective to know when, for example, multi-media presentation was a servant of the gospel and when it became an entertaining substitute for its serious procla-mation. This was just one issue arising in swiftly changing days. This chapter tries to convey something of those changes and how the altered intellectual and moral landscape left a bumpy ride for Christians. The final chapter tells how Christian student witness coped and advanced in this unfamiliar terrain.

A few reminders of events in the sixties will help us get the feel of the times. They began with highlights of outer and inner space – Uri Gagarin orbiting the earth and Francis Crick gaining the Nobel Prize for cracking the DNA code. The Cuban crisis set the world's nerves on edge, and the Berlin Wall cut it more deeply into two. Television brought us the horror of Kennedy's death and the spectacle of Churchill's state funeral. The changes of mood and mind-set are more radical. In 1962 began 'TWTWTW' ('That Was The Week That Was') when BBC television began to preside over the destruction of taste and discipline that had been its own strong point. In 1963 'sound' became a new phenomenon; the Beatles were the first to utilize its power to sway multitudes, and the pop prophet was with us. The way the beat generation 'got across' its message was to unsettle many Christians' views on how to 'get the gospel over'. Communicating Christianity seemed a problem, too, on the academic side. Humanism was assertive, and in 1963 the bestseller *Honest to God* seemed to be saying that humanists and Christians were really one and the same 'man come of age'. In the Easter weekend of 1964 there was the first incidence of public youth violence when 'mods' and 'rockers' clashed in Clacton. It was not a racial or unemployment eruption, for this was a prosperous period. It was caused by inarticulated questions about identity and life's purpose. It was to be shared by university students. At the cultural end of the scale Peter Hall was holding the 'theatre of cruelty' in Stratford and shocking people with avant-garde continental plays. By the following year protest on the streets came to stay, with civil rights marches and then anti-war protest rallies. Television brought it all very close to home.

And it was not long before people were breathing in the air of a new counter-culture with its scent of 'pot' and slogans of change. With student protest and the sexual revolution and the permissive society and the 'lawless' generation, the swinging sixties left its indelible mark on posterity. By the mid-seventies the counter-culture was so pervasive that it was seen, in milder form, in the prevailing youth culture. What is clear is that the student world had been in a sort of ideological vacuum at the beginning of the sixties. It was but a matter of time before these potent forces filled the gap. All this coincided with the very time when there was a hardening of attitude in the nation against Christianity and when the expanding universities opened much wider doors to the nation's morally rootless, though touchingly idealistic, youth in search of itself.

Most of this idealism found Christianity irrelevant. But it was not by any means entirely anti-Christian. The era of 'Christendom' may have come decisively to an end in these years, but some of the counter-culture reaction was itself a protest against the emptiness and hypocrisy of traditional, formal religion and was trying to be and say something better in the name of Christianity. The Martin Luther King and anti-Vietnam War protests in particular had a very moral and often Christian impetus. And because the human heart is inescapably religious, the change of atmosphere was by no means all loss as far as Christian witness was concerned, as we shall see.

In the 1962 annual report of the IVF, a few years before the deluge, Douglas Johnson posed a question: 'What of the future?' At last, someone had noted, Britain had spent more on its universities than on the annual egg subsidy! It was to be expansion from now on. The most striking trend was the determination of many university authorities to go residential and follow the Scandinavian model of mixed halls. 'The wisdom of this remains to be seen,' comments the report. What interested IVF leaders such as Johnson were three things.

First, students would now come from a much wider range of schools, homes and social backgrounds. This new mixture, with its promise of ability drawn from a true cross-section of society, was good. But it would mean that CUs, composed until then of middle-class and often public-school youngsters, would have to work harder to achieve and maintain satisfactory leadership standards.

Secondly, it was an ominous sign for culture in its deeper sense that the rise in technological interests had led to students reading less for pleasure. 'Will this be accompanied by a comparable reduction in spiritual reading?' If so, the danger was that biblical truth would cut even less deeply into twentieth-century Christianity and the trend to superficiality would be reinforced.

The third concern about the future was the evidence of a growing disillusionment in students themselves. 'Wasted Years?

The Purposeless Student', read an educational headline after a long-term survey of fresher intake. 'The fact is', commented Johnson, 'that in the midst of all the planning and the provision of more residences and student numbers, these young men and women are being introduced to a moral and spiritual wilderness. The intellectual life of our nation is becoming "without form and void" and over the chaos broods the spirit of humanism.' This 'is clearly destined to lead only to greater moral and spiritual destitution'. By 1970 Oliver Barclay noted a stark student statement from Durham which represents the outworking of this ethos at its worst. 'To us, life is a meaningless parody, so we occupy ourselves with being cynical, redblooded and quixotic, anything in fact to hide an emptiness and fear . . . most of us are asleep. We simply shut our eyes and try to squeeze enough enjoyment out of life to make it tolerable and are quite content, provided we mostly get our own way. For us the only certainty of life is death. It has to be, to justify the way we live.'

The most dramatic sign of student disenchantment came in 1968, the troubled year of protest. The effects of introducing young people to a moral and spiritual wilderness were picked up by Oliver Barclay: 'Part of the real danger was that those who were most active in student protest were, at least in part, driven by the desire to accomplish something and become someone in a world in which they have lost their identity and their aim in life. In a recent debate on Christianity and humanism the humanist speaker, in winding up, said something to this effect: "It is true, what these Christians say, that for the humanist there is no purpose in life. But we have got to put purpose into it." What better way is there available of putting purpose into life than a student protest about something? Certainly students, of all people, need to be alert to the need of change in society. But the shrillness and vehemence of the protest owes much to the tragic emptiness of life for so many.' That Durham group put it in the raw. 'A few of us have had the guts to rebel against a corrupt society, but all we can do is hate and destroy until we cannot distinguish the good and the bad and in the end we find ourselves and our ideals corrupted by our own human nature.' Christians above all can understand the torment of this and sympathize with the sense of alienation.

If 'freedom', the current slogan, was the answer, the student had a whole curriculum of it. Students were certainly more free to 'do their own thing', and the university ethos now militated against both organization and self-discipline. It was hard to get up, and harder still to get to bed – though 'freedom' meant it was easier to go to bed with a partner. 'The "hall" is really just blocks of flats with very little community. You meet only the ten others on your staircase. The atmosphere is tough – very vulgar pictures on some staircases and some people only move in there so that they can sleep with their boy/girlfriends.' The developing moral situation, first among the minority, and then on a wider scale, was grim. One university handout hardly reflects the brave hopes for the educational pursuit of excellence. 'Venereal disease must be contained since there have been outbreaks. If you should be unfortunate to contract this, again don't hesitate in going to the Family Planning centre. Don't bother giving it to anyone else – they won't appreciate it too much.' The change in moral climate was quite dramatic when it came. Within a few years the rare became the norm and by the early seventies student health services were dispensing the pill to half the women in their third year. With the unchurched generation that grew up after the war there was little knowledge of the moral law of God.

By the mid-seventies the great expansionist plans of science and humanism were in disarray in the university world. Many places in the new polytechnics and new universities were not being taken up. Because of nuclear threat and the ecological realization that the earth is being systematically despoiled, science and technology were no longer seen as necessarily progressive. There was an astonishing new openness to religion. Christian students no longer lived in the religious vacuum of the scientific fifties. The influence of the East was not only behind the drug culture; it bathed it in religious light. The Divine Light Mission and the Hare Krishna movement and variants on transcendental meditation had their outposts on campus. Spiritism, too, prospered as true spiritual values withered in Western minds. Then came stern, demanding, Islam with its own fervent evangelism. 'The fact is,' said Barclay in 1974, 'life without a supernatural aspect seems to be too bad to be true. Some non-material anchor is needed or life seems empty even when luxurious.'

The new counter-culture attitude contributed basic ingredients to this unease with science and, indeed, with the modern materialistic lifestyle. It valued more the pursuit of individuality, community, and artistic creativeness. Inward experience and 'doing your own thing' were more attractive than the desire for academic excellence, which involves disciplined learning and training in a more authoritative context. In 1975 the *Times Educational Supplement* analysed the counter-culture. It noted its essential hostility to structure: 'It attacked ritual, form, boundaries, roles and certainties in every conceivable sphere. The boundaries most frequently under attack were those between public and private, decent and indecent, tabooed and available, sacred and profane, between art and ordinary life, good taste and vulgarity, between human and inhuman, male and female, man, animal and nature. The rejection of control in all its forms showed itself as a preference for randomness or chance over plan, for excess over balance, for the fantastic over the normal, for emotion over reason, for the ephemeral over the lasting, for immediacy over hard-won comprehension, for the purely personal or topical allusion over the historically rooted image.'

That paints it in its darkest colour, but these tendencies had become fairly widespread and it was urgent for Christians growing up amid it all to get a balanced reaction. It all meant that from the sixties onwards the CUs were operating in different climates from the one we have got used to in the previous chapters of this book. There were key questions that arose that were new and difficult to settle. Few generations of Christian young people have ever had to cope with such a crashing tidal wave of change over such a short span of time. A case could be made out for this period as being the third most significant period in modern history. The Reformation period saw a fundamental change in the way people saw their relationship to God. The Industrial Revolution saw an alteration in their relation to the environment. The 1960s and 1970s marked a change in the way people related to themselves – the consequence of a long retreat from Christian truth and values. The seventies have been described as the 'me decade' when the absorbing theme was 'Let's talk about me'. Therapies for inner healing multiplied from secular as well as spiritual sources. Moulded partly by the current preoccupation with inner feelings ('me-ism', some have called it) and partly by teachings on the Holy Spirit, many Christians engaged in much spiritual navel-gazing and lost out on the great objective truths of the faith. This had often left CUs doctrinally weak, with inward-looking leadership, and less interested to understand or relate the faith to what was going on around them than in their own spiritual experiences. Given the temper of the times it became difficult to distinguish between interest in what God has for me and my (understandable) interest in myself.

There was also a much more subtle influence arising which seemed to get to people like a fog. It had the effect of loosening, and indeed, disparaging, the sense of heritage and continuity and history in contending for the faith. It derived from the counter-culture influence we have analysed earlier. Not all of this was bad, but it produced religious confusion at a time of great religious opportunity. It was as if the Enemy of people's souls gave up his rationalistic attack via humanism as evangelicals mustered a believing, revelation-based mind. His tactics changed into the area of religious and sensuous experiences. In terms of preaching gifts, teaching capacity and books to read the evangelical scene had improved out of all recognition since the war. Especially was this the case in terms of literature. Since 1962, when IVP came of age with *The New Bible Dictionary*, it continued to give evangelical students an array of unprecedented armour for the battle. By now the long list of IVF vice-presidents showed how the gospel had made its impact in the academic world, with eighteen or nineteen university professors in place of the brave one or two of pre-war days.

Yet there were forces at work in society, foreseen by Douglas Johnson in 1962, which were to result in a tendency to demote the written word at the very time when evangelical writing had reached the stature worked and prayed for in 1941. Further, preaching and teaching, as well as reading, were going to have to argue their biblical and historic right to priority in the life of Christian fellowship. The shift came from an undercurrent of influence that brought in quasi-spiritual (and therefore attractive) but non-biblical ways of looking at the Christian life.

Those elements in the counter-culture that were corrosive of historic evangelicalism included its hostility to structure, control, certainties and moral boundaries; it preferred randomness to plan, emotion to reason, immediacy to hard-won comprehension, and the purely personal or topical to the historical. These tendencies soon came through in the thinking of Christian students, though in much weaker forms, and under

215

a spiritual guise. To many CU leaders, organizing a programme and planning ahead was unspiritual; a warm, informal unstructured time of worship with a guitar was more spiritual than half an hour's early morning study of *Search the Scriptures;* a talk with a lot of contemporary personal stories would turn people on, whereas a look at the lessons of the past was a bore. There was a resistance to the hard-won comprehension that grappling with issues from a thoroughly biblical standpoint required. The emotional power and immediacy of slogans – what Schaeffer called 'contentless banners' – were much more attractive. Many preferred to speak of Christianity as an alternative theory and practice of peace, love and freedom, not sin and salvation. The 'Why shouldn't we?' attitude was gaining ground as more were stepping over well-marked moral boundaries. Also the idea that the small group was more real than the larger unit became very popular in CU circles. It derived more from the fashionable idea that 'small is beautiful' than from the New Testament teaching on fellowship.

This distinction needed identifying, because the narrowing effects of this current secular idiom began to turn CUs in on themselves. For example, Oliver Barclay asked, did 'small is beautiful' (an attractive and valuable counter to the mass facelessness of the time) mean that 'if we have warm fellowship in a residence or faculty group we do not need to bother about anything else'? 'Why organize a big meeting or speaker if we can just enjoy the "immediate" – spontaneous singing and sharing? The attractions of this for the modern campus are obvious. If one judged by press reports the modern campus can be a centre of protest, confrontation between rival group interests, drug-taking and pushing, immorality and theft. The new Christian student could be forgiven if, on finding other Christians, he retreats into their defensive shell, relieved at their wholesome lifestyle, finding it a haven from the storm, a help to moral decision and holy living. This dimension of fellowship is vital.

'But if it becomes a satisfying end in itself, making people easily content, it cuts out both wider evangelistic responsibility and the missionary vision and even the need for disciplined study. Inward-looking and parochial fellowship is not fellowship in the *gospel*, which leads outwards to witness and proclamation. Richard Baxter, the Puritan leader, had amongst his rules for the preservation of unity in the church this recommendation – "When a small controversy begins to endanger the church, raise a greater yourself." The UCCF is held together and is given direction by what Baxter might have called the greatest controversy. We came into being to bear witness to the great biblical truths of the gospel. We continue to exist to bear witness to that. Fellowship is the base from which that witness is launched. If it does not issue in outreach to a bigger world, in evangelism and missionary "go", is it the fellowship that the New Testament describes?'

Tony Wilmot, who left Oxford for Africa as Barclay began his student days at Cambridge, cannot restrain his sense of concern at this ingrowing tendency. 'It seems to me that British Christians – not only students – have progressively focused closer and closer to the viewer. At Oxford the college group seems more important than the OICCU. In our day we believed in OICCU, OICCU believed in IVF, IVF believed in IFES and in missions – the world was our parish. The Great Commission inspired us. Now we are not thinking of turning the world upside down; the world is dictating our agenda. Should British Christians cease to be world Christians because Britain is no longer a world power? Are we fired still with the top priority of the Bible – to have people everywhere reconciled to God?'

David Lyon, the sociologist, bears out the conviction that the close fellowship community of the early church issued in missionary 'go'. While noting the genuine search for real community in the various experimental communes of the early sixties, he contrasts the early church community movement recorded in Acts:

'These small-scale but rapidly expanding voluntary groups of disciples attempted to live out the teaching of Jesus. They did so, not in isolation like the Qumran community, but in shoulder-rubbing contact with the larger Roman-dominated culture of their day. Their Master had instructed them to be the salt of the earth purifying and giving taste to society. But they were also to be "cities set on a hill"; a communal alternative to surrounding ways of life. They were noted for their mutual love, but this did not operate in a ghetto. Their enemies complained that they had turned the world upside down.'[1]

So, if and where there is a shrinking and localizing of CU interests it may be a reflection of the contemporary cultural

[1]David Lyon, *Future Society*, p. 63.

drift – a subtle combination of the 'me decade' and 'small is beautiful'. But it leads to mediocrity of vision and cannot claim biblical credentials.

Each generation needs to identify which tendencies are part of the fashion of the age. Today's are not necessarily wrong for that reason, any more than the fashions of yesterday were necessarily right. But they need fresh criticism by the standards of Scripture before they become accepted and mould us (Romans 12:1–2). The strong point of CUs over the years is their freedom from being swamped by the fad for the new. For example, the constant base of the Scriptures has given continuity between the speakers from an older generation and the student. Young students have no difficulty in inviting their seniors to speak to them. Why? Because their identification is in the content of the biblical message. The present-day youth culture has, however, been raised on symbols of the generation gap and this can put false strain on evangelical continuity. In the Christian world both sides of that gap have therefore to work hard to make sure that they together seek to hear God's word. There lies the unity of the Christian generations. Without that, fashion will determine whether we accept or reject each other on grounds of style, image, vocabulary. When Christians feel the influences of new mores more than their biblical heritage, tensions escalate and unity goes. Older and younger leaders have therefore had a salutary stimulus since the sixties to identify what was purely traditional or trendy rather than biblical in their lifestyles. This is all to the good in helping to bridge gaps. Comparing the worship features of CUs fifty years apart, David Bentley-Taylor has this to say: 'On the plus side, the freedom of the present time has identified an inadequacy in our earlier CUs. Audience participation was not obvious in our day. Our CUs tended to be rigid and reserved, but then, so was our age and we reflected it. Present CUs have also toned in with the atmosphere of the times and the way of the day. The Scripture would certainly allow us room for some "give" in moderation here, but things can get out of hand.' Different evangelical groupings represented in IVF/UCCF continue to show great resilience in resolving tensions by the constant attempt to shed biblical light on the traditional and the trendy.

There have been two areas in particular where Christian students since the sixties were in danger of swallowing the fashion, if they failed to be true to their biblical heritage. First, Christians tend to be much more experience-centred since the sixties, unwittingly taking their cue more from the 'feelings generation', of which they were part, than from the biblical stress on saving truth as the basis for genuine experience. Truth does not seem to be so emphasized as essential today as it was a generation ago – at least, not articulated, theological truth. Francis Schaeffer's writings warned that a 'Jesus experience' could be just an emotional high if not rooted in the truth as it is in Jesus. An obvious result of indifference to truth has been that many found it hard to see the value of solid Bible study, teaching and preaching. This has a circular effect, for, without the controls of solid biblical foundations, people are even more susceptible to the trendy and eventually the trivial, without even realizing it.

Secondly, it is hardly surprising that experiments in evangelism are always being tried in the kaleidoscopic world of ours. Student freshness and initiative in adapting to their world abounds. The traditional coffee party has diversified into a range of imaginative alternatives – pizza parties, baked-potato parties . . . gateaux . . . cheesecake . . . even banquets. It may not be 'prosperity evangelism' but it smacks of evangelism in a day of prosperity! Music, drama, mime, 'happenings', the evangelistic concert, have become a common feature of some missions and freshers' weeks. To follow the fashion would be merely to dress up current ideas in Christian clothes, which is much easier than thinking through how to present biblical truths in current idiom. Where there is expression of the colour and variety of Christian gifts, illustrating and establishing the truths proclaimed and argued in the course of mission addresses, all is well. This can build an appropriate platform for the preacher. But there are also the influences of the day that lead us to lack confidence in the power of God's Spirit to convert people to himself, through the truth of his Word. We are all subject to the creeping man-centredness that rates the image of the speaker or of the group or singer more highly than the message he brings.

This is accentuated by the shift in communications emphasis in the world about us and is worth analysing further. We have seen many examples in this book of how CUs adopted rational/spiritual means of evangelistic communication. Preaching, teaching and personal evangelism, backed up by reading of suitable literature, were seen as the verbal and intellectual bridge to non-Christians. This, coupled with prayer that the Spirit of God would use the truth passed on to bring people to Christ, kept them in continuity with the biblical message and methods. The dominant ethos of evangelism in the student world was concept-based and essentially serious. Evangelistic meetings would be similar, in that respect, to university lectures; there would be a straight talk and little more. Of course, this is not to say that previous generations necessarily got it right. Much evangelistic preaching has always been weak, because of two tendencies. Some preachers tend to go too quickly to the emotions and the conscience. Others try to satisfy the intellect to such an extent that they neglect to challenge the will and attack the conscience. Perhaps a true biblical approach in evangelism was seen in Stott's letter to the Cambridge assistant missioners in 1952.[2]

Ever since the cultural changes we have been examining have taken hold, there have been attempts to 'get through' by means of an appeal to the senses, rather than, or at least in addition to, rational means. Because this has sometimes been the stress of Christians who have also given high prominence to spiritual gifts, it requires more than the wisdom of Solomon to discern what is coming from the surrounding culture (with its stress on body language) and what the Spirit may be saying to the churches (about how to approach the *whole* person, body, mind and feelings, with the gospel)! In place of the primacy of the verbal and intellectual, the visual and the physical have pressed their potent claims. It has come through drama, dance and mime, electronic sound and beat. Entertainment evangelism strongly uses these approaches. The dominant ethos is experience-based, therefore, and in addition strongly resounds with an atmosphere of celebration. It is not an accident that entertainment has been linked with evangelism in a day when fun is a major motivation to action – for example in charity giving, and even, in some places, in basic scientific research! The fun ethic is supreme; to be boring is one of the great crimes of the age. Though the two other tendencies in modern evangelism majoring on sense needs – power evangelism (physical healing), and prosperity evangelism (happiness and tangible signs of success) – are not, in the nature of the case, likely to impinge

[2]See above, p. 153.

so much on the campus, they contribute to the conditioning atmosphere.

The days call for mature judgment from student leadership. What can they take from the multi-media scene? What does and does not come under Paul's great liberating principle, ' . . . so that by all possible means I might some' (1 Corinthians 9:22)? The crucial word there seems to be 'save'. This brings the crucial issue into the area of the message that the methods convey. The question centres, first, in whether such methods as are appropriate are seen as a supplement to, rather than a substitute for, the preaching/teaching model of the Scriptures. That there can be appropriate supplements derive from the fact that the visual and physical are as much part of God's created world as the verbal and intellectual. The mind and senses are equally God-given, and, as the fall has affected man as a whole, not just sensually, so the Spirit renews man as a whole, not just intellectually. The difficulty arises in that, whereas the intellectual content of the gospel to be taught and believed is crystal clear, there are only general biblical criteria relating to means that supplement preaching. It is in this area that so much of the multi-media operate. The church needs the help of a new look at the biblical teaching on the senses, in the context of our created humanity and of Christ's humanity, so as to establish God-honouring visual and physical back-up to preached communication.

The question centres, secondly, on how we guard the gospel itself, whatever extra means we engage in. We have seen how a previous generation lost the gospel of the cross without any of the multi-media factors. Robin Wells brings out the implications of this for us:

' "The message of the cross" – that is Paul's phrase for his preaching (1 Corinthians 1:18). There will always be attacks on this, for the death of Christ is central to the gospel. In a previous generation the biblical teaching of the death of Christ was explicitly denied. Today's attacks sometimes take different forms. For example, we might be tempted to divert our attention from the cross to other things, things that may be true in themselves. So, God's stark declaration on human sin and the judgment it deserves is quietly diluted. Perhaps the victory of the cross is proclaimed: yes, wonderfully true. But the dark side is there too. Christ is proclaimed as King. We rejoice! But do we forget that he had to die as our representative and substitute? And what of our own discipleship? The cross, and Jesus' call to us to take up our own cross and follow him, stand opposed to the triumphalism that we often meet today . . . which paints the rosy picture . . . and denies the painful problems. Could triumphalism be the devil's work to keep us from being prepared for suffering . . . which . . . judged by the story of the church through the ages, this country has for many years had an unusual freedom from?'

Therefore, in an encouraging situation of enormous opportunities where many thousands of students come, year after year, under the sound of the gospel through the enthusiastic witness of CUs, the supreme task is to ensure that it *is* the gospel sound that they are really hearing. The sheer variety of religious options in today's world shows the still greater need for clarity about the saving truths the CU stands for. Perhaps the main common feature of contemporary religious options is one it shares with our culture as a whole – indifference to the question of objective truth. For the theological fashion designers of today it simply does not matter whether there is historical and doctrinal truth woven into the garment of faith. The common fabric is one of religious/mystical experience and a concern for ethics.

The rich blessings of the post-1945 period were the long-term outcome of the faithfulness of the valiant few to the Word of God. They refused to be taken in by human fashions either in the church or the world at a time when evangelical faith was denied and then simply bypassed. Weight of numbers meant nothing to them in comparison to the Word of truth. The Doctrinal Basis was and is central in this. It provides the fabric of faith's garment, outlines the strong skeleton of the living body and provides the bone and marrow of sufficient Bible truth.

Steve Bruce concludes his study *Firm in the Faith* with the following words: 'The obituary of conservative Protestantism has been written many times, but never with as much conviction as in the period shortly after the second world war. . . . The obituaries were exaggerated. Conservative forms of Protestantism have endured when liberalism has declined. . . . Conservative resilience . . . lies in its ability to resonate with the interests of the secular world while still preserving its own distinct identity.' He notes how its discipline of belief accounts for its constant 'survival over extended periods in the ecclesiastical wilderness and its revival in more promising "perilous times" '.

This chapter has outlined some of the peculiar pressures of the perilous times of the sixties and after. Our concluding chapter looks again at the same period, but this time at some of the positive evangelical responses to those challenges. It will show the continuing survival and revival of CU witness into present times in England, Scotland and Ireland.

Chapter Twenty-One

SURVIVING AND REVIVING

If surviving and reviving is a feature of the evangelical faith, then the CUs are typical. In the 'perilous times' of the last decades they have sought to walk the Way, talk the Truth, live the Life. The previous chapter traced how, as the universities of the sixties came increasingly under the sway of humanism, they began to show some of the tell-tale and ominous signs of moral indifference. 'The IVF has no need to canvass reasons for its existence,' said the 1963 annual report. 'The sole hope of the universities in the midst of this self-made waste is the moving of the Holy Spirit to restore order and renew spiritual life. The IVF will remain useful to the student world only in so far as it can be more the vehicle of the Holy Spirit.'

CUs were aware of the stiffening situation. Many gave much time to prayer that the Spirit would move again, as there were few conversions at the start of the sixties. Ann Wilson went up in 1962 to a London medical school. Perhaps her conversion can be taken as a parable of new life to come out of death, for her story begins over a corpse! At her first session in the dissecting room her partner asked various questions as they cut up the body together. It was the first time she had heard the gospel. As they talked about religious faith she was asked, 'Do you know God?' She was taken aback. This was a completely new one to her. When she returned to her hall of residence she knelt down for the first time ever, but had no idea what to say. Some friends sent her a card. On it she read, 'Seek ye the Lord while he may be found.' In November 1962 she attended a LIFCU meeting at All Souls. She asked for a copy of John Stott's *Becoming a Christian*, and as she read it so her seeking came to an end in Christ. In the meantime, John Goldingay (now Principal of St John's College, Nottingham, and author with IVP), converted through an independent evangelical church in Birmingham, went to Oxford, and gained a 'first' in theology. John and Ann met at a Swanwick conference and became one of the many couples who began the marriage trail there.

During these years specific efforts were made to meet the challenge of humanism. CUs held lectures with such titles as 'Humanism – Is it Enough?' Martyn Lloyd-Jones addressed the Christian Medical Fellowship on 'The Approach to Truth – Scientific and Religious', a lecture that was published in stylish format and had influence well beyond the occasion of its delivery. In Oxford, the Humanist Society, briefly able to claim to be the largest society in the university, whipped up a poster campaign against the Stott mission in 1964, maintaining that Christianity was intellectual suicide. But the Humanist Society in Oxford died rather quickly. It was at Oxford, too, that a Graduates Fellowship group for research students and university staff got off to an excellent start, when Professor Donald MacKay of Keele, by now a considerable apologist for the faith, addressed a gathering of eighty.

By 1966 prayer and perseverance saw an extraordinary turn-around, and the picture in the CUs was one of unbounded opportunity again, though against a background of moral flux. 'It is doubtful if CUs have ever been in such real touch with non-Christians.' Bristol CU was a good example. Take this account which appeared in the student newspaper. 'A graduate student from another university was making his first visit to the Students Union, but soon after entering the building he was found recumbent on the slab in the union bar . . . staring fixedly into the middle distance and sipping a small lime juice.' Was he drunk? No. What then was the matter? He was suffering from 'severe shock'. Asking some humourist the way to the bar he had been misdirected to the hall next door to it, where the CU held its regular Saturday night Bible readings. Bursting in upon 250 people enthusiastically engaged in this activity had been too much for him. He is reported to have said that he had never seen so many Christians in one place in his whole life. 'Why', asks the journalist, 'is Bristol University so strongly Christian? . . . Is it the climate, the geology of the area? the spirit of John Wesley?'

Gig Goulstone (later with the Bible Churchmen's Missionary

Society and the Overseas Missionary Fellowship) arrived to study medicine at Bristol 'as an unsuspecting, contented agnostic, with very little Christian background. I did not know it then, but the first five people I came across were all Christians. One of them, a Chinese fellow medic, became a special friend. Through her witness and the prayers of the hall group I became a Christian about four months later, at a CU house-party entitled 'Dead or Alive?' It made the issue rather black and white. I experienced the touch of God in a very real way, and have not got over it yet, fourteen years on, I'm glad to say. Reading the New Testament for myself in Today's English Version in the first vacation was an important factor. But the faithfulness, patience and love of my Christian friend was vital. Subsequently I led a prayer group, helped with international student events and ran a Christian folk group. These student days were absolutely crucial for me in my Christian growth – and birth.'

Another reaction to a first visit to a CU shows how surprised students can be on hearing the gospel spelled out uncompromisingly in a university context. 'I say,' he remarked, 'that was rather evangelical, wasn't it?' He kept going though, and two terms later was trying to help a fellow student to faith by explaining, 'Although I had often attended church it was not until I got into the CU that I realized that I was really a sinner and that Jesus was a personal saviour.'

Though the situation in the technical colleges had improved, they were still the places where indifference was the rule and it was tough to maintain interest in religious groups of any kind. Yet there were some wonderful examples of brave initiative in some of these colleges, where the work of the Spirit of God was obvious. Birkenhead College of Technology (now Polytechnic), is sited along the Borough Road, which it shares with Tranmere Rovers football ground. In September 1967, Russ Parker (now a vicar in Coalville) left his job as a bus conductor and, at twenty-one years of age, started a course at the college. He had been converted three months before and it had halted his slide into a drink problem. He saw a notice which asked anyone who was interested in forming a CU at the college to get together. He attended the meeting, though he had hardly any acquaintance with Christian institutions. There were nine people present, two of whom were left from the small group of the previous year. To his astonishment he was asked to be chairman! They got together to pray and, uncultured in Christian terminology, asked the Lord that Christians in the college would come out of the woodwork. Quickly their numbers jumped to a few dozen, and a lot of lukewarm Christians got a new vision of serving Christ. They set up a bookstall several floors up in a college building and then prayed that God would open opportunities to preach.

He did.

In the course of a discussion around the bookstall a student dared them to go down to the main refectory building, stand up on a table, and preach. Russ, with the boldness that sometimes lives in the sheer novice, met the challenge and one day stood up among hundreds of students. People responded with questions and gradually conversions began to come. Birkenhead was a centre of the growing drug culture in the north. Some of the students on drugs were saved and were then prayed over that the Lord would deliver them from the habit.

During the year there were some remarkable evidences of a heightened sense of God's presence. Members of the teaching staff were drawn into this. One man stopped in the middle of delivering a lecture, conscious that people's minds were on other things, saying 'I think it's time we talked about Christ.' The class launched into a discussion of God, the Bible and the Christian experience of conversion. Later the lecturer became a Christian. In another lesson the mathematics teacher put down his chalk and then asked, 'Mr Parker, is it enough to be a churchgoer?' He rededicated his life to Christ there in the room. Another member of staff was also challenged and was later ordained.

The students showed a tremendous verve for evangelism. Lots of people attended the CU meetings. With the permission of the deacons, the CU members also took Rockferry Baptist Church on a Thursday night, and many came. On a Saturday morning they bought season tickets at 2s. 9d. apiece on the Birkenhead to Liverpool ferry and sang evangelistic songs and preached on board. They saw the importance, too, of carrying the flame to other colleges. They took teams to Carlett Park in Eastham on the Wirral and to Wallasey, and the work in these colleges was helped on. At one of these meetings a future president of the Liverpool University CU was converted. Some half-a-dozen men were called to full-time service during that extraordinary period when God enabled his people at Birkenhead 'Tech.' to pray and preach with rare fruitfulness.

Undoubtedly these were years of varying degrees of encouragement on a wide front. A steady flow of conversions kept coming all over the country and the sixties ended as a wonderfully fruitful time. Missions were given added impetus through Michael Green's ministry, and his evangelistic books such as *Man Alive!* and *Runaway World* were certainly being read by all sorts of people.

This came at a time when, said an annual report, 'we are constantly being told that the biblical way of talking to man "come of age" about God and the world simply will not do. CUs may be "rather evangelical", but we are bound, at the end of another year, to acknowledge God's way of making this message effective in a new life and character' and 'on an exciting scale'. 'Evangelical Christianity defies many modern intellectual prophecies as to what can and cannot appeal to modern man. This is not to say that we have nothing to learn. The serious concern to understand the non-Christian which some of the "new theology" men demonstrate sometimes reproves us. But it is possible to be so sensitive to modern trends that the message becomes modified and this we must never allow. Intellectually disinfected Christianity will turn out to be spiritually sterilized also. The Bible persistently adheres to personal categories in talking about God and to concepts such as wrath, holiness and atonement. Man's need will always be primarily that he is a sinner rebelling against his loving and holy God. That need can only be met by the NT gospel that Christ died for our sins and rose again. To the biblical writers these were not mythological concepts. The IVF will affirm these teachings, whether witness based on these doctrines is obviously successful or not, because they are involved in the clear teaching of Christ and the apostles.'

During these years evangelical theological students were in great heart. Bob Horn, the TSF secretary, was a warm and clearsighted encourager. In 1966 the TSF conference was the largest ever and was deemed outstanding. It can scarcely be imagined how excitedly students, accustomed to being battered by negative criticism in their colleges, reacted to a turning of the tables when Kenneth Kitchen, of Liverpool University, lectured on pentateuchal criticism and interpretation. After the conference 600 copies of the lectures were sold within hours of their being produced. Help on the New Testament side was now significant. The first of Donald Guthrie's trilogy on New Testament introduction, *The Pauline Epistles*, had appeared in 1961. In December 1963 an eager TSF executive committee requested the appearance of volume two, *The Gospels*, 'before summer exams'. In this case they had to wait till March 1965! The growing number of evangelical theologs were hungry for reliable material. They wanted to answer critical questions in a way intellectually consistent with their conservative convictions.

In these and all sorts of other significant ways the CUs had withstood the overt attack of humanism and the frontal criticisms of the 'Christian' humanists which many of the new theologians were. The seventies had many new open doors. Missioners such as David McInnes and David Watson gained the ear of a new-style generation, utilizing many of the multimedia facilities that were now readily available in the student world, while some 'old hands' such as Leith Samuel did the same without the extras. John de Caesteter, now a medical missionary with the Africa Inland Mission, was converted in his last year at Cambridge through a mission led by McInnes. It was while continuing studies at the Middlesex that he 'grew up' as a Christian and was confirmed in his call to the mission field. Greg Scharf, curate at All Souls, London, 'took me and others under his wing, and patiently, week by week, led us through the basics of the faith'. Richard Hill, of Oxford, now a Church of England minister, went to hear Leith Samuel and 'at about the fifth invitation, understood not a word, but felt there was something there worth having'. Earlier he had walked out of the Corpus Christi College squash before the talk, and had been given up as a no-hoper. He was surprised, however, to find committed Christians in the hockey side. He was led to Christ by a friend after a testimony meeting at the Northgate Hall.

'I had a strong aversion to church but was finally tempted along to St Ebbe's by an invitation to lunch at a Chinese restaurant, after the service. The sermon on Ephesians 6, by Keith Weston, so exactly spoke to my experience that I had no difficulty going afterwards. I began to learn how to live as a Christian. I was the only Christian in the cricket team and I once made myself unpopular by refusing to play on a Sunday. Several students I knew became Christians during my time at Oxford and many others were built up. Some of our later-night discussions, on predestination for example, might have had little practical use, but they taught us all to think biblically.'

The seventies saw exciting growth in the art colleges world. An early arts weekend drew well over 100 – unthinkable only a few years before. One man who attended had drifted into a CU meeting in his college the evening before the conference, where he had a long talk with the travelling secretary. He had been looking for truth for some time and had, in fact, stopped painting while he tried to find an answer to his questions. He hitchhiked down to the weekend and during it professed conversion. Encouragements flowed from many growth points and what had seemed an almost hopeless situation was transformed. For ten years, prayer and hard work had seen little evidence of answers. Professor Rookmaaker's tour of England in 1972 had helped crystallize the change that had occurred among art students.

Though churchgoing by non-Christians had declined sharply, the now more self-contained student community made talking about religion a more 'on the spot' thing. Even the rapid deterioration of morals seemed often to have made the affected students anxious to talk to those friends who 'had something' and who showed signs of real moral stability. The combination of contraceptive machines, the pill, mixed halls and the growing notion that sleeping together was normal created some catastrophic situations. A desire to help was both risky and rewarding. One Christian moved into a group where couples slept together and succumbed to the 'normal'. Another moved in elsewhere and saw four conversions among his housemates. Those who give a Christian lead and example are in need of the constant prayer and support of older Christians in their local church. Walter Trobisch's *I Married You* was helpful to those who were converted from a background that lacked even rudimentary acquaintance with Christian ethics. When the slide became apparent the IVF student executive committee produced a signed handout on *Sex and the Single Student*, which got into all kinds of circles. Missions began to see the largest turn-outs on nights that have dealt with 'God and the sexual revolution'. This need-centred evangelism was valuable when related to truth and Christ-centred answers. David Richards, a midlands traveller of the eighties, gives an up-date of the situation.

'The room was packed with non-Christians. They sat listening, generating aggression with their eyes. The CU had had

231

the bright idea of an evangelistic talk with the title 'Maximum Sex' and of getting the trav. sec. to be the speaker! The title had intrigued non-Christians and Christians alike. The publicity had obviously uncovered a need. Why? What are the attitudes to sex among students today? . . . Today's student is a product of the sexual attitudes prevalent in the 1960s. They are the outcome of the "free" sex and "free" love of the time when seemingly anything went and frequently did.'[1]

Thankfully 'religion' became almost as big a talking-point as morality. One of the most startling features of the arrival of 'scientific man' was his lurch away from the study of science to that of religion. This had plus and minus effects for the CUs. The tendency of university departments in the days of expansion was to switch from studies that, at least theoretically, were based on biblical disciplines, to the study of religions. Evangelical scholarship, which had laboured hard to contribute positively to the former, had given scant attention to the latter (though Robert Brow had written a fine book on *Religion*, published by IVP in 1966). This has a lesson. Mankind is very much a *moving target*. By the time we catch up in terms of his particular problems, he has shifted to others. But that does not mean we ever lose our basic contact point which lies deeper than the latest fashion. Accordingly, it was found that these religious courses were attended by increasingly large numbers of non-Christians, studying theology because they were 'into' religious experience, gurus and God. Formal religion was out, but religious-type questions came flooding in even from the pop prophets. This 'nowhere man in a nowhere land who knows not where he's going to' was really asking religious questions, but in the most unreligious kind of way. The meaning or rather lack of meaning to life, authority or rather the rejection of it, boredom, alienation, parental restrictions, sleeping around – these questions emanating from meaningless existence emerged in the lyrics and gave an open door for Christian contribution and discussion. Some were alert enough to take them. The TSF now found its role widening from that of helping evangelical theological students to that of organizing evangelistic missions, and there were many who came from the study of religion to Christ. The student world and its idiom change so fast that books date, areas of debate take fresh forms and there is always

[1]*Christian Arena* (June, 1987).

need for the contemporary writer. Christians are not immune from future shock. But always and ever the moving target remains man on the run, in need of the God he eludes. The story of the whole of this period of flux is, in this sense, precisely the same as the earlier years of our story: Jesus saves all who turn and come to God through him.

We ought to ask about the basic evangelical attitude to science during this period when many students tended to shun studying it. Why did many shun it, and did evangelicals share that mentality? That there were dangers in the direction science was taking in military and environmental matters was becoming plain for all to see; but there were also signs of greater urgency in the world to readjust, and some of the protest movements take credit for this. Also, subsequent financial constraints have made students nervous of studying non-functional subjects such as religion and there is now far less evidence of resistance to studying science.

The passing years have shown that the main threat posed by science has come mainly as a consequence of the declining acceptance of the Christian view of human nature and morals. Researchers are, in consequence, dominated by a totally mechanistic concept of human beings. It is ironical that the objections of the counter-culture to science in terms of human values have, in the longer run, contributed to the increased dehumanizing of science. That is because its view of humanity, which was romantic and stridently non-Christian, has further weakened the understanding of man as a unique, rational, moral being made in the image of God and inhabiting God's world. It is instructive to see how Theodore Roszak, the main interpreter of the counter-culture, grapples to maintain personal meaning. He has taken a pantheist stance to seek to preserve a spiritual affinity between man and nature, in his more recent book *Person/Planet*. By contrast, Donald MacKay's *The Clockwork Image: A Christian Perspective on Science* remained firmly within the biblical world in facing the problems science posed to the meaningfulness of life. He forcibly argued that the biblical view of the world was the essential complement to science. Without that perspective it threatens to become nothing but 'machine-minded,' the very threat that Roszak so abominates.

Historically, this biblical motivation to responsible science had spurred Christians to have a large stake in academic scientific research (not something the ordinary person has been aware of). It is noticeable that as evangelical life recovered and students were converted in increasing numbers during the years of our story, so the number of evangelicals involved in scientific research leapt during the forties and fifties, a goodly number of them gaining chairs. At least three ex-CU members have become university vice-chancellors. Also, the Research Scientists Christian Fellowship, a professional group within UCCF, received the 1986 Templeton Award for its outstanding contribution to science and Christianity over the past thirty years.

There can be few areas that show greater need of a sustained biblical response than the disease of machine-mindedness. Only the biblical heritage has the rational and the moral base to do that. The new science and the new culture both take us away to look in other directions. The evangelical claims no inherent superior knowledge over others; what he claims is that he has found the place to look for truth – God's revelation. If he does not search hard for it there, he, too, gets it wrong. David Lyon, a Christian sociologist, points out that the widespread diffusion of computers is leading to an upsurge of willingness to conceive of humanness in 'machine' terms and that this is being countenanced lately by some evangelicals. It is a case that illustrates the challenges facing Christian apologetics in a time of 'moving targets'.

This machine-minded approach to humanity can sound very theoretical. But you need not spend long on a modern campus to see that it tends to breed an empty kind of person. There are plenty of students who are made in the image of clockwork man, though they may not see themselves like that. He can be a really antagonistic customer, living, it would seem, in another universe, light-years away from a Christian world-view. Does the gospel touch his kind?

Sometimes it does. And it depends a lot on what example of a real human image, transformed by the Spirit of Christ, that that kind of person is able to discover in the Christian.

David Elliman is a lecturer in mechanical engineering at the University of Nottingham. In his testimony in a recent *University Staffs Christian Fellowship Broadsheet* he tells how, in his first days at university, he grew friendly with Steve, a fellow student, until he discovered that he was one of the hated 'God Squad' – president-elect, no less! From that point, he says, 'Steve might as well have had AIDS or leprosy, as far as I was concerned, and I avoided any further contact with him, pointedly ignoring his greetings whenever we passed. To my surprise, and irritation, Steve remained as friendly as ever, which I put down to his "thick skin".

'Some months later I rushed in late for hall dinner . . . Feeling somewhat antisocial I sat alone . . . gazing rather absently out of the window. I was jarred back to consciousness by the sight of a smiling Steve heading inexorably towards me. In panic I avoided his gaze, and tried to put on such an unfriendly expression that I felt sure he would walk past. Steve appeared not to notice and sat opposite me. He was still smiling, I noticed with disgust, and resolved to "have a go" at his ludicrous and nonsensical beliefs. My mind was busy marshalling five incontrovertible arguments against Christianity, which I felt sure would devastate Steve's fairy-tale beliefs. My hostility began to change to patronizing pity as I anticipated an easy victory in the argument to come. I was about to launch my attack when Steve spoke. "I've been meaning to see you, Dave, as I sensed you have been feeling a bit low lately, and I thought I might be able to help." This was completely unexpected, and I must have sat with my mouth open for several seconds. He was right, of course, I did feel empty and disillusioned, but how could he know? I had plenty of friends, an attractive girlfriend, and was getting deeper into an exciting scene of parties, alcohol and drugs. My other interest was racing motorcycles, and I was eagerly negotiating the purchase of a suitable bike with cash saved from a holiday job.

'In amazement I became aware that Steve was now asking if I had heard of Pascal, the French philosopher . . . "Pascal wrote that each of us has a God-shaped void inside which aches to be filled." I listened with increasing astonishment as he told me I was frantically trying to fill my void with Newcastle brown ale, motorcycles, LSD, sex . . . but that nothing would really satisfy me until I came to know Christ. I felt a heavy weariness and an uneasy, guilty feeling, as though I had been caught stealing. All my arguments now seemed too pathetic to mention, and we finished the meal talking amicably about other things.

'Steve's diagnosis of my "condition" was to trouble me a great deal over the next few months, as the Holy Spirit revealed just how accurate it was.

'My grant began to disappear rapidly as I purchased even greater quantities of drugs to fend off feelings of depression. Christmas came, and I happened to be watching television when Passolini's *Gospel of Matthew* came on. The words of our Lord came home to me with such force and authority that I was transfixed, and only became embarrassed by the tears streaming down my face at the end. An unfamiliar thought entered my head . . . pray . . . "I don't believe in you, God," I stammered, "but if you are there I have tried everything else, and had enough. Can you fill this emptiness, this aching hole inside?" Within moments my whole being seemed filled by such peace and joy, greatly surpassing anything induced by alcohol or drugs, that I was left in no doubt as to the answer. As I grew to know more of our amazing Lord Jesus, I was struck by the likeness in Steve. It was a great joy to join the CU and meet more of the family, but my gratitude to Steve for his witness to me in the face of downright hostility has increased year by year.'

The university has always been good ground for 'friendship evangelism', though Christians so often fail to be 'Steves'. It also continues to be one of the rare places in Western society where the Christian presence may still be 'felt'. 'The biggest event in the university this week seems to be God.' This remark was overheard on the way into a Students Union building during a mission week. In many recent missions the stress has been to get copies of the Gospel of John distributed to people in their rooms before the series of evangelistic addresses. Then, as in a recent CICCU mission led by David Jackman, gospels were also placed on all the seats of the auditorium, and the hearers encouraged to follow the reading from them. Each night about a thousand students crowded into the Guildhall in Cambridge to hear the way of salvation proclaimed. There was a loud rustle of paper as students thumbed through the pages. People were gripped with the Bible message; there is an element of suspense as the story unfolds. The very novelty of the Bible's message to the present-day student has proved an aid to listening. One non-Christian, who was assisting with the relaying of the lectures on closed-circuit television, told his Christian friends that the next night he would prefer to be in the main hall so he could listen without interruption.

Chua Wee Hian, the IFES General Secretary, tells of a thrilling spin-off from this mission for the wider world witness.

236

Three staff workers from East and West Germany were present. One commented, 'I have been struck by the phenomenon of believing prayer. The Christian students here expect God to work. They really pray. I am going back to my home country to motivate German students really to pray for their non-Christian friends.' And in the way that is now so reassuring to so many Christian parents with CU backgrounds of their own, there came a letter from Chua Wee Hian's second son, Daniel, actively involved in his college mission activities. He had never made so many pots of tea and cups of coffee in all his life! Students crowded into his room to discuss the gospel.

Where, then, have we come to, and where do things seem to be going in the world of student witness?

'Some years ago we in the IVF prayed that we might grow to be the main Christian witness. This prayer has in many cases been answered, though it is partly through the decline of other bodies.' By 1970 this was how the annual report read the situation and that is how matters still stand. It calls for a few comparisons.

In 1944 Oliver Barclay spoke at some of his first CU meetings in Nottingham and Durham and was involved in college groups in Cambridge. Forty-two years later he was a speaker in the same contexts. The experience provoked praise and reflection. In terms of sheer size 'the Cambridge college CU was a little disappointed that that year only half the freshers came. In 1942 it would have been only a dozen or so. Nottingham and Durham were very small in 1944, a little beleaguered and attended by non-Christians only for special evangelistic meetings on the whole. Now they are large and flourishing with a percentage of non-Christians coming frequently.' In present-day CUs often a fifth and sometimes a third of the members have become Christians while at college. Many of these will have had little or no evangelical background, and others who attend are not necessarily inclined or equipped to give or maintain strong biblical foundations. Awareness of what IVF/UCCF witness was and is all about is no longer the common possession of the soaring numbers that are now in and on the edges of the CUs. In this respect, the collapse of the SCM has been a mixed blessing. Strong rival groups can have their role in keeping one's mettle up.

On the other hand, there has been benefit in the strong mix

of Christian and non-Christian background now found in the CUs. CUs, in their search for presidents and vice-presidents of stability and maturity, have found themselves repeatedly calling on the sons and daughters of a previous generation of evangelical leaders. These continually appear at universities and it is particularly encouraging to see how many are the children of those converted while students. These have that solid home and church background which so many other young Christians lack. As the key to the holding and growing operation of the thirties was the quality of students sent up through Scripture Union and Crusader camps, for example, so the quality control in CUs today will depend on, and the future will tend to be determined by, home and church base.

But with so high a percentage of today's world unchurched there is much value, too, in having leaders recently out of that background. Some of the earlier generation CUs were very tightly fenced off from real engagement with non-Christians. The combination of the younger Christian with few Christian antecedents, but a closer understanding of the non-Christian community, and the better-instructed person from a non-Christian home, often provides the CU with the best bridge for evangelism. On the whole, CU leadership, with the marked exception of the post-war ex-servicemen, probably compares very favourably with the past. 'Looking back' says Professor Howard Marshall, 'I feel that the EU of my day at Aberdeen was immature, inactive and lacking in outreach compared with its present successor.' However, the direction society has taken means that the task is a lot more demanding and hazardous and there has never been greater need of back-up and reinforcement from travellers and local churches. The battle for biblical maturity and how to attain it is even fiercer, and in such alien days requires constant creative consultation between student leaders and more senior Christians.

There is certainly one respect in which some Christian students are more courageously outgoing than their predecessors ever were, and these are often the ones converted in college who take active part in student politics. In the heyday of amateur sport, now gone, joining in sport was a major outreach and many Christians made their stand clear. Today the nub of the battle often lies in student politics, and this is an arena for a different kind of 'tough'. A thick skin and tough-mindedness are needed, because when people who are known as Christians stand for office they can attract heavy attacks from homosexual or feminist groups and political extremists. Much of their attack is a caricature that dubs good to be evil. The call to be 'salt and light' in the modern world of student politics has a dimension about it that former CU generations never encountered.

Nevertheless, the big question-mark over this generation of CU members is whether they have the appetite to take in enough solid food to build up a good base for life. There is no intrinsic reason why the new stress on singing should detract from this, though it can certainly give visiting speakers the impression of triviality. 'We sang simplistic choruses in our day,' says David Bentley-Taylor, 'but only in the camps, never in the CUs.' Sometimes the CU worship sessions are led with great care and linked to biblical themes of doctrine and practice. 'However,' says Oliver Barclay, commenting on his recent visits, 'I would have preferred to sing nothing more than twice and to have concentrated on those choruses which gave more *reasons* for praising God. I wish more CUs would adopt the practice of having the time of worship as a response to a talk and its message rather than as a "warming up" session.'

It is a reasonable estimate that 15,000 students in Britain attend CU Bible study groups during an average week. If this 'feeding of the 15,000' genuinely brings young people up on the milk and meat of the Word of God, then the future is as bright as the promises of God to those who heed his Word. When youth have faith in the truth the coming generation reaps the benefit to the glory of God.

Keith Weston, president of UCCF in its sixtieth anniversary year, draws out the characteristics of those students in our generation who have learned from home and church and CU to think biblically. 'They test what they see and hear around them by what they find in Scripture. The study of the Bible is a vital ingredient of their student life. They give it priority in the quiet of their own room and in the setting of the CU group. By it they "box the compass" of their attitudes and conscience. They get into line with what God says by obedience to the Word. They adjust the mind with reference to what others affirm. Praise God, every term they are being joined by hundreds more with the same priority. They too entrust their lives to Christ. They too launch out into a new lifestyle centred on God's Word . . . Do you long for the return in our land to biblical standards at every level? Then pray for the students of today. Pray for faithful, relevant and intelligent study of the Bible in their CUs.'

A quick foray over the border will help us to glimpse how the Scots situation has continued to develop. Keith Weston's picture of the Bible moulding the believer describes well the qualities that are aimed for and exhibited in depth in many Scots situations. A word about the *Dundee* CU will focus the continuing influence of strong biblical priorities.

From the sixties onwards the Dundee CU, which had been roused by a time of awakening from a rather dreary period, began to supply some exceptional leaders who contributed substantially to witness in student and then church life. 'For some years Dundee was the most spiritual of the lot,' said William Still. Eric Wright (later a travelling secretary from 1968 to 1975) and Bruce Milne, someone with marked preaching and lecturing gifts, were at the heart of this. 'From 1962 to 1965' says Martin Allen of Chryston, 'Bruce laid quite a foundation. His leadership in the CU, on the Scottish executive committee and on student campaigns was inspirational and instrumental in real blessing. Even after going down to study at Spurgeon's he never lost touch with the Scots scene and maintained bonds of fellowship.'

Dundee CU in the late sixties and early seventies knew blessing, and people like Jock and Jim Robertson, David Dickson, Peter Chirnside and Glynn Harrison were all being prepared for significant and varied ministries. Eric Wright made an outstanding contribution, for he was unquestionably owned and used of God in a very special way. Still adds, 'From the early sixties a very recognizable appetite for the teaching of the Word arose and a generation of men and women emerged who were and are committed to that emphasis. Wright's encouragement to committees to go for solid Bible teaching has had a remarkable product both in ministers and in dedicated school teachers.'

'Parallel to this', says Eric Alexander, minister of St George's Tron Church in Glasgow, 'was the formative influence of an increasing number of congregations where students worshipped. The presidents and others were gently influenced so that CU programmes began to reflect a real desire for consecutive exposition of Scripture. This then contributed to a further revival of such ministry in the Church of Scotland. My personal connections as a student were much more with TSF. A cynical statement was made at one lunch at Trinity College, that the conservative evangelicals would meet in the telephone box. The painful thing was that we could have done – there were so few of us. That whole situation has changed quite dramatically.' A recent TSF representative says, 'A cogent distinctive feature of the Scots TSF scene is that by far the majority of members are studying theology in order to be admitted to the ordained ministry, and many of them are reading divinity as a second degree. Most evangelical students are found in the Aberdeen faculty, where they get a great deal of support from academic staff and postgraduate students. Glasgow and Edinburgh also have well-consolidated groups and extensive speaker meetings.'

In 1971 the Aberdeen CU had a marvellous golden event. The CU president, Alex Morrison, sent a telegram down south which crystallized what had happened across the face of the land: 'Aberdeen CU 50th anniversary conference greet IVF and give thanks to God for its influence in Scotland.' Howard Marshall says, 'It was a remarkable experience to meet at that gathering one or two of the founder members – for example, Dr William Souter spoke on "Initial Steps", to say nothing of some of the giants of the years in between.'

Twenty years before, Henry (Sandy) Tait had been converted at Gilcomston while a student at Aberdeen. He had gone on to minister at Crieff. By the seventies a small group of two dozen or so ministers met at Crieff, many of them young men eager to discuss pastoral concerns. That group, under the leadership of William Still, has now increased over tenfold. It reflects the emergence all over Scotland of evangelical ministries committed to the systematic exposition of the whole Bible, in the persuasion that it is through the whole Word that the Spirit of God works in the human heart for its cleansing and transformation and the making of Christian character. It is perhaps as fine an example as any in the UK of what can happen when the student world and the local church find in that persuasion their common ethos. In many ways it is in Scotland that we now best see a demonstration of the principles that were expounded at the Kingham Hill conference of 1941.

There are, of course, difficulties in Scotland, too, in maintaining such priorities in our age. For example, 'since the growth of halls of residence the work has been somewhat fragmented: such fragmentation has the danger of people hiving off in groups, and in these days when there has been so much charismatic influence, co-ordination of effort is not as prominent as it used to be, and there is less uniformity of view with perhaps fewer young folk thirled to doctrinal standards than twenty years ago.

'However,' continues Still, 'we had a wonderful time in the university chapel, Aberdeen, on Friday, with perhaps 200 students testifying and praising God and listening to his Word with rapt attention. There has never been such spiritual quality in the CU as now, with their lively prayer meetings of sixty or seventy. How these young people love to pray!' We have already noted Howard Marshall's estimate of the outgoing maturity of the present generation. When both spiritual depth and active outreach are together judged by such people to be measurably greater in many of the present generation it surely gives a strong pointer to what priorities best serve the Fellowship in its witness to the world of today.

A closing review of the developing work in *Ireland* will give us renewed encouragement to anticipate God's blessings for future years.

It is common for a work of God to start through the rediscovery the Bible's message. It is perhaps less common for it to happen as a result of someone finding a Bible in a bin! That's where an Irish student, an ex-Dominican, found a New Testament while staying in London. He started to study it and its message gripped him. It was one of the first signals that God was beginning to bring the Bible back into the southern Irish scene. He was a student in an Irish college and he was helped to start a Bible study there by the local representative of a seamen's society.

Until that time (the late sixties) there was, except for Trinity College, Dublin, no evangelical work in the south of Ireland universities and colleges. Robbie Burns, who travelled in the north of Ireland, Manchester and Liverpool, used to take exploratory trips by bus down south. With few contacts anywhere outside Dublin he devised a means of making friends. He would look for a group of students and follow some home in order to see where they were lodging. On his next visit he would stay at that place in order to try and get to know them.

242

It was from such beginnings that much has now happened. Robbie's first real contact was with the ex-Dominican whom he made several trips to see. The Bible study group he had established began to hold occasional meetings, with talks by Herbert Carson, Dr A. Connell of the Royal Victoria Hospital, Belfast, and Professor David Gooding of Queen's, one of the constant influences for good among evangelical students in the university.

Then a Presbyterian student from Co. Derry arrived to study in University College. There was no CU so he went to SCM. The following year, since he was the only one with any spiritual drive, he was elected auditor (president). He arranged a talk on the Holy Spirit, shared by a Presbyterian minister and a Roman Catholic priest. They arranged to meet again, because they found they had emphasized the same things. From this began a weekly prayer meeting, the first of what became countless charismatic groups that swept across the Irish Roman Catholic Church, some of which meet primarily to study the Bible. It was part of a new spiritual climate in the seventies.

Meanwhile a few Queen's graduates began to take further study at southern colleges. Several of the present leaders in the south were converted through the witness arising from this. The concerns are reminiscent of the early moves of CICCU and OICCU members to see evangelical truth established in other universities on the mainland. Of those originally involved in these initiatives in Ireland, one is now a lecturer at University College, married to one of the Roman Catholic students who came to know Christ as Saviour in these years, another became a traveller in north and south and a third is now the Presbyterian minister of a church in Galway that stands beside the university.

In 1979 Clem Hegarty came into contact with these evangelicals. He was in his fourth year at Cork University. 'I had never really read a Bible. But it was during a deep search for the meaning to my life, which I felt was going nowhere, that I met these "Christians" for the first time. I was introduced to some Queen's students by my sister Donna, who herself had been converted to Christ the previous year while Students Union vice-president. At the time Cork University had a small Bible Union of five or six. They have continued for eleven years or so and have seen conversions to Christ each year. The group knew personally an amazing number of students and have now been officially recognized as a society in the university.'

Since becoming a travelling secretary in 1983, Clem Hegarty has brought a significant new plus to evangelical leadership in the south. He is the first southerner, and 'a Catholic by background into the bargain' who has done the work. All his predecessors had much cultural acclimatizing to do. Southern Ireland is in many ways oblivious to the north and vice versa. 'Cassells Morrell, the traveller in my student days,' says Clem, 'told me that when he started he did not even know what Shamrock Rovers, the football team, was. But he learned!'

Perhaps as remarkable a story for its longer-term implications as the finding of a Bible in a London bin is that of the conversion to Christ of an Irish atheist in Barcelona! Mary Farrell,[2] an Irish student, had been contacted in Spain through IFES worker Ruth Siemens and American student Rebecca Manley Pippert. When Mary returned to Ireland she, too, began a Bible study group in her college. This initiative was built on when an evangelical member of staff was appointed. Through her consistent lifestyle many girls took notice of the gospel, and came to Bible study and then to personal faith.

A key feature, reminiscent of the development in England in the forties, has been the increasing number of committed Christians appointed to colleges staffs who have been able to encourage the work on a longer-term basis. One of the best signs has been the young Christians of one or two years' experience who 'are incredibly natural evangelists in general. In one college an older student established a Bible study group and within twelve months eight of his class had come to faith,' reports Clem.

Robbie Burns looks back to the time when his first visit as traveller to a southern university town drew the question from an aging local minister whether he was down for a tiddlywinks weekend! How empty the gospel challenge had become. But the student contacts were growing, and Burns was replaced by Gavin Pantridge and he was replaced by two people – one man for the north and one for the south. The girls have continued to have their traveller. Now a new generation of Roman Catholic students has been saved and they are seeking teaching through Bible study groups. And small new Bible-based churches have

[2]Her story is told in Rebecca Manley Pippert, *Out of the Saltshaker*, chapter 1.

come into being too. The great need of the eighties is depth of biblical belief and life. Currently nineteen groups are operating. It has been truly exciting for these committed young people to watch God at work and to seek to work along with him. The meeting of the annual Irish UCCF conference at Greystones, Co. Wicklow, has helped to focus the unity of the work.

Over the years a kind of unofficial Irish senior committee of Dr George Swann, Dr Sidney McCann and T. S. Mooney (who was treasurer for forty years) grew up in the north. What was an advisory committee has now become the UCCF Irish Council, and its prayers and responsibilities extend north and south. 'With all my heart I can say, "Thank God for all UCCF has meant to Ireland," ' said T. S. Mooney, a few months before his death. Is it too much to pray that the rich inter-mingling of biblical truth that has flowed back and forth, north and south, between England and Scotland could one day be a pattern, under God, for Irish students in the south and Ulster students in the north? Former Ireland travellers such as David Bruce have a great burden to see the reconciling work of the gospel of Christ span the antagonisms of the years. A pipe dream? Or part of a renewed UCCF/IFES vision? The new spring of CU life in the universities of the south is, after all, implicit within the original vision of 1919, when amidst 'prayer like April showers', God began to raise up 'this much better thing'. This latter-day fulfilment south of the border (a border that did not exist when the vision was given!) brings our story full circle and sets it rolling yet again. Each fresh sign that God perseveres with us and through us to the fulfilment of his promises is a stimulus to pray again.

'Again (Elijah) prayed, and the heavens gave rain, and the earth produced its crops' (James 5:18). 'The IVF was born in prayer,' wrote Douglas Johnson in 1953, quoting this text in the report for that year. We echo and reinforce it thirty-five years on. 'Those undergraduates who met for prayer in Mrs C. T. Studd's house at the 1919 Keswick Convention prayed until two in the morning. They affirmed, "We had never before known such assurance in prayer." A few months later one of them was praying again in Trinity College, Cambridge, when the vision came to him of the future IVF. Norman Grubb wrote, "I saw that not only must there be this witness in every university, but that God was going to do it" . . .

'It is evident that God has answered these prayers. But we cannot be complacent. The need for the witness of the CUs is greater than ever. The problems we now face are more complex and the calls upon our resources more numerous. Now is the time for us all to remember Elijah's example and to *pray again*.

'Pray for the students of today' (Keith Weston).

'How these young people love to pray!' (William Still).

In this call to prayer to churches and parents and in this praying concern of the student of today we see grounds to believe that, in the gracious hands of the Lord of the years, evangelical witness will continue to survive and revive in the educational training-grounds of our land.

Bibliography

Annual reports (IVF/UCCF, 1949–86).

Norman Anderson, *The Evidence for the Resurrection* (IVP, 1950); *idem, An Adopted Son* (IVP, 1985).

Oliver R. Barclay, *Whatever Happened to the Jesus Lane Lot?* (IVP, 1977); *idem, For the Faith of the Gospel* (UCCF, 1978).

F. F. Bruce, *In Retrospect* (Pickering and Inglis, 1980).

Steve Bruce, *Firm in the Faith* (Gower, 1984).

W. M. Capper and D. Johnson (eds.), *The Faith of a Surgeon: Belief and Experience in the Life of Arthur Rendle Short* (Paternoster, 1976).

Michael Cassidy, *Bursting the Wineskins* (Hodder and Stoughton, 1983).

Christopher Catherwood, *Five Evangelical Leaders* (Hodder and Stoughton, 1984).

J. E. Church, *Every Man a Bible Student* (Paternoster, [2]1976).

F. D. Coggan (ed.), *Christ and the Colleges* (IVF, 1934).

John Eddison (ed.), *Bash: A Study in Spiritual Power* (Marshall, Morgan and Scott, 1982).

Sinclair B. Ferguson (ed.), *Letters of William Still* (Banner of Truth, 1984).

Geraint D. Fielder, *'Excuse Me, Mr Davies – Hallelujah!' Evangelical Student Witness in Wales, 1923–83* (EPW/IVP, 1983).

Joyce Gladwell, *Brown Face, Big Master* (IVP, 1969).

Howard Guinness, *Journey Among Students* (AIO, no date).

David Hawker, *Kanchi Doctor* (Scripture Union, 1984).

Douglas Johnson, *Contending for the Faith: A History of the Evangelical Movement in the Universities and Colleges* (IVP, 1979).

Brian Kellock, *The Fibre Man: The Life Story of Dr Dennis Burkitt* (Lion, 1985).

Bill and Shirley Lees, *Is it Sacrifice?* (IVP, 1987).

Pete Lowman, *The Day of His Power: A History of the International Fellowship of Evangelical Students* (IVP, [2]1988).

David Lyon, *Future Society* (Lion, 1984).

Donald M. MacKay, *The Clockwork Image: A Christian Perspective on Science* (IVP, 1974).

Sally Magnusson, *The Flying Scotsman: A Biography of Eric Liddell* (Quartet, 1984).

Katharine Makower, *Follow My Leader: A Biography of Murray Webb-Peploe* (Kingsway, 1984).

Bruce Milne, *Know the Truth* (IVP, 1982).

Iain Murray, *D. Martyn Lloyd-Jones, The First Forty Years, 1899–1939* (Banner of Truth, 1982).

J. I. Packer, *Evangelism and the Sovereignty of God* (IVP, 1961).

John S. Peart-Binns, *Living with Paradox: John Habgood, Archbishop of York* (Darton, Longman and Todd, 1987).

Rebecca Manley Pippert, *Out of the Saltshaker* (IVP, 1980).

Helen Roseveare, *Give Me This Mountain* (IVP, 1966).

Theodore Roszak, *Person/Planet* (Granada, 1981).

David Sheppard, *Parson's Pitch* (Hodder and Stoughton, 1964).

John Stott, *The Cross of Christ* (IVP, 1986).

Nigel Sylvester, *God's Word in a Young World: The Story of Scripture Union* (Scripture Union, 1984).

University Staffs Christian Fellowship, *USCF Broadsheet* (Winter 1984–5).

Various contributors, *DJ 80* (Christian Medical Fellowship, 1985).

Tom Walker, *Renew us by your Spirit* (Hodder and Stoughton, 1982).

David Watson, *You are my God* (Hodder and Stoughton, 1983).

John White, *Excellence in Leadership* (IVP, 1987).

Robert Wilder, *Christ and the Student World* (IVF, 1935).

J. Young, *Paul Brand* (SCM, 1980).

The Doctrinal Basis of the UCCF is available by request from the UCCF, 38 De Montfort Street, Leicester LE1 7GP. *Evangelical Belief*, a booklet explaining the Basis, is available from Christian bookshops, or, in case of difficulty, from IVP, Norton Street, Nottingham NG7 3HR.

Index